g

on the road

NEW ENGLAND

Produced by AA Publishing

Written by Kathy Arnold and Paul Wade

Additional research: Lans Christensen, Gael May McKibben, Tom Arnold and Harlan Levy

First published 1997

Edited, designed and produced by AA Publishing.

Distributed in the United Kingdom by AA Publishing, Norfolk House, Priestley Road, Basingstoke, Hampshire, RG24 9NY.

A CIP catalogue record for this book is available from the British Library.

ISBN 0 7495 1487 6

Published by AA Publishing, (a trading name of Automobile Association Developments Limited, whose registered office is Norfolk House, Priestley Road, Basingstoke, Hampshire, RG24 9NY. Registered number 1878835).

Colour separation: Daylight Colour Art, Singapore

Printed and bound by G. Canale & C. S.P.A., Torino, Italy

Front cover: *fall foliage*
Inset: *Waits River, Vermont*

Below: *fall on the Mohawk Trail*

CONTENTS

ABOUT THIS BOOK

This book is not only a practical touring guide for the independent traveler, but is also invaluable for those who would like to know more about New England.

It is divided into the 6 states, each with its own city and driving tours. The driving tours start and finish in those cities which we consider to be the most interesting centers for exploration.

There are special features on Boston and the American Revolution, the beauty of the fall and the rich heritage of the arts and the surrounding seas.

Each tour has details of the most interesting places to visit en route. Boxes catering for special interests follow some of the main entries – for those whose interest is in history or walking or those who have children. There are also boxes which highlight scenic stretches of road and which give details of special events, crafts and customs.

The simple route directions are accompanied by an easy-to-use map at the beginning of each tour, along with a chart showing how far it is from one town to the next in miles and kilometers. This can help you to decide where to take a break and stop overnight. (All distances quoted are approximate.)

Before setting off it is advisable to check with the information center listed at the start of the tour for recommendations on where to break your journey and for additional information on what to see and do, and when best to visit.

Torrington, Connecticut

For information on aspects of motoring in New England see page 161.

INFORMATION FOR NON-U.S. RESIDENTS

Banks
Banks are usually open Monday through Friday between 9am and 3pm. Many have extended hours until 5pm (or even 8 or 9pm on Thursday) and on Saturday from 9am to 2pm or later.

Although foreign currency can be changed at big hotels or airports, U.S. dollar travelers' checks are recommended because they are readily accepted as cash everywhere from restaurants to gas stations.

Credit Cards
Major credit cards are accepted in New England. However, many small bed and breakfasts or remote small shops will accept only cash or travelers' checks.

If you have a major credit or charge card (American Express, MasterCard, Access, EuroCard, or Visa), you may be able to obtain cash from an automatic-teller machine (ATM).

Currency
The American unit of currency is the dollar, consisting of 100 cents. All the notes are green, are the same size and have similar designs, so it is important to distinguish between their values.

They range from one to two, five, ten, 20, 50 and 100 dollars. The coins range from the copper-colored one cent, or penny, through the silver 5 cents (nickel), 10 cents (dime), 25 cents (quarter) and ... rarely, a silver dollar.

Customs Regulations
Non-U.S. residents may take in 200 cigarettes or 50 cigars, a liter of alcohol and $100 worth of gifts. Customs officials are very strict about banning any fresh meat, fruit, plants and, of course, drugs (unless these are on prescription).

Electricity
Standard voltage is 110–120V, 60 cycles AC, using flat two-pin plugs. Bring the right adaptor.

Emergency Telephone Numbers
If you have an emergency, telephone the police at 911 who will put you in touch with the right service. Otherwise, dial "0" and consult the operator.

Entry Regulations
Citizens of most European countries, plus Japan and New Zealand, no longer need visas as long as they are visiting the U.S.

for business or tourist purposes. For a stay not exceeding 90 days, and provided that a return or onward ticket is held, only a valid passport is required. Check with your travel agent before travelling, since American immigration officials are very strict.

Health Matters

It is essential to have adequate health insurance before travelling to the U.S.A. While hospitals are usually excellent, treatment has to be paid for and the costs may be exorbitant. Treatment may be delayed or refused if proof of proper insurance is not available. Your hotel will be able to recommend a doctor or local hospital.

Alternatively, call the local hospital. No special inoculations are required. See also **Health Services**, page 160.

Post Offices

Stamps for postcards and letters are on sale in many shops and hotels; for a larger package, go to a post office. It is cheaper to send postcards and aerograms than letters. See also page 163.

Public Holidays

See page 160 and **New England Calendar of Events**, pages 161–3.

Telephones

Each state has at least one area code, with new ones opening up all the time as telecommunications expand. Pay phones require 5, 10 and 25 cent coins, so use a telephone card for convenience. To call abroad, dial 011, then the country code:
Australia 61,
Canada 1,
New Zealand 64,
UK 44.

Time

New England is on Eastern Standard Time (EST), 5 hours behind the UK, 6 hours behind mainland Europe, and 15 hours behind Sydney, Australia. Daylight Saving Time alters the time by one hour from March or April to October or November.

Travelers Aid Society

The Travelers Aid Society, at 17 East Street, Boston, Massachusetts 02111 (tel: 617/542–7286), is a nonprofit social service agency dedicated to helping travelers solve problems large and small. Professional staff members provide crisis intervention, counseling, referrals to community sources, and emergency financial assistance to travelers in crisis.

Travelers Aid volunteers can be found at Logan Airport (tel: 617/567–5385) and at the Greyhound Bus Terminal at South Station (tel: 617/737–2880) and will help you to find an address, a hospital, lost luggage, a way to get money from home, or the solution to any other travel dilemma.

Useful Addresses

Discover New England, Greatness Lane, Sevenoaks TN14 5BQ (tel: 01732 742777); (in U.S.A.) Unit C-3A, Heritage Place, 205 Worcester Court, Falmouth, MA 02540 (tel: 508/640–8169).

DestINNations (for inn reservations), PO Box 1173, Osterville, MA 02655 (tel: 508/790–0577); (elsewhere in U.S.A. and Canada) 800/333–4667; (in U.K.) North America Travel Service (tel: 0113 243 0000).

Bed and Breakfast Agency of Boston, 47 Commercial Wharf, Boston, MA 02110. Tel: (in U.K.) 0800 895128 (in U.S.A. and Canada) 800/248–9262.

Lobster pots at Mystic Seaport

MASSACHUSETTS

After 350 years of permanent European settlement, Massachusetts has acquired a "little history." Here, the Pilgrims landed and built their communities. A century and a half later, patriotic passion exploded in a series of events culminating in the American Revolution. Not surprisingly, that heritage has been preserved. Conservation has encompassed old houses and bridges, churches and farms, even entire villages.

Massachusetts is known as the Bay State because of the gaping Atlantic gulf enclosed by the flexed arm of Cape Cod. The shape of the state ensures a variety of landscapes. It stretches from the storm-tossed Atlantic to the rolling, wooded hills of the Berkshires, with the rich meadows of the Connecticut Valley in between.

The seasons are distinct: crisp, clear winter days melting into an explosion of spring greenery and flowers, followed by muggy, soporific summers and, finally, the fall with its dazzling multi-colored leaves (see pages 102–3).

Massachusetts, especially around Boston, was also America's cultural cradle (see pages 56–7). Artists and writers, poets and musicians have long been drawn together by the web of academia. Harvard University, founded in 1636, is the oldest American institute of higher learning, but there are numerous other colleges to be found throughout the state, as well as boarding schools (called prep schools because they prepare students for college).

Concord is a beautiful town with a rich and varied history

Outdoor festivals of music and drama are a bonus for visitors during the summer months.

But the region's focus always returns to history. Many of America's most treasured icons are here, from Plymouth Rock to Boston's Old North Church and Concord's historic bridge. Thanksgiving is celebrated with justifiable pride; after all, the tradition of eating turkey and pumpkin pie was "invented" here. They even have the cranberry bogs nearby to provide the accompanying sauce.

Tour I

"Listen, my children, and you
shall hear,
Of the midnight ride of
Paul Revere ..."

Paul Revere is one of the best-known messengers in history, thanks to Henry Wadsworth Longfellow's poem. His ride from Boston to warn the Americans that the British were on the march has become legendary. The patriots assembled and took on the trained soldiers, first in Lexington and then in Concord. All the British wanted to do was capture the rebels' arms cache; they had no idea that the skirmishes of April 19, 1775 would spark the American Revolution. In both towns, historic sites have been preserved, while the visitor information centers provide details of "who did what and when." The route for this tour also has a literary focus. In the 19th century, Concord was the home of some of the best-known writers of the day: Henry David Thoreau, Louisa May Alcott, Nathaniel Hawthorne and Ralph Waldo Emerson.

Tour 2

Although Cape Cod has long been recognized as a playground for Bostonians, the North Shore, with its rugged, rocky outcrops is also a popular place to relax by the sea. Add to that atmospheric fishing villages and the gruesome history of witches in Salem, and this drive is fun as well as scenic. The sparkling light has long attracted artists, especially in Rockport. Castles and underwater rocks, whales, frozen peas and even clam chowder are threads in the rich tapestry of America's history which unravels along this shoreline drive.

Tour 3

Cape Cod enjoys a mystique matched by few holiday destinations. The names of its 300-year-old villages are reminders of English fishing ports, its history peopled with Indians and fishermen, whalers and sea captains. On Cape Cod Bay the sands are

sheltered and the water is warmer than on the Atlantic Ocean shore, where strong waves buffet the dunes of the Cape Cod National Seashore. This 40-mile (60km) coastline stretches from the elbow of the peninsula up to Provincetown, known for its bohemian lifestyle. The popularity of the Cape has taken its toll: roadside development sprawls around Hyannis on the south shore and traffic can be bumper to bumper on summer weekends. Off season, it is easier to get away from it all, and find what aficionados call "the old Cape Cod."

Tour 4

Western Massachusetts has an intriguing mixture of the rural and sophisticated, the historic and eccentric. The rolling Berkshire Hills inspired authors

Chatham Light, Cape Cod.
Lighthouses are a unique part of
New England's heritage

such as Herman Melville and Edith Wharton, and attracted millionaires, who built vacation homes away from the seaside. Now the hills resound to summer festivals of music and theater. Attractive towns and villages range from Deerfield, with its perfectly preserved 17th-century houses, to Williamstown with its excellent college and astonishing art collection. Stockbridge thrives on its "traditional America" image, ably reinforced by *Saturday Evening Post* cover artist Norman Rockwell, whose paintings are on display here. Drive down lazy back roads to old covered bridges arching over rocky streams; there are surprises around every corner.

BIRTHPLACE OF A NATION

The American perspective of the War of Independence is simple: the Colonists were oppressed by King George III and Parliament and justifiably rebelled. The issues were a little more complex. In the early days, there were no "states" as such. The Colonies differed in population and style of government: some depended on fishing and trade, others on farming and tobacco. Although links with the Mother Country were strong, for economic and cultural reasons, the Colonists had become increasingly independent-minded during the century-and-a-half since the first settlers arrived.

Americans, boarded the newly arrived HMS *Dartmouth*. Its cargo of 300 chests of tea was thrown overboard. In response, General Gage and four British regiments were sent to Boston, and the port was closed down in 1774.

Below: the Boston Massacre, in which five Colonists died
Bottom: the "Sons of Liberty," disguised as Mohawk Indians, throw East India Company tea into the water

A turning point in American history was the defeat of the French and the Indians in the war from 1756 to 1763. This gave the New Englanders, and the colonies along the coast to the south, a vision of vast lands stretching westwards and a sense of "new" country to be developed. Relations with Britain, however, became strained when Parliament decided that the colonies should help pay for the seven years of war; after all, the English reasoned, they were defending Colonial lands. Moreover, a 10,000-strong army was still needed to protect the Colonies. A monopoly on trade was proclaimed, restricting Colonists to dealing only with Britain and other British possessions (notably the West Indies). Further, a ban was issued on new settlements west of the Appalachians.

Although these restrictions rankled, what inflamed Colonial passions was direct taxation. Traditionally, Britain had raised money by customs duties on shipping; the Stamp Act in 1765 set a new precedent. This placed a charge on all contracts, deeds, newspapers and legal documents. Protests forced its repeal within a year but other revenue-raisers followed, only to be repealed. Parliament decided to stand firm on one, however. That was the tax on tea.

After the French and Indian War, economic times were hard for the Colonists, and the new rules hurt financially. But the Colonists also protested on prin-

ciple. "No taxation without representation" was the cry at public meetings and in pamphlets. Articles questioned the legality of such taxes, claiming that they infringed the charters of some of the Colonies.

Boston was an important focus of militant feelings, which periodically exploded into riots. One relatively minor event, on March 5, 1770, became a legend. A lone British sentry on duty at the Custom House was harassed by a crowd. Reinforcements arrived, but the mob continued to bait the soldiers, heckling them and throwing stones. Shots were fired; five Colonists died. This incident became known as the "Boston Massacre" and was used by leaders such as Samuel Adams to whip up emotions.

Three years later, in December, came one of the most colorful incidents of the era, the Boston Tea Party. As a protest against the tax of 3 pence per pound on tea, about a hundred men, disguised as Native

The scene was set for the smoldering coals of resentment to be ignited. In April 1775, it was reported to General Gage that farmers in Concord, a small village west of Boston, were stockpiling firearms. He ordered 700 British troops to march out, confiscate and destroy the Patriot's illegal cache. On route, they skirmished with the Minute Men (locals who could be ready "in a minute" to fight) in Lexington before being outnumbered in Concord. Instead of withdrawing in an orderly manner, the British confronted the militiamen, lost three soldiers and had to beat a hasty, undignified retreat to Boston.

cost was hundreds of lives. The psychological victory belonged to the Americans. King George III replied savagely by declaring the colonies to be in rebellion. Mercenaries were hired in Europe and transported across the Atlantic to augment the troops.

Not all the Colonists were ready for war. About one-third remained loyal to the crown and another third were neutral. The rest, however, were vociferous and demanded to sever links with the Mother Country. Further British attacks on Falmouth (now Portland, Maine) in October 1775 and on Norfolk, Virginia in January 1776, only

Boston, never to return. Fighting, however, continued elsewhere. In May, representatives of all 13 Colonies met in Philadelphia, Pennsylvania. Freedom was the agenda of this Continental Congress. A short document drafted by Thomas Jefferson of Virginia set out the grievances and proclaimed that "these united colonies are, and of right ought to be, free and independent states." This was the Declaration of Independence, accepted unanimously by the delegates and signed on July 4, 1776.

Liberty did not come immediately, however. War raged for five years and even after the

Some 20,000 Minute Men rushed to Boston, penning the British forces in. In May 1775, artillery powder and ammunition captured at Fort Ticonderoga in New York State was hauled overland by the Colonists and used to capture Bunker Hill. Although the Redcoats soon stormed and recaptured it, the

served to fan the fury. *Common Sense*, a pamphlet written by Thomas Paine, became a best seller, with 120,000 copies sold in January 1776 alone. Although he was an Englishman who had lived in the Colonies for only a year, he argued strenuously for independence. In March 1776, the British withdrew from

The citizens of Lexington re-enact the events of 19 April, 1775

formal British surrender in 1781, London refused to recognize the Colonies' independence. Finally, in September 1783, a peace treaty was signed in Paris, acknowledging that a new nation had been born.

Lexington
& Concord

Concord and Lexington are two of the most famous towns in the United States, due to the skirmishes between locals and British soldiers in 1775 that triggered the American Revolution. Concord has an additional claim to fame: it was home to some of the great writers of 19th-century America. Today, Lexington feels like a residential suburb of Boston, while Concord retains more of an historical flavor. The main theme of this route is liberty and literature, but at the end of the drive, the focus is strictly contemporary.

The Minute Man Statue on Lexington Green

ITINERARY

CAMBRIDGE	▶ **Lexington** (8m-13km)
LEXINGTON	▶ **Concord** (6m-10km)
CONCORD	▶ **Cambridge** (16m-26km)

1 DAY • 30 MILES • 49KM

FOR HISTORY BUFFS

The Colonists had no regular army. What they did have, however, were militia, small forces of volunteers pledged to be ready at a minute's notice, giving rise to the the name "Minute Men." Although mainly farmers, the men also hunted for game, using "rifled" guns which were more accurate than the British muskets. Like modern guerilla fighters, the Colonists tended to disappear into the countryside, rather than marching along roads as the British did. In any case, British soldiers were easy to spot, because of the bright red coats they wore.

i *Chamber of Commerce, 859 Massachusetts Avenue*

▶ *From Cambridge, take the Fresh Pond Parkway (**Routes 16** and **3**) to **Route 2** west. Take this for 3 miles (5km) and then exit onto **Routes 4** and **225**. At the first stop sign, turn left onto Massachusetts Avenue (always known as "Mass Ave"). This is the route taken by Paul Revere on his way to Lexington. On the left, at No. 1332, is the Munroe Tavern.*

1 Munroe Tavern
On the afternoon of April 19, 1775, this fine old pub (1695) was the site of the temporary hospital and headquarters for British soldiers retreating from the battle at Concord. Fourteen years later, George Washington dined here in an upstairs room, while on a tour of New England. Today it is the headquarters of the Lexington Historical Society.

i *Lexington Visitor Center, 1875 Massachusetts Avenue*

▶ *Follow Massachusetts Avenue straight into Lexington to the triangular green. On the right, the Visitor Center has a diorama giving an overview of*

the events covered by this route. In order to follow events in sequence, bear to the right of the Green and turn right on Hancock Street. At No. 36 is the Hancock-Clarke House.

2 Hancock-Clarke House
At around 1am on April 19, 1775, John Hancock and Samuel Adams were awakened by a knock on the door. Paul Revere had arrived to warn these two important leaders of the patriots' cause that the British were on the march. This 1698 house is furnished as it would have been on that fateful night. Among the memorabilia are Major Pitcairn's pistols (see Lexington Battle Green) and the drums of Minute Man William Drummond.

▶ *Return to the Green. Next to the Visitor Center is Buckman Tavern.*

3 Buckman Tavern
In the early hours of April 19, several Lexington Minute Men had gathered to drink ale in this handsome three-story tavern

Headquarters of the Lexington Minute Men, 1775

(1690). Around 4am came the news that 700 British troops were minutes from the Green. Bells rang, drums rolled and the Minute Men, under the command of Captain John Parker, filed out of the tavern. As the sun rose, they assembled on the Green, more as a protest than looking for a fight. The Tavern looks exactly as it did in 1755, with bar orders chalked on the tap room wall. The front door has a hole in it, allegedly from a bullet shot during the encounter.

▶ *Across the street is the Green.*

4 Lexington Battle Green
The bronze statue of Captain John Parker stands on a stone cairn, facing the line of the British approach. Behind him the Lexington militia would have stood. "Ye villains, ye rebels, disperse!" ordered the arrogant Major John Pitcairn. Faced by the superior numbers

and strength of the British, Parker wisely told his men: "Don't fire unless fired upon, but if they mean to have a war, let it begin here!"

A shot rang out, no-one knows from where. Suddenly fire was exchanged; two British soldiers and eight Minute Men were killed or wounded. Seven of them are buried under the Revolutionary Monument further on the Green. The British, having beaten off this minor attack, marched on towards Concord.

▶ *Leave Lexington on Massachusetts Avenue and follow it west (it becomes Battle Road) for 2 miles (3km). Turn right onto **Route 2A** and drive to the Battle Road Visitor Center.*

Lexington's First Parish Church

5 Battle Road

Although the actual road followed by the British troops has been largely covered over by Route 2A, a small section has been preserved in the Minute Man National Historic Park. About half a mile (800m) beyond the Visitor Center is the site where Paul Revere was captured by a British patrol. His fellow messenger, Dr. Samuel Prescott, eluded them and rode on to Concord. In another half mile (800m), a narrow winding section of the original Battle Road bears off to the right. This is a typical "two rod road," named because of the 32-foot (10m) distance between the stone walls on either side of the road (a rod measures 16 feet). Here, the William Smith House, the remains of the Hartwell House, and the Ephraim Hartwell Tavern all reflect the

SPECIAL TO...

The events of April 19, 1775 are re-enacted each year on Patriots' Day. At sunrise, latter-day Minute Men from communities around Concord march through the woods much as their ancestors did. Historically accurate 1775 uniforms are *de rigeuer*, both for the "farmers" and the "Redcoats". In a brief but moving ceremony near the Old North Bridge, officials from Britain and America pay their respects to those who died, as the *Last Post* rings out. Later in the day, skirmishes are cheerfully re-enacted, with much rattling of drums and piping of fifes. Nowadays, the holiday falls on the Monday closest to April 19, to make a long weekend.

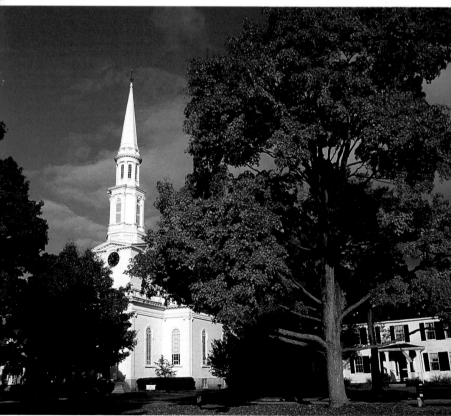

style and methods of construction used in Colonial Massachusetts.

▶ *Drive to the intersection of Battle Road and **Route 2A** and turn right. After 2 miles (3km), the parking lot for The Wayside is on the left. Just before The Wayside is Grapevine Cottage.*

6 Grapevine Cottage

Welch's grape juice and jelly have long been favorites, but their success dates back to a grape developed by Ephraim Bull. This enthusiastic horticulturist spent ten years experimenting, then exhibited his Concord grape in 1853 at the Massachusetts Horticultural Society's show. It was an instant success for Bull, and growers offered as much as $1,000 a seedling. When, in 1869, Dr. Thomas Welch perfected a way of pasteurizing Concord grape juice, a soft drink was born. The headquarters of Welch's is in Concord. Grapevine Cottage is now privately-owned.

▶ *Next door is The Wayside.*

7 The Wayside

The Wayside, with its distinctive red brick chimneys, was the home of the muster master, whose job was to summon the Minute Men if the British attacked. In the 19th century, it became first the residence of the Alcott family, then in 1852, Nathaniel Hawthorne bought it and changed the name from Hillside to The Wayside: He completed *Tanglewood Tales* in his study in the tower at the top of the house.

▶ *Just up the street is Orchard House.*

8 Orchard House

The Alcotts moved to Orchard House after leaving The Wayside, and it was here that Louisa May wrote much of *Little Women*. Researchers for the 1992 movie took photographs and made sketches here, then built a

house in Canada specially for the filming. It was not an exact replica, however, and those taking the guided tour may notice differences, particularly in the bedrooms. Carefully preserved furnishings and costumes reflect the family's 20 years here.

▶ *Follow **Route 2A** towards Concord. After a short distance, turn left onto the Concord Turnpike and the Concord Museum parking lot.*

Orchard House, the home of novelist Louisa May Alcott

9 Concord Museum

This is a fine example of a small museum, with relics of the Revolution including one of the two lanterns hung in the Old North Church in Boston, and the sword of Colonel Barrett, commander of the Concord militia. Louisa May Alcott's tea kettle and doll are here, while among the display of Henry David Thoreau memorabilia are the bed, writing desk and rocking chair from his cabin at Walden Pond (see below).

▶ *Across the street is Emerson House.*

🔟 Emerson House

"But isn't it a lovely blaze!" was the reaction of philosopher Ralph Waldo Emerson to the fire that destroyed his house in 1872. Sent away to recover from the shock, he returned after a year to find that his home had been rebuilt by his friends and neighbors. Emerson's life here was characterized by "plain living and high thinking" but is less remembered for his essays than for quotes such as, "If a man can write a better book, preach a better sermon, or make a better mousetrap than his neighbor, though he builds his house in the woods, the world will beat a path to his door." The reconstructed house is as he left it, though his study has been removed and rebuilt in the museum across the road.

▶ *Continue into Concord and, at the Green, take **Route 62** towards Bedford. After a short distance, take the second entrance to Sleepy Hollow Cemetery.*

⓫ Sleepy Hollow Cemetery

As peaceful as it sounds, with its steep hills and stately trees, the cemetery is a place of pilgrimage for fans of the Concord authors. At one end, high atop "Authors' Ridge," rest the remains of Louisa May Alcott, Ralph Waldo Emerson and Nathaniel Hawthorne. The grave of Henry David Thoreau is marked by a simple headstone, inscribed with only one word: "Henry."

▶ *Return to Concord Green and turn right onto Monument Street. Ignore the parking lot on the right and, after crossing the Concord River, turn left on Liberty Street. Turn left again into the parking lot for the North Bridge Visitor Center.*

⓬ Old North Bridge

Here is "the rude bridge" where, on April 19, 1775, "... the embattled farmers stood, And fired the shot heard round the world." The words are from the *Concord Hymn*, written by Emerson in 1837 to celebrate the completion of the Battle Monument. One of the most powerful American icons, it was sculpted by Daniel Chester French, who also created the figure of Abraham Lincoln for the Lincoln Memorial in Washington D.C.

On the day of the battle, some 400 Minute Men were waiting here to confront the 700 tired and worried British Regulars. As they advanced across the bridge, the famous shot rang out. The sloping fields would have looked much as they do now, though the bridge is a modern replica. Across the river, at the edge of an open field, stands the Old Manse. From the windows of this three-story wooden house, the parson, William Emerson, watched the bloody events. He was the grandfather of Ralph Waldo Emerson, who lived here as a little boy.

▶ *Turn left out of the Visitor Center's parking lot and proceed to the first stop sign. Turn left onto Lowell Road and drive back to Concord Green. Follow the sign for **Route 2A**, then after a short distance, turn right on Heywood Street. Turn left on Walden Street (**Route 126**). Continue for 1 mile (2km), crossing **Route 2**, to the Walden Pond car park. Follow signs for **Route 126** and take it south to Walden Pond.*

⓭ Walden Pond

Henry Thoreau came here and "lived alone, in the woods, a mile from any neighbor, in a house I had built myself, on the shore of Walden Pond." This two-year "back to nature" experience was the basis of his most

famous work, *Walden*, published in 1854. Seeking the solitude that he found may be difficult in summer, when families swim and picnic at "this pond ... so remarkable for its depth and purity ... a clear and deep well, half a mile long and a mile and three quarters in circumference ..." A replica of his cabin is conveniently close to the car park; to avoid the crowds, walk around to the far side of the water, where a cairn marks the site of the real cabin. The pond is surrounded by the 304-acre (122-hectare) Walden Pond State Reservation.

▶ *Follow **Route 126** south for a short distance to Baker Bridge Road and turn left. At No. 68 is the Gropius House, the home of Walter Gropius, founder of the Bauhaus Movement. Born in Germany, he moved to America in 1937 and lectured at Harvard for 14 years. Continue to the end of the road and turn right on to Sandy Pond Road. On the left is the DeCordova Museum.*

The Old North Bridge, actually a modern replica

🖼 DeCordova Museum

Dedicated to the work of contemporary American artists, this museum is located in 35 acres (14 hectares) of open fields and woods overlooking Sandy Pond. Some 60 sculptures are displayed outside in natural settings. In summer there are outdoor jazz concerts, and the museum shop sells original works of art.

▶ Return to Sandy Pond Road, turn left and drive to the first intersection. Cross Lincoln Road, and continue on Trapelo Road 2½ miles (4km) to **Route 128**. Go north on **Route 128** to **Route 2** east, the first exit, and return to Cambridge.

SPECIAL TO...

Around 1845, Concord was the literary epicenter of America, with four of the country's most revered writers living near one another. Ralph Waldo Emerson (1803–82) was a philosopher, poet and magnetic speaker. Today, he is best remembered for the *Concord Hymn*, encapsulating the events of the Old North Bridge (see page 14).
In 1837, he struck up a friendship with Henry Thoreau (1817–62). Thoreau came to live in Concord and spent two years in a small cabin that he constructed himself at the edge of Walden Pond. It was here that he wrote his most memorable book, *Walden*. The Salem-born novelist Nathaniel Hawthorne (1805–64), a Concord resident for a few years, was also part of the group. At that time, though Louisa May Alcott (1832–88) was just a child, she was already writing poems and romantic stories.

RECOMMENDED TRIPS

Canoes can be rented at the South Bridge Boathouse (on Main Street, Concord) for trips through Concord and the Great Meadows National Wildlife Refuge. Although there are 18 miles (29km) of navigable water, the paddle to the North Bridge and back is an easy two hours. Confirmed landlubbers can take the marked nature trail (3 miles/5km) in the wildlife refuge.

FOR HISTORY BUFFS

"March with the Corps of Grenadiers and Light Infantry ... to Concord, where you will seize and destroy all Artillery, Ammunition, Provisions, Tents, Small Arms, and all Military Stores ... but you will take care that the Soldiers do not plunder the Inhabitants, or hurt private property."
Unfortunately the orders of General Gage were leaked to patriots in Boston and, as the British prepared to cross the Charles River on the night of April 18, two lanterns appeared in the belfry of the Old North Church. A waiting Paul Revere saw the signal and set off on horseback to tell the men of Lexington and Concord to be ready.

The North
Shore

One famous seaport after another follows the curve of the coast north of Boston, from the towns of Gloucester and Marblehead, to Salem and Newburyport. There are hundreds of handsome old houses, and dozens of high-quality museums and art galleries.

ITINERARY		
BOSTON	▸	**Marblehead** (17m-27km)
MARBLEHEAD	▸	**Salem** (5m-8km)
SALEM	▸	**Manchester-by-the-Sea** (7m-11km)
MANCHESTER-BY THE-SEA	▸	**Gloucester** (8m-13km)
GLOUCESTER	▸	**Rockport** (5m-8km)
ROCKPORT	▸	**Pigeon Cove** (2m-3km)
PIGEON COVE	▸	**Essex** (10m-16km)
ESSEX	▸	**Ipswich** (5m-8km)
IPSWICH	▸	**Plum Island** (21m-34km)
PLUM ISLAND	▸	**Newburyport** (11m-18km)
NEWBURYPORT	▸	**Boston** (43m-69km)

1 DAY • 134 MILES • 215KM

⬛ *Greater Boston Convention and Visitors Bureau, Prudential Tower*

▶ *Leave Boston via the Callahan Tunnel, and follow* **Route 1A** *to Lynn. After 8 miles (13km), pass a rotary (roundabout), and bear right onto Carroll Parkway. Follow* **Route 129** *along the sea-wall to Swampscott, and bear right onto Puritan Road, for 1 mile (1.5km) until it rejoins* **Route 129**. *Go right on* **Route 129** *to Ocean Avenue and turn right to Marblehead Neck.*

Marblehead attracted fishermen from Cornwall, England, in 1629

❶ Marblehead Neck

On the road across the causeway, look right for a view of the Boston skyline. To the left, a fleet of sailboats sits anchored in Marblehead harbor. Bear right and follow signs for the Bike Route for about 2 miles (3km) to Chandler Hovey Park and the lighthouse. From the park there are spectacular views all the way to Manchester and Gloucester harbors. Marblehead Neck itself is all quiet residential streets, with neither a shopping center nor a historic district.

▶ *Return to* **Route 129** *and turn right to Marblehead.*

❷ Marblehead

The up-hill-and-down-dale style of the Marblehead's old town reflects the West of England origins of the fishermen who settled here in 1629. On Front Street, the oldest houses cluster round the harbor of what was soon known as the "greatest Towne for fishing in New England." As the seafarers roamed further afield and developed a thriving overseas trade, so the merchants built bigger and better houses. Jeremiah Lee

Mansion is a fine example: a splendid Georgian mansion, built in 1768 and now home to the Marblehead Historical Society. Marblehead sailors played a vital role in the Revolution, and a local boat, the *Hannah*, takes pride of place as America's first warship. Today, tourists envy the luxury yachts which fill the moorings.

⬛ *Information Booth, Pleasant and Spring streets*

▶ *Leave Marblehead on* **Route 114** *and* **Route 1A North** *and drive 5 miles (8km) to Salem.*

❸ Salem

One short period of hysteria in the 17th century singled Salem out from the rest of the North Shore coastal ports. Now, more than 300 years later, witchcraft trials and executions have become big business. Those wanting to relive the gruesome spectacles can visit the Witch Museum and Witch House, but there is much more to see in this historic town. The fine mansions were so impressive that future-president John Adams wrote in 1766: "the houses are the most elegant and grand that I have seen in any of the maritime towns." Examples can be found

Statue of Puritan Roger Conant, who founded Salem in 1626, outside the Salem Witch Museum

on Chestnut, Essex and Federal streets.

The Peabody Museum, arguably America's oldest museum, was started in 1799 by a group of sea captains wishing to display their souvenirs from far-flung voyages. The richest and most impressive section is the Asian Export Art Collection which contains beautiful objects from China, Korea, India and Japan which were made specifically for sale to the West.

The town's nautical traditions are portrayed in the admirable Salem Maritime National Historic Site that snakes along the harbor front. A gold eagle perched over the entrance marks the Custom House, where writer Nathaniel Hawthorne once worked as surveyor of the port.

i Hawthorne Boulevard

FOR HISTORY BUFFS

Salem comes from the Hebrew word *Shalom*, meaning peace. But the calm of Salem was shattered in 1692 when several young girls began to have fits and accused three women of casting spells on them. Panic followed, other accusations were made, and before common sense prevailed, 19 people had been hanged, and one man, Giles Grey, was crushed by rocks. The hysteria was stamped out the following year, when the governor ordered all the so-called witches to be released from prison, probably because his wife had been one of the accused!

▶ Take **Route 1A North** across the bridge over Beverly Harbor, and follow **Route 127** through Beverly for 4 miles (6km) to the Prides Crossing railroad station.

❹ Prides Crossing

When the railroad from Beverly was extended to Manchester in 1840, it crossed land once owned by the Pride family, who supposedly received the grant in the early 1700s from the King of England. The route was used by wealthy Bostonians who left the city and came out to spend the summers by the water in their large mansions. The railroad depot still has separate benches marked for use by Democrats and Republicans. Now, residents of this small village make the trip in and out of Boston every day by car.

▶ Continue on **Route 127** for 3 miles (5km) into the center of Manchester-by-the-Sea.

❺ Manchester-by-the-Sea

Originally settled by Englishmen from Manchester, the town's name was amended recently to emphasize its position at the head of a pretty harbor, graced with its flotilla of sailboats. On one side of the town square is First Parish Church, built in 1807, with a clock face on each side of its distinctive steeple. Visitors come in summer, not just to walk along the waterfront, but also to spend the day on Singing Beach, where the wind "sings" as it whistles along the sand.

▶ *Continue on **Route 127** for 3 miles (5km), then bear right for Magnolia. Continue for 2 miles (3km) through the town center and up the hill on Norman Avenue to Hammond Castle.*

⓺ Hammond Castle Museum

Whenever you use a remote control button to switch television channels or open the garage from your car, the man to thank is Dr. John Hammond (1888–1965). This genius thought up over 800 inventions and was granted 400 patents, mainly to do with electronics. His quirky mind is reflected in the clifftop mansion he built in 1926, which incorporates bits of European buildings: there is an archway built with lava rock from Mount Vesuvius, and a Roman bath. There are even secret passages and a laboratory. His vast 8,200-pipe organ stands in an impressive hall where concerts are given at weekends. Hammond is buried on the grounds with two of his cats and, as requested, poison ivy grows over his grave.

▶ *Return to **Route 127** and continue for 2 miles (3km) to Gloucester.*

⓻ Gloucester

The first landmark in town to meet your eye is *The Man at the Wheel*, the statue of a ship's pilot staring out towards the mouth of the harbor. Perhaps he's looking to find the channel between the lighthouse on Ten Pound Island and Eastern Point Light. The statue was set in place in 1923 to commemorate Gloucester's 300th birthday, and as a reminder that the town continues to be a working port, America's oldest. Although fishing boats still chug in, ready to sell their catch, the fleet has decreased in recent years.

FOR CHILDREN

Rudyard Kipling lived in New England for a few years. In 1897, he published a thrilling tale of derring-do called *Captains Courageous*, based on the then-famous Gloucester fishing fleet. In it, a Portuguese sailor, one of many who came to seek their fortunes on the Massachusetts coast, rescues the son of a wealthy family who has fallen overboard from a liner. Now read on ...

The pier at Gloucester
Inset: *The Man at the Wheel*

However, the maritime tradition attracts tourists, not just for the annual Schooner Festival in early September, but throughout the summer for whale-watching excursions. The Cape Ann Historical Museum is a tribute to artist Fitz Hugh Lane, who lived out his life here. Not surprisingly, he specialized in seascapes.

SPECIAL TO...

There really was a Cap'n Birdseye. As early as 1912, Clarence Birdseye of Gloucester was intrigued to see how the Inuit people of Labrador preserved their food by freezing it. By 1924, he had perfected the bulk deep-freezing technique that is taken for granted today. The Freezing Company concentrated on fruit and vegetables in the early days, but as demand for his products grew, Birdseye needed to speed up the process, so he invented the multiple plate freezer, which is still used. In the 1950s, the company developed fish sticks, or fish fingers, a great favorite with children.

127CC

WHALEWATCHING...

Up and down the coast of New England, boats still set off to hunt for whales. Unlike the 19th century, however, the purpose is not to shoot the majestic mammals with harpoons, but with cameras. Tours depart regularly from Boston, but they also go from Gloucester on the North Shore, from Portsmouth, New Hampshire and from Cape Cod towns such as Provincetown. The favorite places for spotting whales are the Stellwagen Bank and Jeffreys Ledge, both popular feeding grounds. Harbor porpoises and Atlantic white-sided dolphins, relatives of the whales, are also abundant, and have teeth rather than the baleen plates of the whales.

RIGHT WHALES
Named by Yankee whalers, because they were the "right" whales to catch, this is the most endangered species in the world. They are easily recognized by the callosities, crusty growths, on their backs. Reaching up to 50 feet and 60 tons (16m and 61,000kg), these whales can be spotted offshore from April to January.

HUMPBACK WHALES
The name comes from their habit of arching their backs before diving. They are also known to "breach," leaping clear out of the water, a particularly impressive sight, since humpbacks grow up to 50 feet (16m) long and 30 tons (30,500kg) in weight. They are resident off New England from spring to fall.

FIN WHALES
The largest whales in New England waters are also the most common. Reaching 70 feet (21m) in length and 50 tons (51,000kg), fin whales can be identified by their dorsal fin, as well as the white chevron on their backs. Like the humpbacks, they are resident from spring to fall.

SPECIAL TO...

May 22 is Motif No. 1 Day in Rockport. It celebrates an old fishing shack, dating from the mid-1800s, that stands at the end of Bradley Wharf in Rockport Harbor. Local lore has it that, back in the 1920s, art teacher Lester Hornby was confronted by yet another student's sketch of this dark red hut, festooned with lobster traps and colorful lobster floats. "What? Motif number one again!" he exclaimed despairingly to the pupil. Would-be photographers and painters should walk to the end of the wharf to compose their own version of this picturesque icon.

[i] *33 Commercial Street*

▶ *Follow Route 127 for 1 mile (2km), then bear right onto East Main Street for Rocky Neck.*

8 Rocky Neck and Beauport
Rocky Neck is a small settlement of working artists. The oldest such colony in the country, it has survived here since 1916. Some 30 people live on the tiny peninsula, with their studios in wood-shingled shacks. The roads are all one way, narrow and busy on weekends.

Further towards Eastern Point lighthouse is Beauport. From the turn of the century, big spenders such as R. T. Vanderbilt and J. D. Rockefeller, as well as such stars as Joan Crawford, came out here to

Rockport's harbor epitomizes coastal New England

consult Henry Davis Sleeper (1878–1934), *the* interior decorator of his day. In Beauport, his own home, he gave each of the 40 rooms a design theme, from the Lord Byron and Paul Revere Rooms to the China Trade and India Rooms. The house is now a museum, full of his collection of antiques and art.

▶ *Return to Gloucester and follow signs for Alternate Route 127A to Rockport.*

9 Rockport
As its name implies, Rockport's early fame was founded on rock, in particular the granite quarried for many of America's 19th-century monuments, bridges and civic buildings. For the past century, however, Rockport has been better known for its artists' colony, which still flourishes and exhibits at the Rockport Art Association's galleries on Main Street. Despite this bohemian

air, Rockport is "dry," so no liquor may be sold. Years before Prohibition, Hannah Jumper led 200 women of Rockport in the Hatchet Gang Raid of 1856. These militant teetotallers imposed their own ban on booze by smashing every cask, bottle and flask they could find, and the men of Rockport haven't had the courage to ask for a drop ever since. Visitors need not despair: drinks may be enjoyed with a seafood meal – as long as diners bring their own bottles.

The heart of the action in this popular resort is Bearskin Neck, where old fishing lofts have been turned into studios and galleries, restaurants and shops selling souvenirs.

[i] *3 Main Street*

▶ *Leave town, rejoining Route 127, and follow signs for Pigeon Cove (2 miles/3km).*

10 Pigeon Cove
Just off Route 127, this small community boasts an unusual building. At No. 52 Pigeon Hill Street stands the Paper House, built between 1922 and 1942 by Elis Stenman and his family. It took two decades and both the house and the furniture have

been constructed out of 100,000 old newspapers. The walls are 215 sheets thick, the desk is made from the Christian Science Monitor and a bookshelf uses only foreign papers!

▶ *Continue on Route 127 and after 1 mile (1.6km) is the turning for Halibut Point State Park. Route 127 continues past rocky points of land and art galleries to the rotary (round-about) at Route 128. Go west on Route 128, then turn right onto Route 133 west for Essex.*

⓫ Essex

The 40 or so antique shops that line Main Street in this small, sleepy-looking town draw dealers and amateurs from all over America for the quality and excellent value of their wares. The small Shipbuilding Museum, also on Main Street, recalls the town's heyday in the days of sail.

SPECIAL TO...

Woodmans of Essex is credited with inventing fried clams back in 1916 and is still one of the best-known clam shacks in New England. "Woodie's" is known for serving fresh, delicious fried clams, clam cakes, and New England clam chowder made with milk, butter, lots of potatoes and clams.

▶ *Continue to Ipswich. Route 133 north joins Route 1A.*

⓬ Ipswich

Ipswich has several fine 17th-century houses, particularly the 1640 John Whipple House (53 South Main Street), one of the oldest Puritan homes still standing. The main draw here, however, is out of town, some 6 miles (10km) along Argilla Road. In 1925, Chicago industrialist Richard T. Crane set his summer home right on the crest of Castle Hill. This 59-room Great House recalls the stately homes of England, with its 63-foot

(18.9m) long gallery and 16-foot (4.8m) high ceilings. It is open for tours, and there are also concerts and an antique auto show in the grounds each summer. Down below, the 5-mile (8km) long pristine beach is one of the most beautiful north of Cape Cod. Beware, however, of "greenhead time," the three weeks at the end of July and early August when the voracious, biting "greenhead" flies take over the strand.

▶ *Continue north on Route 133 and Route 1A north for 11 miles (18km) to Hanover Street. Turn right for Plum Island and the Parker Refuge.*

BACK TO NATURE

Located one mile north of the turn-off to Crane's Beach on Route 133, Wolf Hollow is home to 17 North American wolves. After listening to a presentation about this nearly extinct animal, visitors can watch the wolves as they respond to commands from their trainers. Fear not, for although they are at close range, a strong fence separates observers from the observed.

⓭ Plum Island and the Parker River Wildlife Refuge

With its vast expanse of salt marsh, this is a major stopping point for birds migrating north and south each year. Early spring and late autumn are the ideal times to see some of the 300 species. Stand on the observation platform built along the roads to observe cranes, herons and the inevitable Canada geese.

Plum Island, first visited by Samuel de Champlain in 1601, is a 6-mile (10km) long beach that acts as a breakwater to the coastal towns. Stop on the access road and follow the boardwalks across the dunes, but remember that swimming is dangerous here because of the cold water and the strong undertows.

▶ *Return to Route 1A and continue into Newburyport.*

⓮ Newburyport

As in so many New England towns, the charming wooden houses of Colonial times were destroyed by fire and have been rebuilt in brick. A renovation program in the 1970s and 1980s tidied up the rundown sea front and restored the line-up of fine Federal and Greek Revival architecture. Now this ship-building town at the mouth of the Merrimack River is an attractive, if busy, place to spend time. The Custom House on Water Street is given over to a museum of all things maritime, including a re-creation of a ship's bridge.

Two centuries ago, the town commissioned Charles Bulfinch, the architect of the State House in Boston, to design the Courthouse on High Street. This street is often called "sea captain row," with mansions such as the three-story Cushing House, built in 1808 by John Cushing. His son, Caleb, was the first emissary sent by the United States to China, and his collection of fine porcelain, paintings and cabinetware from China fills the 21 rooms.

ⓘ *29 State Street*

▶ *Leave on High Street (Route 113) and follow signs to I–95 south and Route 128. (Do not take Route 1.) Take I–95 south, then west. After about 30 miles (48km), turn south onto I–93 for Boston.*

RECOMMENDED WALKS

Halibut Point State Park is a delightful place to stop and stretch your legs, with well-maintained nature and walking trails. The point is not named for fish; it was originally called "Haul About Point" because sailing ships had to "come about" here and tack to sail around Cape Ann.

Cape Cod

2 DAYS • 241 MILES • 387KM

This 62-mile (99km) long peninsula is one of the country's eminent vacation playgrounds. Route 6A, the Old King's Highway, passes through 300-year-old communities where every other house seems to be a craft shop, antique store or bed and breakfast.

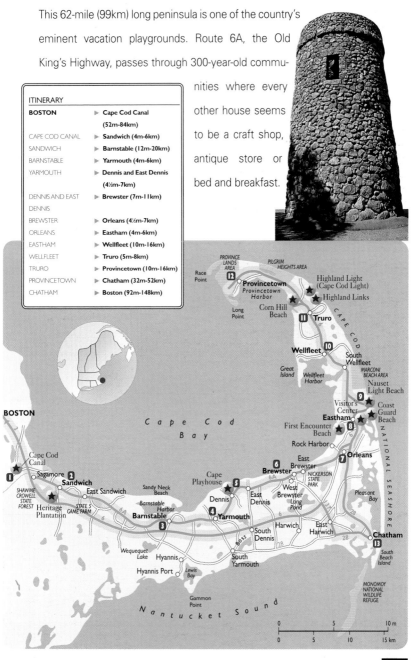

mile (216km) journey. Traders welcomed the opening of the canal in 1914, 300 years after Myles Standish of the Plymouth Colony first proposed the idea. Running 17 miles (28km) from Cape Cod Bay to Buzzard's Bay, the Canal is surprisingly 160 yards (150m) wide. Nowadays, recreational yachtsmen take the short cut, watched by fishermen and cyclists on the Cape Cod Canal Bikepath.

▶ Now on *Route 6A, continue to Sandwich (4miles/6km).*

② Sandwich
Sandwich reeks of old-world charm, due to its fine collection of 18th- and 19th-century houses, the Wren-like spire on the First Church of Christ and tree-lined streets. Overlooking Shawme Pond is shingled Dexter Grist Mill, still in working order, and one of the oldest houses on the Cape, the 1654 Hoxie House. In classic 'salt box' style, with diamond window panes, it contains 17th-century furniture, tools and tableware inside. The Eldred House, next door, is now a museum dedicated to the children's author Thornton W. Burgess, best remembered for his *Peter Cottontail* stories. Despite its 300 years of history, however, Sandwich is no living museum: its lobster boats are actually working vessels, handled by real fisherman.

▶ *Continue on Route 6A to Barnstable (12½ miles/20km).*

③ Barnstable
Off the road to the left, 4 miles (6km) before Barnstable, Sandy Neck is a rich nature reserve where the dunes were trampled by U.S. soldiers training for the North African Desert campaign during World War II. When a north wind blows, watch for windsurfers skimming across Barnstable Harbor.

In town, drop into the Sturgis Library to see the original home of the Reverend John Lothrop, one of the first residents of the 1639 settlement. The library's genealogical records are useful for those searching out family roots, especially if they are descended from the Lothrops, who occupy much of the cemetery. The main industries in the 19th century were growing cranberries and making bricks, some of which are now collector's items.

▶ *Continue on Route 6A to Yarmouth.*

④ Yarmouth
The Captain Bangs Hallet House reflects the affluence and sophistication of a successful sea captain's life in the 19th century.

Fine example of Sandwich's famous glass, highly valued by collectors
Page 23: Scargo Hill Observatory

[i] *Greater Boston Convention and Visitors Bureau, Prudential Tower*

▶ *Leave Boston on **Route 93**, **Route 3** south to the Sagamore Bridge, crossing the Cape Cod Canal.*

⓪ Cape Cod Canal
Sailing from Boston around the outside of Cape Cod has always been dangerous. Indeed, even just a century ago, some 25 ships a year foundered on the 135-

Situated near the Yarmouthport Post Office, its handsome Greek Revival façade hides the original 1740 structure. It is now the headquarters of the local historical society, and the starting point for pleasant walks through a nature preserve along the Botanic Trails of Yarmouth.

The 1780 Winslow-Crocker House, now run by the Society for the Preservation of New England Antiquities, is filled with high-quality furniture and household objects made in Colonial and Federal times by New England craftsmen. Near by, children can pet animals at the 200-year-old Taylor-Bray Farm.

▶ Continue on **Route 6A** to Dennis and East Dennis.

5 Dennis and East Dennis
Few men can match Josiah Dennis' claim of having five villages named for him. This 17th-century Congregational minister is immortalized in East, West and South Dennis, as well as Dennisport and Dennis itself. In his home, the Josiah Dennis Manse, visitors can see his portable pulpit, watch weavers at work in the attic and browse round the small maritime museum. There is a 200-year-old schoolhouse on the grounds. Not quite as ancient, but still the oldest summer theater in the U.S.A., is the Cape Playhouse, where Bette Davis worked as an usherette before treading the boards. Gregory Peck and Henry Fonda also started their acting careers here. Don't miss the Cape Museum of Fine Arts in the grounds, or the church-like building nearby which is actually an art deco cinema, complete with leather seats and a mural by 20th-century American artist Rockwell Kent.

Take time to see the lie of the land from the Scargo Hill Observatory where, on a good day, you can see Provincetown, 20 miles (32km) to the north.

ℹ️ *Dennis Chamber of Commerce, 242 Swan River Road, West Dennis*

▶ Continue on **Route 6A** to Brewster (7 miles/11km).

6 Brewster
On and behind Route 6A, which doubles as Main Street in Brewster, stand the elegant clapboard houses of 19th-century sea captains. At the height of New England's trading with China, as many as 100 lived here, and many are buried in the graveyard next to the "Captains' Church," the First Parish Church. Memories and records of that era are in the Brewster Historical Society Museum at Spruce Hill, East Brewster.

Other museums worth a visit include the New England Fire and History Museum, which has a unique 1929 Mercedes-Benz fire engine, and reconstructions of a blacksmith's and an apothecary's. More souvenirs of yesteryear include the old Post Office and Barbershop at the 200-year-old windmill at West Brewster.

ℹ️ *Brewster Chamber of Commerce, 74 Locust Lane*

You can watch the process of corn being ground at Brewster

> #### FOR CHILDREN
>
> The Cape Cod Museum of Natural History at Brewster is popular for its aquarium and lively exhibitions, lectures and tours explaining the Cape's bird and animal life, and its geological beginnings. As well as two short trails in the wildlife sanctuary, the longer John Wing Trail is a fine walk to the unspoiled beach. Remember, though, to check times of tides before setting out. The museum also organizes nature trips by boat to the Monomoy Islands, a wildlife refuge off Chatham.

▶ Continue on **Route 6A** to Orleans roundabout.

7 Orleans
The name rhymes with "beans," even though it commemorates the French Duke of Orléans,

BACK TO NATURE

The alewife is a type of herring that spawns in fresh water every three or four years. In spring, these silvery fish swim up the narrow Stony Brook creek, using the fish ladder to bypass the water-powered Grist Mill on Stony Brook Road, just north of Brewster, off Route 6A, and return to the ponds where they were conceived. This is one of nature's miracles that can be seen close up in April and May.

who fled here from the French Revolution in 1797. This busy town, near the junction of Routes 6 and 6A, has been the "hub of the Outer Cape" for two centuries. Back then fish, and salt for preserving the catch, were shipped direct to Boston from tiny Rock Harbor on Cape Cod Bay.

i *Orleans Chamber of Commerce, Post Office Square*

▶ *Continue north for 4 miles (6km) on what is now* **Route 6** *to Eastham. Just before the town, the road to Fort Hill, on the right, provides panoramic views above the cupola-crowned Victorian house of whaling captain Edward Penniman.*

8 Eastham

The windmill opposite the Town Hall in Eastham, pronounced East-Ham, was built in Plymouth in 1688, rebuilt in Truro, then moved to its present site in 1808. The oldest windmill on the Cape, it is celebrated on Windmill Weekend in September. Samoset Road leads to Cape Cod Bay. Here, First Encounter Beach is the legendary site of the first meeting between the Pilgrims and the Native Americans. A metal plaque explains how arrows and musket fire were exchanged when the newcomers encountered the Indians, who remembered a slave trader kidnapping some of their people six years before. Don't expect to find any arrowheads, though; the Pilgrims gathered up the arrows and sent them back to England as curiosities.

From here to Provincetown, the Cape is a landscape of steep dunes tufted with grass. On the Atlantic side, breakers pound the flat beaches while lighthouses emphasize the sense of solitude.

At the Salt Pond Visitor Center, beyond Eastham, displays and films explain the ecology and wildlife of the 27,000-acre (10,800-hectare) Cape Cod National Seashore, a stretch of unspoiled coastline some 40 miles long (64km). A road leads to Coast Guard Beach where, in 1929, Henry Beston spent a year writing his classic nature journal, *The Outermost House*. The book is evocative, and perhaps more readable than Henry Thoreau's *Walden*. The beach is superb.

Eye-catching façade on Cape Cod

The Nauset Light serves as a reminder of the region's sea-faring heritage

ℹ️ *Eastham Chamber of Commerce, Route 6A, Eastham*

▶ *Detour east to Coast Guard Beach, on Doane Road, then turn left on Ocean View Drive to Nauset Light Beach.*

SPECIAL TO...

The local Indians taught the Pilgrims how to cook shellfish and New Englanders still use the same method for a clambake on the beach. Dig a shallow pit into the sand, line it with stones and build a wood fire. When the wood has burned down, cover the hot stones with layers of damp seaweed, clean clams, more seaweed, corn on the cob and bluefish. Seal with a tarpaulin. Leave for an hour to steam, then uncover and eat.

9 Nauset Light Beach

As you drive through the typical scrub oak and pine that is the natural vegetation of Cape Cod, you will catch glimpses of the ocean to the right. You can venture down to a stretch of seemingly unending sandy beach, where the Atlantic thunders and you can get away from other people simply by taking a walk.

SCENIC ROUTES

The Cape Cod Scenic Railroad, complete with commentary, runs by cranberry bogs and marshes between Hyannis and the Cape Cod Canal. This should not be confused with the Cape Cod Rail Trail, where there is no longer a train. The Rail Trail follows the former Boston to Provincetown railroad route between South Dennis and Wellfleet. Here, the bed has been replaced by a smooth, 25-mile (40km) path. Its flatness makes it ideal for joggers, hikers and cyclists.

▶ *Loop back to Route 6 via Cable Road and Nauset Road to Wellfleet (7 miles/11km).*

10 Wellfleet

Famous for its oysters since Samuel de Champlain's Gallic taste-buds were tickled in 1606, this charming town, complete with picturesque harbor and photogenic old houses, now attracts artists whose works fill its 22 art galleries. Fishing still goes on, and the clock on the First Congregational Church

Wellfleet was once a Colonial whaling and cod fishing port

reflects Wellfleet's nautical tradition by following ships' time, confusing landlubbers by chiming, for example, two bells at one, five and nine o'clock. It is reportedly the only clock in the world to do so.

[i] *Wellfleet Chamber of Commerce, off route 6, South Wellfleet*

FOR HISTORY BUFFS

"... I extend on behalf of the American people most cordial greetings and good wishes to you and all the people of the British Empire." President Theodore Roosevelt's transatlantic message to King Edward VII of England in 1903 was the first sent from Guglielmo Marconi's Wireless Telegraph Station in South Wellfleet.

At Orleans, the French Cable Station had already linked up with Brest in France in 1891. The stations were situated here because the Cape is one of the closest parts of the U.S. to Europe.

▶ *Continue north on **Route 6** for 5 miles (8km) to Truro.*

RECOMMENDED WALKS

The Great Island Trail is an 8-mile (13km) round-trip walk along a narrow spit of sand. The trail is covered at high tide, and has views up to Provincetown and down to Brewster. To get there, follow Holbrook Avenue from Wellfleet Center. Turn right on to Chequesset Road and drive past the dunes and salt ponds to the car park.

🔟 Truro

Originally named Dangerfield, this is a small, quiet neighborhood. On the way to North Truro, the Highland or Cape Cod Light is on South Highland Road. Standing on the site of the Cape's first lighthouse (1791), it has been damaged and restored, moved and rebuilt. The oldest golf course on the Cape, Highland Links, is nearby.

Back on Route 6, turn down Corn Hill Road for Corn Hill Beach where, in the car park, is a little taste of Pilgrim lore. Soon after the Pilgrim Father's arrival, Captain Myles Standish came across a cache of corn buried by an Indian in the sand. Desperate for food, he took it, but on meeting with the owner about a year later, Standish repaid him what was owed.

Further north, park the car and hike the short Pilgrim Spring Trail to the spot where legend has it that the Pilgrim Fathers first found "springs of fresh water" after their gruelling transatlantic crossing.

[i] *Truro Chamber of Commerce, Route 6A*

▶ *Continue north on **Route 6** to Provincetown (10 miles/16km).*

🔟 Provincetown

Although the Vikings are reckoned to have landed here long before, in AD1004, this is where it all started for the Americans on November 11 or 21, 1620, depending on which calendar you use. The *Mayflower* dropped anchor in what is now Provincetown Harbor, after a 65-day voyage. Of the 102 passengers, one had died, but a baby had been born. Myles Standish, a soldier of fortune hired by the Pilgrims for protection, rowed ashore. These days, a rather unimpressive plaque on Commercial Street marks the event. After five weeks, the Pilgrims continued on their way, hoping to find a more hospitable site for settlement. They are remembered with the Pilgrim Monument, found in the center of town. Built in 1910, the granite tower soars 252 feet (76m) high. The stairs are a real test of stamina, but climbers can read the plaques noting the founding dates of Massachusetts towns and *Mayflower* descendants. The reward is the observation platform at the top. The museum at the base tells the story of Provincetown.

The town's main industry of deep-water fishing for cod, mackerel and whales was established in the early 18th century. Although the fishing passed over a century ago, 35 boats still go out each morning to supply New York and Boston with fresh fish, and whale watching is a popular excursion in wintertime.

Today, in Provincetown, known almost universally as P-town, the fun really begins after the day-trippers have gone home. Artists have been coming here since Charles Hawthorne arrived in 1899. He taught for 30 years and his painting, *Fish Cleaners*, can be seen in the Town Hall. Edward Hopper and Jackson Pollock are among the famous who joined the amateurs, working in the dazzling light on the shore. Playwright Eugene O'Neill wrote and produced his earliest plays in what was, and still is, a surprisingly bohemian town where everyone comes to have a good time.

i 307 Commercial Street at MacMillan Wharf

▶ Return on **Route 6**, but before the Orleans rotary (roundabout), turn off on **Route 28** for Chatham (32 miles/52km)

🅱 Chatham
Sitting right on Cape Cod's "elbow," Chatham relies on more than just tourism, thanks to its busy fishing fleet. The bounty of the sea is represented by the striking 1992 sculpture *Provider* on Fish Pier. Here, each afternoon, crates of flounder and haddock, cod and halibut are transferred straight from the boats to waiting trucks. Take a walk along Main Street, with its clapboard houses, restaurants, shops and 175-year-old Mayo House, the headquarters of the local historical society. Train buffs should head for the Railroad Museum in the 1887 depot, where a diorama of the railroad yard as it was in 1920 is a recent addition.

i 533 Main Street

▶ Take **Route 28** out of Chatham. Turn north on **Route 137** and rejoin **Route 6** at Exit 11. Follow **Route 6** back to the Sagamore Bridge, then **Route 3** to **Route 93** and back to Boston.

Provincetown, overlooked by the Center Methodist Church
Inset: cranberries at Plymouth

2 DAYS • 181½ MILES • 292KM

The Berkshire
Hills

The Berkshires were once the exclusive playground of the rich. Now these forested slopes are a vacation destination for everyone, particularly music lovers who are drawn to the numerous summer festivals.

ITINERARY	
SPRINGFIELD	▶ **Monterey (32m-51km)**
MONTEREY	▶ **Great Barrington**
	(9m-15km)
GREAT BARRINGTON	▶ **Sheffield (7.5m-12km)**
SHEFFIELD	▶ **Stockbridge (20m-32km)**
STOCKBRIDGE	▶ **Lenox (7m-11km)**
LENOX	▶ **Pittsfield (6m-10km)**
PITTSFIELD	▶ **Williamstown (22m-35km)**
WILLIAMSTOWN	▶ **Shelburne Falls (32m-51km)**
SHELBURNE FALLS	▶ **Deerfield (11m-18km)**
DEERFIELD	▶ **Northampton**
	(16m-26km)
NORTHAMPTON	▶ **Springfield (19m-31km)**

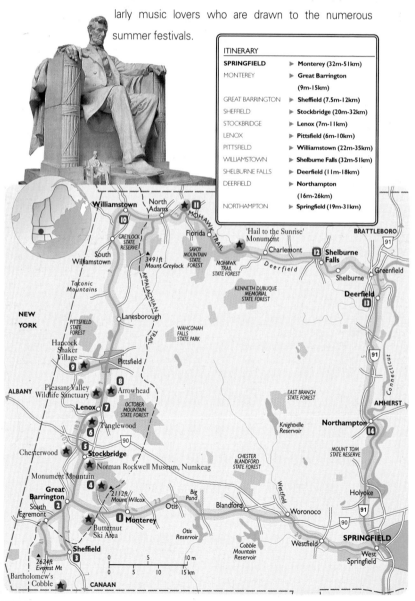

ℹ️ *34 Boland Way, Springfield*

▶ *From Springfield, take **Route 20** west across the Connecticut river, through West Springfield, passing the Exposition grounds, site of the huge "Big E," New England's largest fair, held every September. Bear left on **Route 23** west at Woronoco. Drive through Blandford and Otis to Monterey.*

❶ Monterey

The Mexican name of this town honors General Zachary Taylor, a hero in the Mexican-American War (1846–8). So popular was "Old Rough and Ready" Taylor after his victories at Monterey and Buena Vista, that one Kentuckian predicted (correctly) that the general would win the 1848 presidential election "by spontaneous combustion." Born in Virginia, Taylor had no known connections with the village.

▶ *Continue on **Route 23**, past the Butternut Ski Area.*

❷ Great Barrington

Local inventor William Stanley assured that this small town would have its place in the history books. He first demonstrated the potential of using alternating current here in 1886 by lighting up 24 shops on the main street. Stanley's system, more efficient than Edison's cumbersome direct current lighting, led to more widespread use of electricity. A lamp and plaque in the small park at the corner of Main and Cottage streets tells the story.

On five Saturdays in summer, St. James Church hosts the Aston Magna Festival. It is the oldest festival in America devoted to baroque, classical and early romantic music, all played on period instruments. Chamber concerts, sometimes involving members of the Boston Symphony Orchestra, are another summer feature, held at Searles Castle (1886), on Main Street.

ℹ️ *Chamber of Commerce, 362 Main Street*

▶ *Leave town on **Route 7** and head south for 7½ miles (12km) to Sheffield.*

Monterey's One Room School
Opposite: Abraham Lincoln's statue, Chesterwood Studio

BACK TO NATURE

About 1½ miles (2km) south of Sheffield, is one of several small, flat-topped hills known locally as 'cobbles.' Barthlomew's Cobble is a 500-million-year-old lump of limestone and quartzite, doubling as a nature reserve. The Ledges Interpretative Trail (20 minutes) winds through rugged, glacially formed rocks. Here, some 45 species of fern, many of them rare, grow in the summer. A small museum records some of the 900 types of plants and wildlife in the area.

3 Sheffield

Back in the 18th century, two minor events helped shape American democracy. In 1773, the Sheffield Declaration demanded freedom for the individual, while in 1787, Shays' Rebellion ended here. Poor farmers, many of them Revolutionary War veterans, thought they were being over-taxed and rebelled under Captain Daniel Shays. The seven-month protest brought the end of imprisonment for debt, and also strengthened the case for federal and state laws. A century or so ago, local people carved a large slab of local marble into a monument honoring the rebellion. It stands in a farmer's field north of the town. Today, antique shops line the main street and the Sheffield Pottery sells ceramics made by artists from all over New England.

▶ *Leave Sheffield west on Berkshire School Road to* **Route 41** *and turn north. Join* **Route 23** *and take it through South Egremont to Great Barrington. Rejoin* **Route 7** *and head north to Monument Mountain.*

4 Monument Mountain

This jumble of huge boulders has long been a favorite for picnickers and hikers. Back in 1850, two of New England's best-known authors, Herman Melville and Nathaniel Hawthorne, first met here. Caught in a thunderstorm, they took shelter, drank champagne with their companions, and listened to a recitation of *The Story of the Indian Girl*. The poem relates the local legend of a love-lorn girl who leapt to her death from this mountain.

▶ *Continue north on* **Route 7** *to Stockbridge.*

5 Stockbridge

Stockbridge was created in 1722 as a well-meaning experiment by the London Society for the Propagation of the Gospel in Foreign Lands. The local Indians were invited to settle alongside the English colonists in the hope that they would become "civilized" and follow Christian and English customs. Despite the support given by the Indians during the Revolutionary War, the Colonial ambitions of the settlers put paid to the experiment.

Even today, the Berkshires remains picture-postcard pretty, with tall maples and elms. There isn't a telephone or electricity pole in sight, all the cables have been buried underground. The Red Lion Inn is the heart of the town, as it has always been since pre-Revolutionary days. Although this old coaching inn burned down last century, the Victorian replacement retains the wide porches, with rocking chairs for watching life pass by.

FOR HISTORY BUFFS

Nearby is the charming wooden Ashley House, named after Colonel John Ashley who campaigned for The Sheffield Declaration equal rights in the late 18th century. His slave, Mum Bet, is better remembered, since she used her master's arguments to gain her own freedom in 1783. The woodwork and paneling in Ashley's upstairs study show the skill of the craftsmen who built the house in 1735.

RECOMMENDED WALKS

Two trails lead to Squaw Peak, the 1,735-foot (520m) summit of Monument Mountain. The easier trail takes about an hour; follow the sign for Indian Monument. The longer hike (3 miles/5km) climbs through oaks, white pines, laurels and chestnuts, revealing mysterious caves under overhanging rocks and rushing streams. A fine view can be had from the top.

Norman Rockwell's studio, in Stockbridge

This beautiful area has long been a favorite with artistic types. The third movement of *Three Places in New England* includes *The Housatonic at Stockbridge*, which was inspired by an early morning walk along the Housatonic River by New England composer, Charles Ives. Two other artists are honored by museums: Norman Rockwell (1894–1978) and Daniel Chester French (1850–1931).

Installed in the old Linwood estate, the Norman Rockwell Museum has 600 of the illustrator's works, and contains his studio, which was moved here lock, stock, palette and paintbrush. Rockwell's *Saturday Evening Post* magazine covers made him a household name, and all 321 are here. Freckle-faced boys, cuddly grannies and Thanksgiving turkeys all appear bathed in the glow of nostalgia, yet Rockwell did not use professional models. His scenes of everyday life in 20th-century America show "sincere, honest, homespun types." Those types included friends, neighbors and even himself.

Near by is Chesterwood, the summer home and studio of sculptor Daniel Chester French. The best known of his 1,000 works on display are national symbols: the solemn, seated figure of Abraham Lincoln in the Lincoln Memorial in Washington D.C. and *The Minute Man* statue at the Old North Bridge in Concord, Massachusetts. He rolled his plaster and clay models out into the garden on a short section of railroad tracks to study the effect of natural light and shadow upon them.

Besides attracting artists, the Berkshires became a resort for turn-of-the-century millionaires. Up Prospect Hill is Numkeag, the Choate family's magnificent estate. The 23-room mansion vies for attention with the landscaping. Besides collecting Chinese ceramics and porcelain, Mabel Choate also helped

---

SPECIAL TO...

The 1969 film, *Alice's Restaurant*, was based on an incident that has become a legend. After folk singer Arlo Guthrie and friends had enjoyed their Thanksgiving dinner in an old church in Housatonic, they deposited the leftovers outside the Stockbridge town dump. Guthrie was arrested by Officer Obie, and ended up in jail. The conviction meant that Guthrie, a Vietnam protester, could not be drafted for the war. As for Alice and her restaurant, she had several in the area; one is now Naji's, off Stockbridge's Main Street.

Fletcher Steele design the impressive gardens. The birch walk alone is worth the entrance fee.

▶ Leave town on **Route 102** west. Turn right on **Route 183** north at the Berkshire Botanical Garden and continue north for 6 miles (10km) to Tanglewood.

🌀 Tanglewood

The former country estate of the Tappan family is now synonymous with music. Although the New York Symphony first performed here in 1934, it is the Boston Symphony Orchestra that has made Tanglewood its summer home since 1936. Over the years, millions have come to picnic on the grounds before listening to concerts in the 6,000-seat Koussevitzky Music Shed. Great conductors such as Leonard Bernstein and Seiji Ozawa have directed here. In 1994, the 1,200-seat Seija Ozawa Hall was added: the rear wall opens on to a grassy hillside. Jazz, folk and pop are also on the program, along with recitals by students from the prestigious Tanglewood summer music school. Also in the grounds is a reproduction of author Nathaniel Hawthorne's Little Red House, the summer cottage where he wrote *The Tanglewood Tales* and *The House of the Seven Gables*.

Tanglewood's new 1,200-seat Seiji Ozawa Hall

Williamstown's Gothic cathedral
Inset: Hancock Shaker Village

▶ Follow **Route 183** to Lenox.

7 Lenox

Because of the film *The Age of Innocence*, there has been renewed interest in the Pulitzer Prize-winning writer Edith Wharton (1862–1937). Visitors come to this attractive town which was the haunt of some of America's richest families more than a century ago. The Vanderbilts, Carnegies and other stars of New York's upper crust summered in what they referred to as "Berkshire cottages." Some of these grand estates still exist, others are charming small hotels such as the Wheatleigh and the Blantyre. The Mount, Wharton's own 35-room mansion, was built to her own rigid specifications. She spent her happiest years here (1902–11), writing such novels as *Ethan Frome* in bed each morning. She delighted in looking east over the "outdoor rooms," the splendid gardens and pond that she designed. The grounds are now used for the popular alfresco productions of the resident performers, Shakespeare and Company.

ⓘ *Chamber of Commerce,
75 Main Street*

▶ *Continue north on **Route 7A/7** towards Pittsfield. On the right, just before the town, are signs for Arrowhead.*

8 Arrowhead

Author Herman Melville (1819–91) was inspired by the Berkshires. Between 1850 and 1863, he lived on this farm where the views reminded him of his seafaring days: "I look out of my window in the morning when I rise as I would out of the porthole of a ship in the Atlantic." He could see the humpbacked, whale-like shape of Mount Greylock, a constant influence as he wrote *Moby Dick*. The novel did not sell, so Melville was forced to leave Arrowhead and take a job as a customs officer in New York. He died a poor man.

ⓘ *RSVP Tourist Information Booth, Park Square, Pittsfield*

▶ *Continue north for 2 miles (3km) to Pittsfield, turn left on **Route 20** and drive 3 miles (5km) to Hancock Shaker Village.*

9 Hancock Shaker Village

The Shakers, a socialist Christian sect, are remembered for their use of dance in religious services, and their exquisitely simple but practical furniture and architecture. The last of the Shakers left Hancock in 1960, after 170 years, but their homes, workshops, herb gardens and farm have been restored and revived.

Typical is the three-story round barn, built in 1826, where one man standing in the center can feed 54 cows with ease. Shaker food is served on Saturday nights in summer. The tranquility of the 1,200 acres (480 hectares) of meadows and woodlands clearly reinforces Hancock's original Shaker name: the City of Peace.

▶ *Return to Pittsfield and **Route 7**. Continue north for 22 miles (35km) to Williamstown on **Route 7**.*

10 Williamstown

Revolutionary soldier Colonel Ephraim Williams' gift of money ensured that both the town and college would bear his name. With that, he outdid earlier educational benefactors such as John Harvard and Nicholas Brown, who only have schools named for them. Today, Williams College is one of the country's most distinguished small colleges, and the town is one of the most attractive in New England.

There is plenty here for culture addicts. First on anyone's list should be the Sterling and Francine Clark Art Institute, housed in a stunning white, marble, temple-like building. The art collection was created by the Singer sewing machine heir and his French wife and features works by European and American painters. Included are *At the Concert*, one of 30 paintings by Pierre Auguste Renoir; a study of Rouen Cathedral by Claude Monet and *Rockets and Blue Lights* by J. M. W. Turner.

Next is the college's own Museum of Art, which concentrates on non-Western and Ancient art. Contemporary works, such as Andy Warhol's yellow and black self-portrait are on display. Also on the campus is the Chapin Library of Rare Books and Manuscripts. A special celebration is held on the Fourth of July, as copies of the Four Founding Documents of the United States are displayed here: the Articles of Confederation, the Declaration of Independence, the Constitution, and the Bill of

BACK TO NATURE

Halfway between Lenox and Pittsfield is the Pleasant Valley Wildlife Sanctuary. With its hummingbirds and beavers, this is a delightful place for a stroll. Some 7 miles (11km) of marked trails meander through the 1,400 acres (560 hectares) of meadow and forest.

Rights. For over 40 years, the Williamstown Theater Festival has attracted such star names as Paul Newman and Joanne Woodward to participate in the summer season.

▶ Drive east on **Route 2**, which becomes the Mohawk Trail. Follow this to Shelburne Falls.

▣ The Mohawk Trail

Three hundred years ago, Native Americans crossed the Berkshire Hills by walking a footpath cut through the forest. Later, pioneer settlers broadened the route on their way through to what is now New York State. Opened in 1914 as one of America's first "scenic highways," the Mohawk Trail is a popular drive these days, especially in the fall (see pages 102–3). The Mohawk tribe is remembered with *Hail to the Sunrise*, the statue of a serene Indian brave, his arms raised to the east.

▶ Continue east on **Route 2**.

▣ Shelburne Falls

Hamlets dot this rugged road as it passes through forests and along the edges of gorges. Although little seems to have changed in Shelburne Falls since the gushing water drove the mills, members of the local horticultural society did have the ingenuity to disguise a 400-foot (120m) long trolley bridge with a hanging flower garden, the Bridge of Flowers.

▶ Continue to Greenfield and turn south on **Route 5** to historic Deerfield.

▣ Deerfield

Called simply "The Street," Deerfield's main thoroughfare is

The "Hail to the Sunrise" memorial at the entrance to the Mohawk Trail State Forest lined with the most impressive collection of original Colonial houses in New England. The surrounding fields and absence of advertising completes the film-set effect. A dozen of the 65 18th- and 19th-century houses are open to the public, revealing a potted history of early American interior decorating, from furniture to textiles and silverware.

For those in a hurry, the Memorial Hall Museum explains much of the town's rich, if violent, history. In 1675, Indians massacred farmers as they paused to eat grapes, giving a nearby stream its present name of Bloody Brook. In 1704, the French and Indians ravaged the town in the depths of winter, carrying off 112 prisoners to Canada. The Indian House Door, with its gaping hole hacked by a tomahawk, is preserved in the Memorial Hall. The Hall was once used by students at the 200-year-old Deerfield Academy, a well-known boarding school. By contrast, the colors and restoration work in the Wells-Thorn House recall happier days. In 1774, residents raised a liberty pole, and declared their independence nine days before the historic Fourth of July, 1776.

▶ *At this point you have a choice. Continue south for*

*16 miles (26km) on **Route 5** to Northampton or use the faster route, **I–91**.*

14 Northampton

With its mixture of industrial and educational heritage, Northampton is a pleasant, balanced sort of town. Little evidence remains that it was first settled in 1654. In the 1980s, a vigorous program of downtown renewal sprouted restaurants and boutiques.

It is the home of one of America's first women's colleges, founded in 1875 by Sophia Smith, and Smith College is still one of the nation's most prestigious schools.

▶ *Return to **I–91** south and drive to Springfield.*

FOR CHILDREN

Cowabunga! Northampton has a thriving, if small, video industry which was responsible for the Teenage Mutant Ninja Turtles. Kevin Eastman and Peter Laird, who invented the subterranean terrors at their Mirage Studios, are also responsible for the Words and Pictures Museum of Fine Sequential Art in the Round House, on Main Street. In normal speak, this is a comic book store and museum.

Dwight House is a delightful example of early 18th-century architecture in Deerfield

FOR HISTORY BUFFS

"This is my letter to the world, that never wrote to me ..." penned the poet and recluse Emily Dickinson (1830–86) who lived in Amherst, northeast of Northampton, on Route 9. Of her 1,700 poems, only 11 had been published by the time she died. Hundreds were later found in her bedroom. Dickinson rarely left the house, but was a favorite with local children, lowering baskets of her home-baked gingerbread to them from her window. Most of her papers and belongings are kept at Harvard University and Amherst College, but her white dress hangs in her house. The garden at Amherst is a delight.

SPECIAL TO...

Sylvester Graham of Northampton was a health food fanatic and gave his name to Graham flour, a type of wholewheat flour which is more familiar when made into Graham Crackers.

BOSTON

With its unique blend of history and modern development, its "walkable" downtown and efficient public transport system, Boston is a delight for the visitor. Words like "sophisticated" and "civilized" are often used to describe this city that feels European but is the birthplace of American liberty. Balancing all this is a lively student population of over 250,000, from around 60 colleges and universities.

The city owes its foundation to the sea. When the Puritans settled here in 1630, they found poor soil, but a fine harbor. By 1700, only the ports of London and Bristol outranked Boston. Until 1755, Boston was the largest city in North America. Its place on the American stage, however, was guaranteed less by wealth and more by its independent thinkers, who had been in the forefront of the Independence movement (see pages 8–9).

Boston's great strength is that it has moved with the times. Soon after Independence, the rich merchants moved to the elegant estate developed on Beacon Hill where families such as the Cabots, Lodges and Lowells established an almost European aristocracy in the land of democracy. These "Boston Brahmins," as historian Oliver Wendell Holmes dubbed them, considered themselves the "hub of the solar system," and the term "Hub" is one of many nicknames for the city.

When the city's vitality faded in the 1960s, a bold plan of urban renewal revitalized the downtown. Faneuil Hall Market, once a decaying group of waterside warehouses, became a throbbing tourist attraction, with shops and restaurants.

The USS *Constitution*

As well as theater, music and art galleries, sport plays a major part in the life of the city. The professional teams boast proud histories in the nation's four favorite sports: baseball (the Red Sox), ice hockey (the Bruins), basketball (the Celtics) and football (the New England Patriots). As for getting around, that is easy. "The T," as locals call the MBTA (Massachusetts Bay Transport Authority), was the country's first such subway system, opened in 1897.

Tour 5

The Boston Freedom Trail is a "must" for anyone interested in American history. A red line on the pavement leads visitors along the world's first self-guided walking tour of its kind. Along the route are buildings that played an important role in the uprising against British Colonial rule over 200 years ago. This is no dry re-run of history, however.

There are also tantalizing trivia, from America's oldest restaurant to the nation's oldest commissioned vessel. Plaques and cemeteries, sculpture and bullet marks are also pointed out to give an insight into the history of the city, known as the Cradle of the American Revolution.

Tour 6

There is more to Boston than Revolutionary history. This walk shows off the contrasts in Boston, starting down by the water and the modern aquarium and ending at the top of the John Hancock Tower, with its panoramic views over the city. In between are the cobbled streets and Georgian front doors on Beacon Hill, the chic shops of Newbury Street and the open-air elegance of the Public Garden. Always a city that has welcomed strangers, there are also moving tributes to Afro-Americans and victims of the Holocaust.

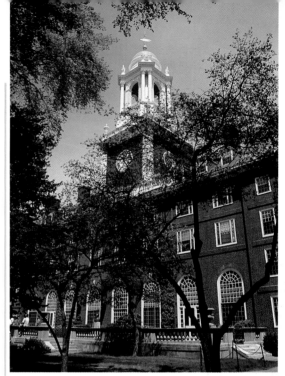

Tour 7

Harvard University is one of the world's great educational institutions. Its libraries and museums boast some of the finest collections in the world, housed in magnificent examples of architecture, from the 17th century to the present day. At the same time, the student body, which now includes the women of Radcliffe College, adds zest to Cambridge, where coffee shops and boutiques, bookstores and

Harvard University is one of the pre-eminent Ivy League establishments in the country

art galleries are a pleasure for students and visitors alike. With huge mature trees along the Charles River and New England clapboard houses, Cambridge retains its own character, totally distinct from Boston, just a bridge or two away.

Boston's impressive skyline at night

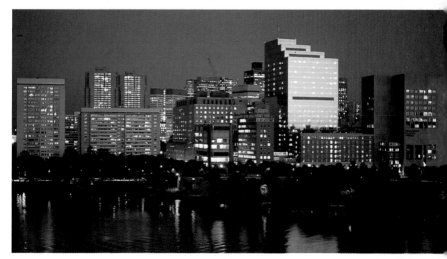

The Boston
Freedom Trail

A local journalist, William Schofield, came up with the simple but effective idea of linking Boston's historically important sites with a walking trail. That was back in 1951. Since then, millions have taken the route, marked sometimes by a painted red line, at other times by red bricks.

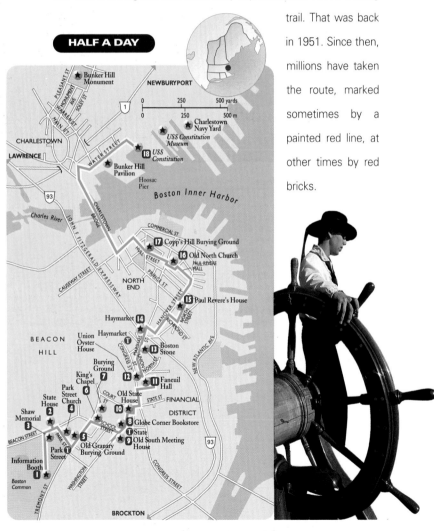

HALF A DAY

Allow half a day, longer if you want to explore the Charlestown Navy Yard, located at the end of the Trail, home of the USS *Constitution*. Remember that in summer long lines build up to see this historic ship.

▶ *Start at the information booth on the Tremont Street side of Boston Common, near the Park Street MBTA stop.*

❶ Boston Common

Often called America's first public park, this common land was set aside in 1634 for "the feeding of Cattell" and as a "trayning field" for militia. Once the cattle left around 1830, the Common was used for recreation and oration. In 1851, Amelia Bloomer, wearing her manly "bloomers," campaigned for women's rights.

In the coming century, charismatic speakers such as Martin Luther King, Jr. and Pope John Paul II have also addressed large crowds here. Today it is an area of lawns, trees and even baseball diamonds.

▶ *Follow the red line to the State House.*

❷ State House

Built in 1795, this "new" seat of state government replaced the Old State House of 1713. The original red-brick structure was designed by Charles Bulfinch, the most able and sought-after architect of his day. His original dome of wood was replaced first with a copper one, then gilded with 23-carat gold leaf in 1874. There are regular free tours.

▶ *Just across Beacon Street is a large monument.*

❸ Shaw/54th Regiment Memorial

The lively bronze bas-relief by Augustus Saint-Gaudens pays tribute to the local black soldiers who volunteered to fight for the North in the American Civil War. Prejudice confined blacks to the ranks, but wealthy white Bostonian, Robert Gould Shaw, led what became the 54th Massachusetts Regiment. He was killed, along with 32 of his soldiers, in the assault on Fort Wagner, South Carolina. Their heroism inspired the 1989 film, *Glory*, which won three Academy Awards.

The Robert Gould Shaw/54th Regiment Memorial acknowledges the role played by the first black regiment in the Civil War

▶ *Walk through the Common to Park Street Church.*

❹ Park Street Church

Founded in 1809, this is where anti-slavery campaigner William Lloyd Garrison made his first speech in 1829. Two years later, the hymn *America* was first sung here on the steps, and it remains part of the church's Fourth of July tradition. It is ironic that the melody is the same as the British national anthem, *God Save the Queen*.

▶ *Adjacent to Park Street Church, facing Tremont Street, is the Old Granary Burying Ground.*

❺ Old Granary Burying Ground

Buried here are some of the best-known leaders of the patriot cause: John Hancock, Samuel Adams, John Otis and Paul Revere (see page 11). One of the most popular graves is that of Mary Goose, also called Elizabeth Vergoose, and supposedly the original Mother Goose. The mother and step-mother of

---

FOR CHILDREN

The most prized ornament in the State House is a fish, the Sacred Cod, made of carved and gilded wood. It hangs above the Speaker as a permanent "memorial of the Importance of the Cod Fishery for the Welfare of the Commonwealth." Harvard students shocked the city in the 1930s when they "codnapped" the symbol as a prank.

---

a total of 20 children, she was buried here in 1757. Her son-in-law was supposed to have published *Mother Goose's Melodies* (*Songs for the Nursery*).

▶ *Turn left on Tremont Street. Cross to King's Chapel, on the corner of School Street.*

❻ King's Chapel

Dating from 1749, King's Chapel was seen as a symbol of British rule in North America. The colony's governors worshipped in a special canopied pew. George Washington also used it in 1789; perhaps one reason that it has survived. Today's congregation follows a curious mixture of Church of England and Unitarian liturgy.

▶ Walk down School Street. Behind the chapel is the graveyard.

7 Burying Ground

This cemetery contains the graves of several historic figures, including Mary Chilton, the first of the *Mayflower* pilgrims to reach Plymouth Rock, and John Winthrop, first governor of the colony. Others buried here include William Dawes, who joined Paul Revere in his "midnight ride," as well as Elizabeth Pain, who provided the inspiration for Hester Prynne in Nathaniel Hawthorne's *The Scarlet Letter*. The oldest gravestone in Boston remembers William Paddy, who died in 1658.

▶ Continue on School Street, passing Old City Hall.

8 Globe Corner Bookstore

Formerly the Old Corner Bookstore, the name was changed after the *Boston Globe* newspaper bought the building, one of Boston's oldest. What started out as an apothecary shop in 1712, became famous in the mid-19th century as the publishers, Ticknor and Fields. Their

The Globe Corner Bookstore was once the literary hub of Boston

best-selling authors included Nathaniel Hawthorne, Henry Wadsworth Longfellow, Henry David Thoreau and Julia Ward Howe, who penned *The Battle Hymn of the Republic*, the anthem of the North during the Civil War.

▶ Turn right on Washington Street.

9 Old South Meeting House

Standing in the quiet simplicity of this 1729 Congregational church, it is hard to imagine the fiery debates that inflamed political passions and led to the Revolution. Back then, "Old South" was the largest space available for public assemblies. After the Boston Massacre in 1770, protesters marched from here to confront the lieutenant-governor. Over three years later came the meeting that triggered the Boston Tea Party (see page 8). Today, the second-oldest church in Boston is a museum recording those tumultuous days.

ℹ *Boston National Park Visitors Center, 15 State Street*

▶ Turn back and follow Washington Street past the Globe Corner Bookstore. Just

before the Old State House, a walkway to the right leads to the Old State House.

10 Old State House

The lion and unicorn symbolize the connection with the Mother Country, a link which James Otis demanded be cut as early as 1761. Five years later, the hated Stamp Act was debated here and, on July 18, 1776, Colonel Thomas Crafts stepped on to the balcony to read the Declaration of Independence. Two hundred years later, Queen Elizabeth II stood on the same spot and spoke in celebration of the American bicentennial. Note the ring of cobblestones outside the seat of the Massachusetts Assembly, recording the Boston Massacre of 1770, when five Bostonians were shot by British soldiers (see page 8).

▶ Cross Congress Street diagonally.

11 Faneuil Hall

In Boston, Faneuil rhymes with Daniel, and the name recalls the French merchant who funded the construction of Boston's marketplace in 1742. In the meeting hall above, freedom of speech was a prerogative. Locals congregated in 1764 to object to the Sugar Act. In the following

Boston's oldest public building,
the Old State House dates
back to 1713

lawyer Daniel Webster used to
sit at the mahogany bar, consum-
ing up to six glasses of brandy
and three dozen oysters at a
sitting.

▶ *Turn onto Marshall Street.*

13 Boston Stone

Myth insists that this millstone
marked the true center of
Boston, and that all distances
were measured from here. This
is a tribute to the public relations
skills of a tavern owner who set
the stone up as a publicity stunt
back in 1737. The stone itself
was used originally for grinding
pigment by a painter from
London, Thomas Child.

▶ *Turn right into Haymarket.*

14 Haymarket

Stall-holders still set out their
fruits and vegetables here on
Fridays and Saturdays as countless others have done for 300
years. Massive road building and
the construction of a tunnel
under the city is disrupting
much of the downtown area, so
Mags Harries' clever sculpture,
usually set flat in the street, has
been removed temporarily.
Called *Asaroton*, the Greek word
for rubbish, it is a bronze version
of market-day leftovers.

FOR HISTORY BUFFS

Among the pages of history
devoted to the men of the
Massachusetts Bay Colony, Ann
Hutchinson is only a footnote.
Yet this woman dared to
discuss her own views of what
was, then, the "official" religion.
The punishment for such a
challenge to the Puritan hier-
archy was exile. In 1638 she
left her home and, with her followers, moved south. They
founded the second settlement
in New England in what is now
the state of Rhode Island.

---

years, their topics of protest were
taxation and English troop
movements. Samuel Adams'
rebellious speech in 1772, stir-
ring up anti-British feelings, was
particularly provocative. But
debate did not stop with
Independence.

Over the centuries,
Bostonians have spoken their
minds here on issues such as
slavery, alcohol, the Vietnam War
and women's rights. Like the
Old State House, there is a
reminder of England: the
grasshopper that tops the building is thought to be a copy of the
weathervane on the Royal
Exchange in London.

▶ *Follow the red line across
North Street to Union Street,
and No. 41.*

12 Union Oyster House

This place enjoys the title of the
"oldest continuously operated
restaurant in America." It started
life as a shop, but became a
place to eat in 1826. Orator and

Paul Revere's House, restored to its original appearance, now operates as a small museum

▶ Follow the red line through the construction to Hanover Street. Turn right on Richmond Street, then left on North Street to North Square.

15 Paul Revere's House

Revere's talent as a silversmith, bell-maker, engraver, and even false teeth-maker fade away in the light of his fame as messenger. He rode to Lexington and Concord on the night of April 18, 1775 to warn that "the British are coming!" (see page 11).

His tiny wooden home, at 19 North Square, is the oldest in Boston (1680) and is as plain and simple inside as Revere left it.

▶ Leave North Square on Prince Street, turn right on Hanover Street, then left on Paul Revere Mall to the Old North Church.

16 Old North Church

Sexton Robert Newman had to flash lanterns ("One if by land, and two if by sea") to fellow patriots across the Charles River to warn them of British troop movements. He hung up two

from the 191-foot (58m) steeple that is still visible in many parts of the city. Supposedly, one John Childs *flew* from the steeple in 1757, though contemporary reports do not explain how. Officially named Christ Church, it is the oldest in Boston (1723), and remains a place of worship. Boston Harbor Tea is sold here to boost funds, and a sign by the collection box suggests that "if it weren't for the Old North Church, you might be making donations in pounds."

▶ Go uphill on Hull Street.

17 Copp's Hill Burying Ground

This is not a resting place of famous historic figures, though Sexton Newman is buried here, as is early black community leader, Prince Hall. Nonetheless, the old headstones are worth a look, particularly that of Daniel Malcolm. Used for target practice by the British soldiers who camped here, the scars are still clear to see.

▶ Continue downhill on Hull Street; turn left on Commercial Street, then right across Charlestown Bridge on the right-hand sidewalk. At the

north end of the bridge, follow the red line down the steps and along Water Street.

SPECIAL TO…

One of the most bizarre accidents in Boston's history took place on Copp's Hill Terrace. In 1919, 21 people were swallowed up and killed by a tidal wave of molasses when a giant tank burst open releasing 2.5 million gallons (11 million litres) of the sticky liquid.

---

18 USS *Constitution*

Like HMS *Victory* in England, this is still a commissioned ship and an icon for the navy. A magnificent example of a wooden warship, her greatest glory came in the War of 1812 against the British who were then masters of the sea. She destroyed four enemy frigates and sloops and earned the nickname, "Old Ironsides," when, as cannonballs bounced off her hull, a seaman shouted "Huzzah! Her sides are made of iron!" In fact, the ship is made of live oak, a particularly tough wood from southeastern U.S.A.

Boston
Old & New

Boston's development started by the water, then moved inland to Beacon Hill where the wealthy lived. Later it included Back Bay, which was reclaimed land. Allow a full day for this tour which traces highlights of that growth, from narrow streets to grand boulevards, with Georgian houses and modern skyscrapers.

Map labels:

LONGFELLOW BRIDGE

Charles/ MGH

Harrison Gray Otis House

Old West Church

Bowdoin

NEW SUDBURY ST

Boston City Hall Plaza

Holocaust Memorial

Christopher Columbus Park

African Meeting House

CAMBRIDGE ST

Quincy Market

Long Wharf

Charles River Basin

BEACON HILL

PINCKNEY ST

TIERNE ST

JOY ST

BOWDOIN ST

SOMERSET ST

Government Center

STATE ST

COURT ST

CONGRESS ST

UNION ST

NORTH ST

COMMERCIAL ST

Aquarium

New England Aquarium

Louisburg Square

MT VERNON ST

ACORN ST

CHESTNUT ST

Nichols House Museum

Custom House

Faneuil Hall Marketplace

Frog Pond

TREMONT STREET

BEACON STREET

MARLBOROUGH ST

ARLINGTON ST

CHARLES STREET

Public Garden

Boston Common

CHINATOWN

JOHN F. FITZGERALD EXPRESSWAY

ATLANTIC AVENUE

NORTHERN AVE BRIDGE

BACK BAY

COMMONWEALTH AVENUE

BOYLSTON ST

BERKELEY ST

Boylston

93

Channel

New Old South Church

NEWBURY ST

Arlington

STREET

Copley

CLARENDON ST

STUART ST

SUMMER ST

BRIDGE

Fort Point

Public Library

John Hancock Tower

Trinity Church

Copley Square

0   250   500 yards
0   250   500 m

SCENIC ROUTES

For an unusual view of Boston, hop aboard one of the Boston Duck Tours' amphibious vehicles. Designed for the Allied landings on the Normandy beaches during World War II, they lumber over land and surge through water. During the 80-minute ride, a conDUCKtor describes the 40 points of interest en route. Best of all is splashing down into the Charles River for excellent views of Boston and Beacon Hill. The tours start in front of the Aquarium.

▶ *Start at the Aquarium MBTA stop. Walk to the New England Aquarium on Central Wharf.*

❶ New England Aquarium

By 1960, Boston's waterfront was an area of vacant warehouses and unused wharves. The decay was reversed in the 1970s by a renewal program that re-established and emphasized the city's age-old role as a port. One of the first projects was the New England Aquarium, at the end of Central Wharf (1817). At low tide, the smell of the sea and the tidal flats permeates the open-air plaza in front of the Aquarium, where seals swim in the open-air pool and the *Discovery*, an auxiliary boat, hosts shows by trained sea lions. Indoors, the aquarium boasts a three-story-high glass salt-water tank (187,000 gallons/41,555 litres) where sharks and eels prowl up and down past Myrtle, a 500-pound (227kg) green sea turtle who likes to have her back scratched by the aquarium's divers. Whale-watching cruises leave daily from Long Wharf (April to October).

▶ *Return to the Aquarium MBTA Stop. Cross under the expressway to State Street. At the corner of India Street is the Custom House.*

❷ Custom House

This massive 1847 granite building was described as "one of the noblest pieces of commercial architecture in the world" by 19th-century poet Walt Whitman. Certainly it is one of the biggest Greek Revival structures in the country and took ten years to build, with 3,000 pilings each weighing over 40 tons (36,363kg) being driven into the soggy soil. In 1915, the 495-foot (148.5m) high tower was added. This shattered the city's height limit and won it the title of the "tallest building in New England." The four clock faces are notorious for showing different times.

▶ *Turn right on Commercial Street and continue into Quincy Market.*

❸ Faneuil Hall Marketplace

The well-travelled visitor may see nothing remarkable about this array of shops and restaurants in restored 19th-century buildings. Yet this 1976 urban redevelopment was the first of its kind and its success has been copied all over the world ever since. In Colonial days, when sailing ships tied up at Long Wharf, the Marketplace was used by vendors of fruits, vegetables and other commodities. By 1825, Faneuil Hall was too small, so Mayor Josiah Quincy authorized the construction of the Quincy Market and its two offspring, the North and South markets. Today, restaurants, pubs, and fast-food counters satisfy the hunger of over 14 million visitors a year.

▶ *Go through the Market, then cross North Street to Congress Street. Turn right and continue to the Holocaust Memorial.*

❹ New England Holocaust Memorial

This memorial, both dramatic and intimate, is a recent addition to the Boston skyline. Located on a busy traffic island between City Hall Plaza and the 18th-

Quincy Market, a lively collection of eating places and shops

century Blackstone Block, the six glass towers are lit from within at night. Each is six stories high and etched with six million random numbers, symbolizing the victims of the concentration camps. On the base of each tower are quotes from survivors, which tell of love, hope and despair. One, from Gerda Weissman Klein, recalls a 13-year-old's gift to her best friend in the camp: "Imagine a world in which your entire possession is one raspberry, and you gave it to your friend."

▶ *Cross Congress Street and continue up the steps to the City Hall Plaza.*

❺ Boston City Hall Plaza

The area around City Hall was once the red-light district, with its attendant slums, burlesque theaters and boarded-up shops. Known officially as Scollay Square, it once deserved its "Combat Zone" nickname. In the 1960s, the run-down buildings were demolished and replaced by the John F. Kennedy federal office buildings and a new City Hall, a pyramid standing on its head, designed by I. M. Pei. In winter the plaza looks barren, but in summer it becomes a lively meeting-place, with pushcart vendors, office workers and free evening concerts on the stage behind City Hall.

▶ *Continue through the Plaza to Cambridge Street and turn right.*

❻ Harrison Gray Otis House

Beacon Hill, with some of the most elegant homes in Boston, dates back to just after the Revolution, when Harrison Gray Otis started to build houses here. This lawyer, mayor of Boston and U.S. senator was also a property developer, so he could afford to have Charles

Bulfinch, the noted architect of the day, design his home at 141 Cambridge Street. Often called the First Otis House, its perfectly proportioned, if rather dull brick exterior hides a sophisticated and surprisingly colorful interior. At the top of a handsome staircase, the grand drawing-room looks much as it did 200 years ago. Today this is the headquarters of the SPNEA, the Society for the Preservation of New England Antiquities, with an architectural museum in the basement.

Nearby, the original Old West Church was reduced to rubble by the British in 1775, to curtail the Colonists from using the tower to signal messages to their militia. The present church dates from 1805.

SPECIAL TO...

Beacon Hill looks like a film-set for a costume drama, with brick sidewalks, gaslights and handsome houses with shutters and window boxes. Acorn Street, one of the last remaining cobbled thoroughfares in the city, is the narrowest on the hill, yet wide enough to comply with building regulations of the period, which insisted that two cows must be able to pass by one another. Note the odd purple panes of glass. Back in 1818, a batch of window glass shipped over from Hamburg was tainted with manganese oxide which gradually turned purple after exposure to light.

▶ Cross Cambridge Street, go up Joy Street and turn into Smith Court.

🟢 African Meeting House
In Colonial days, many black Americans lived on the back, or north slope, of Beacon Hill. Rather than be relegated to the galleries of white churches, they worshipped at the African Meeting House, at 8 Smith Court. The oldest such church (1806) still standing in the coun-

try, it was the home of the New England Anti-Slavery Society. The congregation was such a force in the Abolitionist Movement that the building became known as the Black Faneuil Hall. Today, it houses the Museum of Afro-American History, which traces the civil rights movement, and is at the start of the Black Heritage Trail.

The neighboring Smith Court Residences at Nos. 3, 5, 7, 7A and 10 were built as low-cost clapboard and brick housing in the 19th century when Boston's black population expanded between 1880 and World War I.

FOR HISTORY BUFFS

The Black Heritage Trail, a walking tour of 14 historic sites, celebrates Boston's long-standing black community. Set up after the Fugitive Slave Law of 1850, this was an organized route with safe houses, to help slaves from the South escape to freedom into the Northern states or Canada.

▶ Continue up Joy Street and turn right on Mount Vernon Street. At No. 55 is Nichols House.

🟢 Nichols House Museum
Red-brick houses line Mount Vernon Street, one of the loveliest streets in Boston. The museum is a time-warp, where nothing has been changed since the owner, Rose Standish Nichols, died in 1960. Her will ensured that "people from around the world without a letter of introduction could see the inside of a fine house." From a wealthy Boston family, she is remembered as a landscape gardener and a fervent worker for international peace. Her needlework and paintings lend a personal touch to the 1804 mansion, which also has bronzes by her uncle, the sculptor Augustus Saint-Gaudens. Also on display is a chair owned by John Winthrop, founder of

Boston and first governor of the colony of Massachusetts.

▶ Continue west along Mount Vernon Street to Louisburg Square.

🟢 Louisburg Square
The name of this square recalls the struggle between France and Britain for supremacy in North America. Even though local troops had fought successfully for the Crown against the French at Fort Louisburg, Nova Scotia, back in 1745, this elegant square, named after their victory, was built a century later. Much like a London square, the grassy quadrangle is a private park for owners of the surrounding posh homes. Architect Charles Bulfinch changed his rather plain English style of design to Greek Revival to match the architecture of these houses, lived in by celebrities such as writer Louisa May Alcott (No. 10), who spent her last two years here. Opera singer Jenny Lind, the "Swedish Nightingale," was married at No. 20.

▶ Retrace your steps on Mount Vernon Street and turn right on Willow Street, then zigzag right onto Acorn Street, go left

---

SPECIAL TO...

The early 19th-century equivalent of smoking a joint after dinner was sniffing ether. Dr. William Morton, a dentist, noticed that participants in these "ether frolics" felt no pain if they bumped into the furniture. He experimented with ether, using it on patients before extracting a tooth. On October 16, 1846, in Boston's Massachusetts General Hospital, he supervised an operation that successfully removed a tumor from a patient, using ether as an anaesthetic. This major breakthrough for surgery is commemorated with the statue *The Good Samaritan* in the Public Garden.

on West Cedar Street, then right on Chestnut Street and, finally, left on Charles Street. Across Beacon Street is the Public Garden.

10 Public Garden

Boston can thank a group of public-spirited green thumbs for America's first botanical garden. From 1837 until their success over 20 years later, they battled to protect the city's green heart from developers. Today, their triumph provides a retreat for locals and visitors alike. In spring and summer, flowers bloom by the paths, while the swish of fountains masks the noise of the traffic. Children plead for rides on the slow, stately, foot-pedalled swan boats, introduced in 1877, and peer at the fountain sculpture of Bagheera, the panther immortalised in Kipling's *Jungle Books*. A home-grown favorite is the sculpture of Mrs. Mallard and her six ducklings, at the corner of Charles and Beacon streets. Robert McCloskey's *Make Way for Ducklings* is a much-loved children's tale of a mother duck stopping Boston traffic as she shepherds her brood from the Charles River to the pond in the Boston Public Garden. A children's parade each spring retraces the route of the ducklings.

▶ *Cross the Garden using the suspension bridge and exit through the Arlington Street gate onto Commonwealth Avenue. Walk one block, then turn left on Berkeley Street, then right on Newbury Street.*

11 Newbury Street

Water covered this area of Boston until the second half of the 19th century when Back Bay was filled in and transformed into a residential district. The backbone is Commonwealth Avenue, a Parisian-style boulevard, lined with fine trees and grand statues of long-forgotten worthies. Running parallel to "Comm Ave" is Newbury Street, known for its up-market and trendy art galleries, boutiques and cafés. Yet, the apartments on and around the street create a neighborhood atmosphere. Old buildings have new uses: between Berkeley and Clarendon streets, the Church of the Covenant (1867), renowned for its stained-glass windows, is now an art gallery; Boston's first Museum of Natural History is full of expensive menswear; and the severe face of the New England Insurance Company fronts a trendy fashion shop.

Boston's Public Garden was the first botanical garden in the country Inset: Robert McCloskey's *Make Way for Ducklings*

rectified and now the glass acts as a mirror, reflecting Trinity Church. From the viewing gallery of the John Hancock Observatory, 740 feet (225m) up, you'll be rewarded by a panorama stretching for 100 miles (160km) on a clear day.

▶ *Copley Square is a huge city block, bounded by the Boston Public Library, Trinity Church, New Old South Church, the Copley Plaza Hotel and the John Hancock Tower.*

⓮ Copley Square
Copley Square (1883), another result of the reclamation of Back Bay, was described by one observer as a "desert of dirt, dust, mud and wind." Now it is a pleasant place of fountains, benches ... and zooming skateboarders. The Boston Public Library, the first in America to lend books for free, is Charles McKim's adaptation of an Italian Renaissance palazzo. Constructed with a quarryful of yellow Siena marble, the 1895 building was decorated with works by then-contemporary artists and sculptors such as John Singer Sargent and Daniel Chester French.

▶ *There is an MBTA stop at Copley Square to return to the Aquarium or travel elsewhere in the city.*

Trinity Church reflected in the John Hancock Tower

▶ *After one block, turn left on Clarendon Street and continue to Boylston Street. Turn right and left and into Copley Square.*

⓬ Trinity Church
Two of America's finest architects, Charles McKim and Henry Richardson, worked on Trinity Church in the late 19th century. Richardson's design was inspired by medieval Europe, while the interior coloring was a tribute to William Morris's pre-Raphaelite movement. On the Boylston Street side of the church, the statue of the Rev. Phillips Brooks commemorates the passionate preacher, who used to ride his horse at breakneck speed. He also wrote *O Little Town of Bethlehem*.

▶ *Across Stuart Street is the John Hancock Tower.*

⓭ John Hancock Tower
Once the tallest building in New England, the headquarters of the John Hancock Life Insurance Company has had its problems. Architect I. M. Pei's unusual rhomboid shape was beset by air currents that sucked many of the original 10,344 glass panels off the 62-story skyscraper. The difficulty was

SATURDAY, NOV. 13
5:00-7:00 PM
BAKED BEAN SUPPER
ADULTS $5 CHILDREN $2
CHRIST CHURCH, UNITED METHODIST

Cambridge &
Harvard University

Established as Newtowne back in 1630, this was the first capital of the colony. Two years after Harvard College was founded in 1636, the town changed its name to Cambridge, to give it the same kudos, no doubt, as the English university city. Today, the mixture of grand museums, historic houses, wealthy residents and student *joie de vivre* make it one of the most vibrant and attractive places in New England.

TOUR

7

[i] *Cambridge Discovery Inc,
Harvard Square*

▶ *Start at the Harvard Square
MBTA stop.*

❶ Harvard Square

All around the traffic island is
the bustle and noise of "the
square." Here you can buy international newspapers at the
kiosk, eat international cuisine at
the numerous restaurants, then
buy all-American sportswear at
the Harvard Cooperative, the
large department store, known
as "the Coop" (rhymes with
hoop).

▶ *Walk up Massachusetts
Avenue and turn right through
Johnson Gate, the entrance to
Old Harvard Yard.*

❷ Old Harvard Yard

Harvard is not only the oldest
university in America, but also
one of the most influential.
From its earliest days, it has
symbolized the independent
attitude of the Colonists and,
significantly, America's first
printing press was set up here in
1640. Harvard Yard, the center of
the campus for over 350 years, is
really two vast, open quadrangles, totalling 22 acres (8.8
hectares). The first yard is the

FOR HISTORY BUFFS

America's oldest university is
also one of its most
prestigious. One of the seven
so-called Ivy League schools
(so old that ivy grows on their
hallowed walls), Harvard
emphasizes academic
excellence, shunning the sports
scholarships and razzmatazz of
the country's younger universities. The 7,000 undergraduates
now include the women of
Radcliffe (see page 55), but
there is also an impressive
graduate program ranging from
the prestigious Harvard Law
and Medical Schools to newer
disciplines such as Business
Administration and
Government.

home of the Freshmen (first-
year students) who live in the
red-brick dormitories. On the
right is Massachusetts Hall, the
university's oldest surviving
building. Established as a laboratory and dormitory in 1720, it
housed American troops at the
start of the Revolution.

[i] *Harvard Information Center,
Holyoke Center*

❸ Statue of John Harvard

Directly across the yard, in front
of the granite University Hall
(1815), this seated statue is
labelled "John Harvard, founder
1638." The sculpture is wittily
referred to as the "Statue of the
Three Lies." Harvard was a
benefactor rather than a founder,
the foundation year was 1636,
and the statue is actually of
Sherman Hoar, a Harvard
student who modelled for 19th-
century sculptor Daniel Chester
French.

▶ *Continue past University Hall
and enter New Yard.*

Lowell House, typical of Harvard's
elegant Georgian buildings

❹ New Yard

The second, larger portion of the
Yard is also called Tercentenary
Theater because it was here that
the 300th graduation ceremonies
were held in 1936. Criss-crossed
by walking paths, a figurative
bridge links the spiritual and
intellectual centers of the
university. To the left is
Memorial Church, "Mem
Church." It was completed in
1932 as a tribute by Harvard
alumni to classmates killed in
World War I, and had to be
updated for victims of World
War II and, later, the Korean
and Vietnam conflicts.

▶ *To the right is Widener Library,
the world's largest university
library.*

❺ Widener Library

In this temple to the written
word, information spans the
centuries, from a first folio of
Shakespeare and a Gutenberg

Bible, to microfilm files and computer screens. Some 11 million books are accessible not only to students and faculty, but also to the general public, who may use the desktop computers in the public reading room. Built between 1913 and 1915, the library was given in memory of Harry Elkins Widener, a wealthy graduate who drowned on the *Titanic*. One clause in the endowment insisted that Harvard students had to pass a swimming test to graduate, a rule that was only revoked in the 1960s.

▶ *Straight ahead is Quincy Street.*

⑥ Carpenter Center for the Visual Arts
This glass and concrete block at No. 24 Quincy Street is the only example in America of a building by the 20th-century Swiss architect Le Corbusier. Its film archives are famous for their variety and depth. Film shows of unusual or historic movies are often held here.

⑦ Fogg and Busch-Reisinger Art Museums
Many institutions of higher learning have their own museums. Harvard has eight on campus, of which the Fogg, Busch-Reisinger and the Arthur M. Sackler have world-class reputations.

The Fogg, which opened in 1895, is the oldest of the three. Behind the neo-Georgian façade on Quincy Street is a courtyard modeled after a 15th-century Italian palazzo. The collection concentrates on European art from the Middle Ages to the present, with a strong line-up of Italian Renaissance paintings, as well as a self-portrait by Van Gogh, and *Red Boats* by Claude Monet.

Directly behind the Fogg is the Busch-Reisinger Museum, in the Otto Werner Hall. Here, the main focus is works by the Expressionists, Europeans such as Franz Marc, Paul Klee, Wassily Kandinsky and Emile Nolde, rebels against the Impressionistic style, along with decorative arts and sculpture.

▶ *Go north on Quincy Street, cross Broadway, and the Arthur M. Sackler Museum is on the right.*

⑧ Arthur M. Sackler Museum
This is the university's third art museum, in British architect James Sterling's strikingly contemporary building, opened in 1985. Famous for its exquisite collection of Chinese ceramics, bronzes and jades, it specializes in Ancient Greek, Islamic and Asian art, from Indian miniatures to Japanese prints. On the fourth floor, among the Greek art, are several large ceramic vases, dating from about 340BC. There are also jade dragons, bronze ritual bells, and a large bronze wine container, over 3,000 years old, from China.

▶ *Continue along Quincy Street, crossing Cambridge Street. Memorial Hall is on the left.*

Well-displayed period furnishings complement the Fogg's paintings and sculptures

9 Annenberg Memorial Hall

Memorial Hall re-opened after a major restoration in 1996. Built in 1878 to honor the Harvard men who died in the Civil War, it epitomizes the Gothic Revival style, with a Great Hall soaring up to a jig-saw puzzle roof of carved beams and timbers. Here, Winston Churchill was given an honorary degree in 1943. The stained-glass windows portray stories and heroes from the Bible, American history and Greek mythology. In a controversial move, "Mem Hall" has been made into a dining room. Where nervous undergraduates once took exams, first-year students gossip at mealtimes under the chandeliers. To one side is Sanders Theater, an intimate auditorium finished in dark wood. It was the setting for Harvard graduations up until 1911, but is now used for the performing arts.

▶ *At the end of Quincy Street bear left across Kirkland Street, then turn right onto Oxford Street.*

10 Museums of Natural History

Don't be put off by the fustysounding names of the four museums: there is plenty to fascinate adults and children alike in this brick building. Highlights include the 22-pound

(10kg) meteor which fell from the sky in 1992 and landed on a car in Peekskill, New York, and the life-size skeleton of a 42-foot long (12.5m) *Kronosaurus*. This gigantic crocodile lived 135 million years ago.

Best known of all is the unique Ware Collection of Glass Flowers, 3,000 scientifically accurate, life-size models of flowers and plants made out of blown glass.

▶ *From Oxford Street, go into Harvard Law School. Pass under the arch to the right of Pierce Hall, and bear left on the path along Langdell Hall.*

11 Harvard Law School

The Law School was started in 1817, with six students. Today, each new class of 540 students has been selected from over 7,000 applicants. Langdell Hall, on the right, has the largest law library in the world and a public reading room on the fourth floor that stretches the length of two football fields. Next is Austin Hall, a small brownstone building completed in 1881 by Henry Hobson Richardson. Each spring in the Ames Courtroom, on the second floor, finalists in the third-year competition argue their cases before a Justice of the U.S. Supreme Court. The sessions are open to the public but seating is by ticket only.

Longfellow House: this clapboard building was abandoned by its Loyalist owner in 1774

▶ *Bear right upon leaving Austin Hall and follow the path between Hemenway Gymnasium and Gannett House. Cross Massachusetts Avenue at the traffic light and walk across Cambridge Common.*

12 Cambridge Common

This small green park is all that remains of the fields and pastures where the American army assembled after the 1775 battles of Lexington and Concord (April) and Bunker Hill (June). On July 3, George Washington took command of the American army here and a plaque marks the location of the Washington Elm beneath which this event took place. At least, that is the story ...

▶ *On the far side of the Common, turn right on Garden Street, then left on Mason Street. Turn right on Brattle Street and continue to No. 101.*

13 Hastings House

All along Brattle Street are fine houses, built before the American Revolution. Since most were then occupied by supporters of the crown, it was called "Tory Row." The owners left hastily, and all that remains are their names, recorded on blue plaques. Hastings House, No. 101, is a fine example, as are Nos. 113 and 115, which belonged to the daughters of Henry Wadsworth Longfellow, who lived at No. 105.

14 Longfellow House
The Tory, or British sympathizer, John Vassall lived in this yellow clapboard mansion. He built it in 1759, in anticipation of his marriage to Elizabeth, the sister of the last Royal Lieutenant Governor. In 1775, he was thrown out by the patriots, who moved in with the wounded from the Battle of Bunker Hill. Next, the hospital became George Washington's headquarters for nine months. Washington enlarged it to make room for guests.

In the following century, the celebrated American poet, Henry Wadsworth Longfellow rented a room here. Later, he received the house as a wedding present and lived here from 1837 to 1882. During that period he wrote *Hiawatha* (1855) and *The Village Blacksmith* (1839) here, and completed his translation of Dante, among other works. Here, also, he entertained Dickens, Emerson, Hawthorne, Twain and Wilde. Longfellow was particularly fond of the view across to the Charles River, and it remains unspoiled, thanks to his children, who gave the land to the City of Cambridge in 1913.

▶ *Retrace your steps on Brattle Street and turn left into Radcliffe College.*

15 Radcliffe Yard
Radcliffe College started out in 1879 with just 27 women students in a small two-story house. It was named in honor of Londoner Lady Anne Radcliffe, who gave £100 to Harvard back in the 17th century. Admissions to Radcliffe have always been highly competitive, and many "Cliffies" have become well known, including Helen Keller,

whose life was portrayed in the film *The Miracle Worker*. Nearly a century after its founding, Radcliffe merged with Harvard, and now students receive a Harvard degree embossed with the seals of both colleges. In Radcliffe Yard, the Federal-style Fay House was built in 1807 and was the first building acquired by the college. Today it is the site of the Admissions Office.

▶ *After crossing the Yard, exit onto Garden Street, and bear right to Christ Church.*

16 Christ Church and the Old Burying Ground
In the foyer, just inside the outer door of Christ Church, a plaque on the right marks a bullet hole made, so the story goes, when the British were marching to Lexington in April 1775. Later

Christ Church, designed by Peter Hamson, the architect of King's Chapel in Boston

that year, George and Martha Washington attended services here, using the pew directly below the pulpit, on the left. Between the Christ Church and the First Church is Cambridge's oldest cemetery, God's Acre. The earliest existing grave is that of Anne Erinton, an early settler who passed away on December 24, 1635. Eight presidents of Harvard are also buried here.

▶ *Continue down Garden Street to Massachusetts Avenue and bear right to Harvard Square and the MBTA stop.*

SPECIAL TO...

Close by the sidewalk is a stone milestone, carved in 1734. Look carefully at the words: "Boston 8 miles." Today that distance is covered in 8 minutes on the MBTA.

CULTURAL CRADLE

America's culture, as well as its sense of history, started in New England. The 19th century, in particular, saw the development not just of American themes but of a distinctive American "voice" and viewpoint. What binds the most talented artists and writers together is their sense of New England, in print and on canvas, set to music or presented on stage. Names such as Robert Frost (poet), Nathaniel Hawthorne (novelist), Winslow Homer (painter), Norman Rockwell (illustrator) and Eugene O'Neill (playwright) conjure up bleak landscapes and clapboard houses, glistening seas and "salt-of-the-earth" families, while Charles Ives' music interprets the moods of the countryside.

Literature

The first New England writer to make an international name for himself was Henry Wadsworth Longfellow (1807–82), a poet who was also a professor at Harvard. Hugely popular, his narrative poems told home-grown tales, from *The Song of Hiawatha*, an Indian story, to *The Midnight Ride of Paul Revere*, which encapsulates the start of the American Revolution. Nathaniel Hawthorne (1804–64) also took inspiration from New England history, though he explored the psychological effects of Puritanism in novels such as *The Scarlet Letter* and *The House of the Seven Gables*. His friend Herman Melville (1819–91) received little critical acclaim in his lifetime. A New Yorker who wrote at Arrowhead in Western Massachusetts, Melville's most famous novel was *Moby Dick*, an allegory of good and evil which drew on his experiences aboard a New England whaler as a young man.

While Hawthorne and Melville relied on the realism of history, two authors, Emerson and Thoreau, took a more spiritual path. Transcendentalism was a movement led by Ralph Waldo Emerson (1803–82), a charismatic speaker and writer whose philosophy is best summed up by his often quoted saying: "who so would be a man must be a non-conformist." He appealed to Americans to throw off the yoke of European tradition and to look at their individual experiences. His friend, Henry David Thoreau (1817–62) did just that, going "back to nature." The result of his simple life by Walden Pond, on the edge of Concord, was the idealistic book, *Walden: Or Life in the Woods* (1854).

Both men spent time in Concord where Louisa May Alcott (1832–88) also lived and wrote *Little Women*, a huge best-seller, based on

family life. Another woman writer, Harriet Beecher Stowe (1811–96), brought the issue of slavery to thousands of homes with *Uncle Tom's Cabin*. The book, which was originally published as a weekly serial, sold 300,000 copies. While Stowe wrote to further a cause, Emily Dickinson (1830–86) wrote for herself. A recluse whose poems were only discovered after her death, she lived her entire life not just in Amherst in Western Massachusetts, but also in the same brick Federal house where she had been born.

New England also attracted writers from elsewhere in the States. Samuel Longhorne Clemens, better known as Mark Twain (1835–1910), was born in

Left: Henry Wadsworth Longfellow
Below: Topsy, from Harriet Beecher Stowe's *Uncle Tom's Cabin*

"SLAVE LIFE." OR "UNCLE TOM'S CABIN."
(Mrs Keeley as Topsy. "Is dreffut wicked.")

Missouri. Many of his best-loved stories, such as the antics of Huckleberry Finn and Tom Sawyer, were written in his Hartford home. His tales of the American West, written with humor and an easy style, brought him a wide audience. By contrast, high society was the subject of novelist Edith Wharton (1862–1937). The author of *The Age of Innocence* did much of her writing at The Mount, her retreat in Lenox, Massachusetts.

The quintessential New England poet was Robert Frost (1874–1963) who spent most of his life in New Hampshire and Vermont. So great was his stature that he was the first poet to participate in a presidential inauguration. In 1961, he read his poem *The Gift Outright* at President John F. Kennedy' swearing-in. His descriptions of a Vermont snowstorm and swinging on birch trees are easily remembered; his forthright expression of universal truths have a darker side.

Theater

New York was always the cradle of American theater, but America's first major playwright, Eugene O'Neill (1888–1953), learned his craft in New England. The New Yorker studied at the 47 Workshop of George Pierce Baker in Harvard before making an impact with the Provincetown Players on Cape Cod. Ten of his plays were produced from 1916 to 1920. A Nobel and Pulitzer prize winner, O'Neill is remembered at the theater bearing his name near New London, Connecticut. The cottage where he spent his boyhood summers was the setting for *Long Day's Journey into Night*.

Music

While Puritan influences restricted early New Englanders to music in churches, the region has been a powerhouse of classical music in the 20th century. The best known composer is the avant-garde Charles Ives (1874–1954), born in Danbury, Connecticut, the son of a bandmaster. Fiercely proud and inde-

The Boston Symphony Orchestra performs at Symphony Hall from the beginning of October to the end of April

pendent, Ives bucked European tradition to draw on traditional American folk songs, hymns and marches. The result was his *New England Symphony, Three Places in New England* and *Sonata No. 2* for piano and flute. The last was nicknamed *Concord, Mass 1840–1860*, perhaps because of its dedication to the town's literary circle of Emerson, Thoreau, Hawthorne and the Alcotts.

New Englander Colonel Henry Higginson enjoyed the Austrian attitude to music so much that he set up the legendary Boston Pops in 1885, based on the romance and fun of Viennese orchestras. In 1929, the Pops went outdoors to perform, as they still do to this day. The Boston Symphony, now one of the world's great orchestras, has extended its popularity and fame thanks to the summer season in Tanglewood, in western Massachusetts.

CONNECTICUT

Connecticut is rarely recognized as a vacation destination. Although popular with Manhattanites for weekends, many Americans and overseas visitors overlook it when planning a trip to New England. Yet it has a history dating back to 1635, a rich tapestry of villages and towns, countryside that looks softer than elsewhere in the northeast and miles of unspoiled shoreline. Contrasts are to be found everywhere. Although well over half the state is heavily forested, Connecticut is also heavily populated. Most residents live in the conurbations, on the southwest coast and alongside the Connecticut River that cuts through the middle of this rectangular state.

From the early days, the state has been the home of a host of inventors whose ideas still provide employment. Eli Whitney's cotton gin brought mass production techniques to the world. Sam Colt, inventor of the Colt 45 revolver, set up an arms and ammunition industry that survives today. Clocks and door locks, tires and the pay telephone were all developed here. Now, chemicals, jet engines and insurance are major employers. One of the wealthiest states in the country, in 1988 it also boasted the highest per capita income.

Norfolk is one of the best preserved villages in the northeast

The affluent southwestern corner of Connecticut is virtually a suburb of New York City. Further north, the Litchfield Hills, idyllic for artists and craftsmen, are also a retreat for show business celebrities. Two hundred years ago, the same wooded hills were stripped to fuel the furnaces and forges that processed iron for the guns used during the Revolution.

The coast, especially the eastern strip, is the most popular with visitors. Mystic, an admirable re-creation of an early 19th-century seafaring village, is replete with sailing ships.

There is a rich cultural heritage, because of the influence of Yale University and writers such as Mark Twain, Harriet Beecher Stowe and dictionary-writer Noah Webster. Painters and actors have also made their homes here, and antique shops and art galleries abound.

Tour 8

Hartford is known as the "Insurance Capital of America." The business began in 1794. It is also a city of "firsts" and "oldests." It claims the first municipal rose garden and development of the first American dictionary; the oldest newspaper, the *Hartford Courant* and oldest state house. Two of America's most revered writers also lived here: Mark Twain and Harriet Beecher Stowe, who was Twain's neighbor. Twain's Victorian house is one of the most intriguing you'll see, deliberately designed to be unusual.

Tour 9

When it comes to universities, Yale and Harvard go together like Oxford and Cambridge, in England. Just as Harvard and Cambridge are in attractive towns, so Yale and Oxford are in industrial cities. Yale, with its ivy-covered buildings, is one of the finest academic institutions in the country, with impressive museums and art galleries. Countering all this culture, the Frisbee was supposedly invented here, along with two of America's most popular fast foods: the hamburger and the pizza.

Tour 10

Western Connecticut has bumpy, wooded hills dotted with villages that don't seem to have kept up with the 20th century. Although New York City is within commuting distance, urban frenzy is banned here. This is the countryside the way urban folk prefer it, with waterfalls and covered bridges, pleasant shops and small art galleries. As for history, Litchfield boasts the first American law school, which was set up in a tiny house over 200 years ago. The innocent-looking town of Lakeville turned out tons of arms to fuel the battle against Britain, winning itself the nickname of the "Arsenal of the Revolution."

Tour 11

Connecticut's coast was settled in the early 17th century by British emigrants who named the small towns after their homes: New London, Guilford, Essex and Old Lyme. The oldest stone house in New England, complete with fortifications, was built back in 1640. Later, locals turned their hand to building ships and submarines. The finest maritime museum in the States is at Mystic, where boats and docks re-create the romance, if not the reality, of life aboard the sailing ships of the 18th and 19th centuries.

Later, the seaside attracted artists and writers, while the Eugene O'Neill Theater Center outside New London gave actors such as Al Pacino and Meryl Streep their early opportunities. Despite the popularity of the bigger towns, there are still sleepy corners where visitors can sit and munch a sandwich in peace, overlooking tranquil Long Island Sound.

Mystic Seaport is a re-creation of a 19th-century seaport

Hartford

One of the oldest cities in the country, Hartford was founded in 1636 by a native of Hertford, England. There is an English flavor to the narrow streets and parks of Hartford, downtown is easily navigable, and skyscrapers rise high above the Connecticut River. In this state capital are well-preserved historic places, the nation's oldest public art museum, world-famous rose gardens and the homes of two of America's best-known and best-loved writers, Harriet Beecher Stowe and Mark Twain.

HALF A DAY

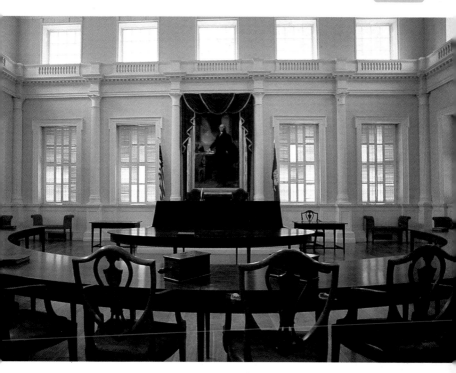

The Senate Chamber of the
Old State House

[i] 1 Civic Center Plaza

▶ Park your car in the Civic
Center garage, entrance on
Asylum Street.

❶ Civic Center

Under a circular dome in the
heart of downtown Hartford,
the Civic Center is a shopping
center, restaurant and professional sports arena, all in one.
Three professional teams share
the Center: the Hartford
Whalers (ice hockey), the
Connecticut Pride (basketball)
and the Connecticut Coyotes
(arena football). There is also the
Connecticut Sports Museum
and Hall of Fame, which highlights local heroes such as former
world featherweight boxing
champion, Willie Pep.

▶ Leave the Civic Center and
walk east on Asylum Street to
Main Street. Cross and enter
the Old State House.

❷ Old State House

Painstaking restorations have
revived the oldest state house,
designed in 1792 and completed
in 1796 by New England's star
architect Charles Bulfinch. It
stands on Meeting House
Square, where the Colony was
founded in 1636. Every day, the
ceremonial firing of a cannon by
uniformed "Continental troops"
precedes the 10am opening.
Guides in full period dress give
the facts and relate anecdotes
about rooms such as the Council
and restored Senate Chambers.
The highlight in these high-
style, Victorian masterpieces is
the original version of Gilbert
Stuart's famous portrait of the
first president, George
Washington. Also in the Old
State House is Mr. Steward's
Museum of Art and Curiosities,
plus an interactive center of
state history. The Museum Store
specializes in state products,
crafts and foods. Outside, a
farmer's market follows in the
Colonial tradition of setting up
stalls by the meeting house.

▶ From the Old State House,
walk south one block to
Travelers Tower, on the corner
of Gold Street.

FOR CHILDREN

Joseph Steward (1753–1822)
was a portrait painter who had
a studio in the Old State
House. When business was
slow in 1797, he assembled a
collection of oddities which
included "a calf with two complete heads, also a pig of the
same description having two
perfect heads to one body ...
an African dog who never had
a hair ... articles of dress and
ornament from China ..."
according to his newspaper
advertisement. In those days,
people loved such curiosities
and the museum was a huge
success, especially with
children. The calf, a stuffed
piranha and a tarantula are
among the objects still on
view today.

❸ Travelers Tower

Soaring 527 feet (1,584m) above street level, the "free Renaissance"-style, pink-granite Travelers Tower is capped by a prominent beacon light. From the observation deck atop the tower, visitors are rewarded with a breathtaking view of downtown Hartford, the Connecticut River and the entire Connecticut Valley from Mount Tom to Meriden Mountain in the south.

▶ *Across the street, on the corner of Main and Gold streets, is the Wadsworth Atheneum.*

❹ Wadsworth Atheneum

One of New England's leading "must-see" museums, "the Wad" was founded in 1842, so it takes the title "the nation's oldest public art museum." Housed in an impressive neo-Gothic building, it boasts masterpieces from the 16th through the 20th centuries, including classics by Picasso (*Harlequin*) and Van Gogh (*Self Portrait*). The most intriguing painting is *House Fronting New Milford Green* by Ralph Earl, painted in 1796. The house still stands. Other home-grown talent includes members of the Hudson River School, the 19th-

FOR HISTORY BUFFS

Connecticut was proud of the royal charter it was granted by King Charles II, in 1662. When the next monarch, James II, wanted to revoke the colony's liberties in 1685, he sent Governor Andros to collect the document. Mysteriously, the candles blew out at the handover and the charter disappeared. Legend insists that Captain Joseph Wadsworth snatched it, ran off and hid it in a hollow oak tree, later called the Charter Oak. The privileges were restored four years later, after William and Mary came to the English throne. When the U.S. Constitution was drawn up, the Connecticut Charter served as a model.

The Gothic Revival Wadsworth Atheneum. Inset: statue of Nathan Hale, local schoolmaster and patriot

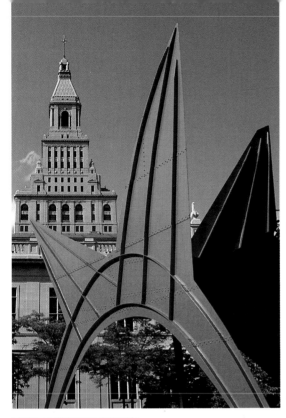

show dates of birth from the 1590s to the early 1600s, in Hertford, England.

▶ *Continue walking down Gold Street to Bushnell Park. Turn right along the border, Jewell Street. Opposite Ann Street, across from the YMCA, the Bushnell Park Carousel is in the park.*

7 Bushnell Park Carousel

The carousel is a Stein and Goldstein, hand-carved merry-go-round built in 1914, with 48 prancing horses and chariots rollicking to the tunes of a 1925 Wurlitzer band organ. At only 50 cents a ride, it is one of New England's bargains. Hot dogs and other snacks are available when the park is open, on weekends only from mid-April to mid-May, and Tuesday through Sunday through August.

▶ *Walk a few steps west to Trinity Street. Look right to the Sailors and Soldiers Memorial Arch, built in 1886 to honor the 4,000 Hartford citizens who served in the Civil War. Turn left and proceed up the hill half a block to the State Capitol. A statue of the French General Lafayette, ally of George Washington, sits on horseback in the middle of the street at the driveway entrance.*

Travelers Tower was once the tallest building in New England

5 Stone Field Sculpture

"$250,000 for a pile of rocks? That's ridiculous!" That was the reaction of many locals when the Hartford City Council voted to fund the sculpture created by Carl Andre in 1977. His work of art consists of 36 large stones laid out in rows to form an isosceles triangle. A similar furor erupted in England when London's Tate Gallery bought "a pile of bricks," a total of 120 bricks in two layers which the American sculptor entitled *Equivalent VIII*.

6 Ancient Burying Ground

Center Church, built in 1632, is Hartford's oldest church. Behind it, the Ancient Burying Ground is one of the city's few surviving historic sites from the 17th century. In the small, green, fenced-in graveyard, some 400 brownstone markers stand to attention, marking the final resting places of Hartford's founding families. Epitaphs record lives that were only occasionally lengthy, more often short. Many

century group of landscape painters who achieved a definite American style. There is also a fine assembly of pilgrim-century, Colonial and 19th-century furniture.

▶ *Cross the street diagonally to the north side of Gold Street and proceed down Gold Street, stopping at the Stone Field Sculpture and the adjacent Ancient Burying Ground.*

8 State Capitol

Another refurbished landmark (built 1789), the Capitol is the home of the House of Representatives and Senate, Connecticut's legislature. Against a backdrop of white Connecticut marble are Gothic spires, a gleaming gold dome, statues, medallions and bas-reliefs commemorating important people and events in state history. Gaudy to the point of being brash, architect Frank Lloyd Wright called it "The most ridiculous building I know of." Open to the public, the assemblies are in session from February to May in even years and February through June in odd years. More statues and historical relics decorate the interior.

▶ *Cross Capitol Avenue to No. 231.*

9 Museum of Connecticut History

The State Library and Supreme Court share this museum, which contains the Fundamental Orders of Connecticut and the Colt Firearms Collection. The latter showcases Samuel Colt's genius for the invention, making and marketing of his patented revolvers and rifles. The museum also has a variety of political, industrial, and military artifacts, with an emphasis on the Civil War era.

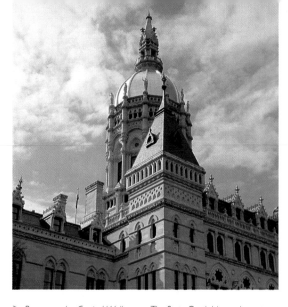

The State Captiol; its exuberant design reflects Victorian pride

▶ *Return to the Capitol. Walk through it (round it if closed) to the rear exit and continue north down the hill and through the park to Asylum Street. Turn right and walk one block back to the Civic Center to retrieve your car. Leave downtown, driving west on Asylum Street under the railroad bridge. Bear left at the fork onto Farmington Avenue. After 1 mile (1.6km), on the left is the home of Mark Twain.*

FOR HISTORY BUFFS

On the Mississippi River, when a boatman called out "Mark Twain," the pilot knew that the depth was two fathoms. This was the pseudonym taken by Samuel Clemens, in 1862, when he became a newspaper reporter. Born in Missouri in 1835, Twain popularized life in the West with books such as *The Adventures of Tom Sawyer* (1876) and *The Adventures of Huckleberry Finn* (1884). Despite his folksy stories, he was no hayseed, but a well-traveled man, awarded an honorary degree by Oxford University in 1907.

---

10 Mark Twain House

The internationally known writer and wit Samuel Clemens, alias Mark Twain, lived in this spectacular orange and black brick Victorian mansion for 17 years. He commissioned this Gothic eccentricity in 1871, when he settled in Hartford with his family. In 1881 he had the 19-room home completely refurbished by Louis Comfort Tiffany. The library is the epitome of Victorian opulence, with carved wood, patterned carpets and lavishly decorated walls and ceilings. Guides describe the life of the writer, his soirées with guests such as English writer Rudyard Kipling, and the way he retired to the billiard room to write books such as *A Connecticut Yankee in King Arthur's Court* and *The Prince and the Pauper*, because his children had commandeered his study. One of the first private citizens in Hartford to have a telephone, Twain had so many problems with the new-fangled instrument that he kept a chart to record its inefficiencies. Symbols representing noise on the line range from "artillery can be heard" to "artillery and thunder can be heard."

▶ *Next door to the Twain house, at Forest Street, is the home of Harriet Beecher Stowe.*

11 Harriet Beecher Stowe House

The "little lady who started the big war" (Civil War, 1865–70), was how President Abraham Lincoln referred to the author of *Uncle Tom's Cabin*. Published in 1852, the book was a blockbuster, selling over 300,000 copies in the first year alone. A stage version was even performed. The sentimental story of slaves in the south was unabashed, though successful, propaganda for the Anti-Slavery Movement. Nowadays, no-one remembers any of her other 30 books. Moreover, the term "Uncle Tom" has come to mean a black person who does not stand up for the rights of his race. This house, in what was quiet farmland a century ago, was Stowe's home from 1873 until she died in 1896. Her home is now restored and paintings by her own hand and her writing table, plus memorabilia of her career and her family lend a personal touch.

Mark Twain's House, in the Nook Farm district of Hartford

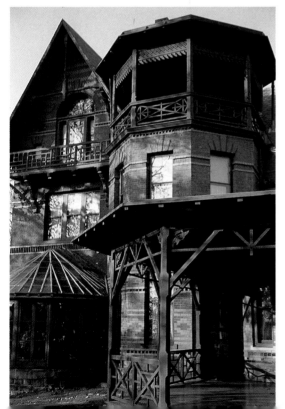

▶ *Continue west on Farmington Avenue for half a block. Turn right on Woodland Street, then take the first left onto Asylum Avenue. Just before the first traffic light, the Connecticut Historical Society is on the left.*

12 Connecticut Historical Society

Inside, the museum offers rotating exhibits on state history, plus permanent displays of furniture and the decorative arts from Connecticut craftsmen of the 17th, 18th and 19th centuries. Browse through the bookshop, with its extensive genealogy collection, enabling people to trace their roots back to England and other nations of origin.

▶ *Back on Asylum Avenue, continue through the traffic light and take the right fork. After a mile (1.6km), having passed through two more traffic lights, the Elizabeth Park Rose Garden is on the left.*

▶ *Return to Asylum Avenue and drive for 1½ miles (2.2km), through two traffic lights. At the third light, turn left on North Main Street and go 2 miles (3km) through the West Hartford Center shopping district. North Main becomes South Main. Continue to No. 227, on the right.*

13 Noah Webster House

Born in 1758, Webster graduated from Yale and became a teacher. He soon saw the need to standardize spelling, so published his *Bluebacked Spellers*, which sold some 70 million copies and became the basis for elementary education throughout the country. The "Schoolmaster of the Republic" did not stop there. He recognized that the language of America was evolving from the original English words, spelling and pronunciation, and spent 20 years compiling a dictionary. Published in 1828, the two volumes contained some 70,000 words.

Inside the house are a first edition of his dictionary, his spellers and some 200 editions of his works. Guides in 200-year-old Colonial dress lead the way through the authentically furnished rooms. There are demonstrations of carding wool, weaving on the massive loom, cooking, bread baking and butter churning.

▶ *Continue south on South Main Street and turn left onto I–84 eastbound at exit 41 to return to downtown Hartford.*

HALF A DAY

New Haven &
Yale University

Founded in 1638 by a group of settlers, the town first depended on seafaring. In the 19th century, thanks to inventors such as Eli Whitney, assembly lines turned out clocks, carriages and guns by the thousands. More recently, New Haven has had to face the urban problems of unattractive development and crime, though efforts to renew and restore civic pride are paying off. At the heart of the city is Yale, one of America's leading universities, adding an enviable cultural dimension to the city.

Neo-Gothic Harkness Tower,
a New Haven landmark

i *Visitor Information Center, 149
Phelps Gate, Yale University*

▶ *Start on The Green on the
corner of Temple and Elm
streets.*

❶ The Green

New Haven has been called
"the first planned city in the
U.S.A." because of its original
grid-like street design, visible
from the 16-acre (6.4-hectare)
Green. Here, residents came to
gossip, to debate and to pray at
the trio of handsome churches,
each with its different architecture, but all built in the early
1800s.

The United Church, often
compared with London's St.
Martin-in-the-Fields, has long
held public meetings and
debates on topics ranging from
slavery in the 1800s to Civil
Rights in the 1970s. It is also
sometimes referred to as the
North Church. In the middle of
The Green is Center Church,
and ever since the mid-1600s, a
meeting house or church has
stood on this site. Cool and
elegant within, handsome
Tiffany stained glass fills the
arched window above the altar.
Trinity Church, the third, was
the first Gothic Revival church
in the country, and was
constructed with materials

allowed to pass through the
British blockade of New Haven
harbor during the War of 1812.
Compared with the white cupola
and steeple of it neighbors, its
tower seems heavy and ponder-
ous. Two impressive buildings,
City Hall and the Post Office,
overlook the Green.

▶ *Walk diagonally north across
the Green towards the impos-
ing battlements and towers of
Yale University and enter the
Old Campus through the
Phelps Gate.*

Yale University is an architectural showpiece

2 Old Campus

Phelps Gate, the front door to Yale, leads to the Old Campus, a typical university quadrangle. The oldest building here is also the oldest in town. Connecticut Hall, with its handsome windows and brick, was built between 1750 and 1753. Nathan Hale, Class of 1773, whose green patina statue sits outside, lived here during his student years. Three years later he was hanged in New York by the British who caught him spying. His last words: "I only regret that I have but one life to lose for my country" became a rallying cry. He was only 21. The right foot of Timothy Woolsey's statue is particularly shiny thanks to superstitious students giving it a rub before exams.

Off to the right, before leaving the quadrangle, is a rough-hewn granite bench. Here, A.

Bartlett Giamattei, a former president of the college would sit, philosophizing about life and comparing it to a baseball game. His best loved essay, *Green Fields of the Mind*, is baseball-oriented. So keen was he on baseball,

SPECIAL TO...

Among the contributions Yale students have made to the world, nothing is quite as much fun as the Frisbee. Since 1947, students supposedly have whizzed flat aluminium pie dishes at one another across the Old Campus. When Wham-O, inventors of the hula-hoop, bought the patent for a plastic flier, they called it a Frisbee, because those dishes came from Bridgeport's Frisbie Baking Company. Such major inventions are often in dispute: Middlebury College in Vermont (see page 117) also claims to be the home of the Frisbee.

FOR HISTORY BUFFS

Like its perennial rival Harvard, near Boston, Yale is one of America's Ivy League schools. Originally started by the Puritans in 1701 to train clergymen and administrators, the first Collegiate School moved to New Haven 15 years later, and changed its name to Yale in recognition of wealthy benefactor, Elihu Yale. Students were nicknamed the "Elis" in honor of the English merchant, whose donation of books was sold to finance the institution. The roll call of famous Yale students ranges from dictionary compiler Noah Webster and architect Eero Saarinen to film star Jodie Foster, Class of 1984. From the renowned graduate schools, especially the Law School, recent celebrities include President Bill Clinton and his wife Hillary, who first met here.

America's favorite summer game, that he gave up academia to become the Commissioner for Baseball and run the professional sport. Sadly, he died soon after taking up the appointment.

▶ *Cross the quadrangle and exit onto High Street.*

3 Saybrook College and the Harkness Tower

Above the elaborate wrought iron gate as one exits is an inscription: "For God, For Country and For Yale." The seal of the college has the Latin words *Lux et Veritas* (Light and Truth), but these jollier words are the last lines of Yale's student song, *Bright College Years*, composed in 1888.

Across the street are the twin buildings of Saybrook and Branford Colleges, reminders of the school's locations before it moved to New Haven. Yale consists of a dozen separate and self-governing colleges. Their buildings were funded by the Harkness family, commemorated by the tall, dark, Gothic Harkness Tower which soars 221 feet (67m), and houses a 54-bell carillon, one of the largest in the world. Its partner, the Wrexham Tower, is modelled on the church steeple in Wrexham, Wales, where Elihu Yale is buried.

▶ *Turn left and continue on High Street.*

4 Skull and Bones Society

Just before walking under the arch, the windowless and ominous-looking stone building on the right is the Skull and Bones Society. Founded in 1832, it is Yale's oldest secret society. Although the membership is never publicized, it supposedly included former president, George Bush. Among many "Bones" legends is one that the remains of the great Apache chief, Geronimo, are interred within its walls.

▶ *Pass under the arch linking the Yale School of Fine Arts (left)*

with the Yale University Art Gallery (right), whose entrance is at 1111 Chapel Street.

> ### SPECIAL TO...
>
> Call them secret societies or senior societies, only half a dozen of the most famous, such as Skull and Bones, are known. Each has only 15 members, all of them seniors who choose their successors from the junior class. Only members have keys to the unmarked windowless buildings where, rumor insists, Masonic-like rituals take place. Some clubhouses resemble grand English manor houses, others echo Greek mausoleums, giving rise to the nickname, "the tombs." All are totally independent of the university.

5 Yale University Art Gallery

The nation's oldest college art gallery dates back to 1832 and is one of several fine museums here, some of which offer free admission. A replica of the original gallery is named for John Trumbull (1756–1843), the founder, and exhibits his work. This artist depicted major moments of the Revolution, such as the Battle of Bunker Hill in Boston, and the signing of the Declaration of Independence. Today, the museum boasts an enormous international collection. From the past are Greek, Roman, Egyptian and pre-Columbian antiquities. From 19th- and 20th-century Europe are paintings by Manet, Millet, Matisse and Magritte. Of the museum's two buildings, the 1953 addition is the work of architect Louis Kahn. He also designed the Yale Center for British Art, across Chapel Street.

▶ *Cross Chapel Street.*

6 Yale Center for British Art

The center's enormous collection, the gift of Paul Mellon in 1966, traces the development of

> ### SPECIAL TO...
>
> America's second-favorite fast-food is the pizza, and that, too, belongs to New Haven. In 1925, Italian immigrant Frank Pepe started selling his special "tomato pies" from a horse-drawn cart. As their popularity grew, he opened Pepe Pizzeria on Worcester Street in New Haven's Little Italy. His trademark *focaccio*-like crust is still cooked in a brick oven, after almost 60 years.

> ### SPECIAL TO...
>
> "Bulldog, Bulldog, Bow wow wow. Eli Yale!" goes the chant. For over a century, the bulldog has been the mascot of Yale's sports teams. Some say an English student introduced the dog; others credit Professor Andrew Graves, whose pooch accompanied him everywhere. The dog was so clever, the story goes, that he barked whenever Yale scored in a football game. Since 1933, there has been a succession of bulldog mascots, all called "Handsome Dan." The 1996 version, Handsome Dan the 14th, is known to his friends as Whizzer.

British art over the centuries and includes a roll call of the great: van Dyck, Gainsborough, Reynolds and Turner. For more specialist tastes are the works of visionary William Blake and animal painter, George Stubbs (*A Lion Attacking a Horse*).

▶ *Continue on Chapel Street, passing the Atticus Bookstore. Here browsers and buyers are joined by sippers of exotic teas and coffees served in the small café. Walk to the corner of Chapel and York streets.*

7 Yale Repertory Theater

Since 1966, a small professional company, boosted by students from the graduate school, has presented avant-garde, cutting-edge work in this 500-seat converted Victorian gothic church.

▶ *Diagonally across from the theater on York Street is the Yale School of Architecture. What looks like nine stories on the outside actually hides 36 floors, and caused much discussion when it was put up in the 1960s. Turn right on York Street.*

8 Yale Drama School

This is one of Yale's many illustrious graduate schools; students who have attended a three-year course here include Paul Newman and Meryl Streep. Contrary to popular myth, Jodie Foster did not attend the Drama School: she was a liberal arts undergraduate.

▶ *Continue on York Street to Elm Street. Turn left, then veer right onto Broadway. Look up to the right.*

9 Payne Whitney Gymnasium

Dominating the skyline is the tower of what looks like a Gothic cathedral. Inside, however, are neither pillars nor pews but "Yalies" in sweat pants and sneakers. Although the university does not award athletics scholarships, sports facilities are as good as anywhere in the

FOR HISTORY BUFFS

Eli Whitney, the Yale graduate who became "father of mass production" made his name by inventing the cotton gin, which separated cotton fibers from the seeds. Although he patented the design in 1794, it was much-copied, so he did not make his deserved fortune.

Next, his analytical brain turned to the making of guns. By standardizing components, he produced guns faster and cheaper in his factory than craftsmen could by traditional methods.

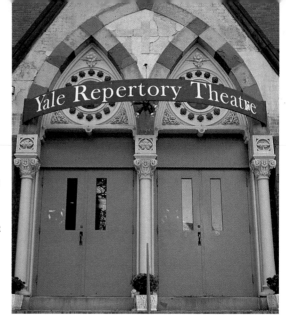

Home of the renowned Yale Repertory Company

country, and "The Game," the annual football game against Harvard, is both a passionate match and a social occasion.

▶ *Return to York Street and turn left. Halfway down the block, at No. 300, is Toad's Place, well known to rock music fans. The Rolling Stones, Bob Dylan and U2 have all played here. Next door is Mory's, one of the best-known spots in New Haven.*

10 Mory's

Today, Mory's is a private club for eating and drinking, but it started out as a bar and inspired a famous ballad, the Whiffen-poof song:
*"To the tables down at Mory's
To the place where Louis dwells ... "*
    Louis Linder was the club's proprietor back in 1909 when four students, members of the Yale Glee Club singers, formed the barbershop-style Varsity Quartet. They took the name of the Whiffenpoof, a mythical half-bird, half-dragon that was a character in a contemporary Broadway show. Now, the 14-strong Whiffenpoofs are the oldest a cappella choir in the country, giving 150 concerts a year. They still meet at Mory's every week.

▶ *Turn right on Wall Street and walk to the corner of Wall and High streets.*

11 Beinecke Rare Book and Manuscript Library

This three-star building alone is worth the journey to New Haven: the exterior, the most memorable of the university's modern buildings, looks like an unbroken cube of white Vermont marble supported at four corners by the lightest of steel pads. Even more memorable is the interior, glowing with bronze-hued light filtering through the translucent marble. The central stack is a six-story glass tower of rare books. On the mezzanine level are two large cases: one holds a rare 1455 Gutenberg Bible, the other a complete edition of *Birds of America* by naturalist John James Audubon (1785–1851).

▶ *Continue on Wall Street, to the corner of College Street.*

12 Scroll & Key

Enigmatic and bearing no name or sign, this stone building, with minarets and mystical carved figures, is home to another of the select and private secret societies.

▶ *Turn right on College Street, left on Elm Street and return to the Green.*

The Housatonic
Valley

1 DAY • 151½ MILES • 245KM

The rolling Litchfield Hills and the Housatonic River give a special character to the scattered villages that dot the peaceful northwest corner of Connecticut, amongst the thick woods.

ITINERARY

HARTFORD	►	**Litchfield (34m-55km)**
LITCHFIELD	►	**New Preston (11m-18km)**
NEW PRESTON	►	**New Milford (8m-13km)**
NEW MILFORD	►	**Kent (16m-26km)**
KENT	►	**Cornwall Bridge (9m-15km)**
CORNWALL BRIDGE	►	**West Cornwall (4m-6km)**
WEST CORNWALL	►	**Salisbury (12½m-20km)**
SALISBURY	►	**Norfolk (14m-23km)**
NORFOLK	►	**Hartford (43m-69km)**

Litchfield, a classic example of the perfect New England town

| i | *Hartford Civic Center*

▶ *Leave Hartford on **Route 44** west. After 16 miles (26km), **Route 202** branches off to Torrington. Continue through Torrington and drive 6 miles (10km) to Litchfield.*

❶ Litchfield

Rather as a judge surveys his court, so Litchfield dominates the local landscape. Appropriately, the Tapping Reeve House on South Street was owned by Judge Tapping Reeve who had America's first law school built in the grounds. Opened in 1773, it produced judges by the score, as well as three justices of the U.S. Supreme Court, 17 senators and two vice-presidents. During that era, Litchfield was also famous for its leather goods, mills and factories. A century later, the affluent townspeople deliberately redesigned their homes and the common to re-create the classic New England village seen today.

The Housatonic River valley

The First Congregational Church, with its white columns, has a stately position at the head of the Green with North, South, East and West streets reaching out in their appropriate compass headings. North Street, often labelled one of the country's most beautiful, boasts textbook examples of late 1700s Georgian and Federal architecture, such as the Sheldon Tavern. The sturdy red-brick building at the corner of North and West streets was customers, from politics to the movies.

ⓘ *Information booth, The Green*

▶ *Drive west for 11 miles (18km) on Route 202.*

❷ New Preston

The road climbs abruptly to New Preston, alongside the tumbling waterfalls of the Aspetuck River which give a clue to the town's industrial background. In the early 1800s, 21 water-driven mills operated between New Preston and Marble Dale, barely a mile away. The mills haven't survived the change to steam power, but New Preston thrives on a new economy of chic antique shops.

▶ *Continue through New Preston for ½ mile (1km) to Lake Waramaug.*

❸ Lake Waramaug

To the Indians, this was the "place of good fishing." Today visitors come to catch the view, often from Hopkins Vineyard, where the red-painted Yankee barn houses the winery and shop.

▶ *Return to New Preston and take Route 202 south for 8 miles (19km) to New Milford.*

SPECIAL TO...

Skitch Henderson, Broadway veteran and director of the New York Pops Orchestra, lives in a typical New England country home called The Silo, located halfway between New Preston and New Milford. Now a cooking school, art gallery and gourmet store of limitless variety, it attracts friends of the Hendersons and neighboring celebrities such as Bill Blass, Whoopi Goldberg and Tom Brokaw.

---

❹ New Milford

The Town Hall on the Green stands on the site of Roger Sherman's birthplace. He is the only Connecticut native whose signature appears on all the significant documents concerning America's independence. Near the bandstand is a tank whose small scale and Victorian styling make it an unusually decorative armed forces memorial.

▶ *Drive through New Milford on Routes 202 and 67 southwest, cross the Housatonic River bridge, turn right at the traffic lights onto Route 7 north and continue for 10 miles (16km) through peaceful countryside to Bull's Bridge.*

❺ Bull's Bridge

Bull's Bridge, one of just two covered bridges in the state which still see daily use, is barely longer than a large car. Beneath, the Housatonic River rushes through a particularly rugged gorge. Raging waters and winter ice jams destroyed four successive bridges until the present one, which has lasted since 1842. Back in 1781, a horse in George Washington's party fell into this gorge while making the crossing. Washington's own financial accounts record "getting a horse out of Bull's Bridge falls, $215.00." The high price suggests that the horse was special to the American general, perhaps his own.

▶ *Continue on Route 7 to Kent.*

SCENIC ROUTES

From New Milford north to Canaan is one of Connecticut's prettiest drives. Running parallel to the Housatonic River the entire way, Route 7 is bordered by the Litchfield Hills to the east and the Taconic Mountains to the west. Housatonic is an Indian word meaning "place beyond the mountains," and the route offers numerous tempting photo opportunities.

SPECIAL TO...

White Flower Farm, 3½ miles (5.6km) out of Litchfield via South Street, is an emporium of flower gardening. Its *Garden Book*, a weighty catalog published twice a year, offers a wealth of horticultural information. Visitors from mid-June through August are treated to the technicolor extravaganza of the begonia displays, a high point in the season.

---

the Litchfield County Jail. Built in 1812, it was in use until the 1990s.

Also on North Street is the red saltbox house that was the home of two 19th-century personalities: the charismatic preacher Rev. Henry Beecher and his sister and author, Harriet Beecher Stowe. The Litchfield Historical Society on the Green has a fine collection of early paintings, decorative arts and furniture, and the Green is lined with trendy shops, galleries and restaurants. The West Street Grill is known for its star

6 Kent

Just as Litchfield was once industrial, so Kent was known for its iron foundries. Where pig iron was smelted in the early 1800s, the Sloane-Stanley Museum now stands. All over New England, coffee tables display at least one of Eric Sloane's art books. A dedicated historian and fine artist, Sloane chronicled all aspects of early American life, from the building of barns to his favorite subject, the making and using of tools. The museum, housed in a big barn, includes a dog-powered butter churn, an authentic frontier cabin, and a re-creation of his art studio, right down to his paint-splattered telephone. Ruins of the furnace stand on the grounds.

▶ *Stay on **Route 7** north for 5 miles (8km) to Kent Falls State Park. Continue for 4 miles (6km) to Cornwall Bridge.*

RECOMMENDED WALKS

Kent Falls State Park is one of a dozen or so state parks and forests in this corner of Connecticut. All are popular spots for picnics and hiking. Here, the special attraction is a broad view over Connecticut's wild terrain.
For a grand view, climb the steep 200-foot (60m) path beside the falls, which are often used for advertisements and feature in the TV soap opera, *The Guiding Light.*

---

7 Cornwall Bridge

From here north, the valley narrows and the hills steepen. Hardly more than an intersection and the bridge, the hub of this little community is Baird's General Store, a well-known stopping point for Appalachian Trail hikers. The "world's longest continuous footpath" stretches 2,050 miles (3,280km) from Georgia to northeast Maine. It crosses Route 7 only a few steps from the front porch where weary walkers stack their backpacks.

FOR CHILDREN

In Canaan, train enthusiasts of all ages can ride the old Housatonic Valley Railroad along the scenic tracks south to Cornwall Bridge.

▶ *Cross the Housatonic again; bear right after the bridge*

*and continue north for 4 miles (6km) to West Cornwall on **Route 7.***

SPECIAL TO...

In West Cornwall, the Cabinet Shop showcases the work of craftsman Ian Ingersoll, who uses native maple and cherry woods, turning them into classic reproductions of streamlined Shaker furniture. Expect reverential accuracy and high-quality workmanship.

Water tumbles down a 200-foot (60m) flight of natural steps in Kent Falls State Park

8 Cornwall Bridge to West Cornwall

This is one of the prettiest stretches of the Housatonic, known as a fly-fisherman's paradise. Throughout the summer anglers stand practising the elegant art of casting and placing the fly delicately on the water.

Somewhat rougher are the sports of white-water canoeing and kayaking. Paddlers meet at Clarke's Outdoors, a log cabin on the left. Although U.S. Olympic teams make this their home base, Clarke's also outfits day trips for recreational paddlers and provides a shuttle service to and from the entry/exit points. The favorite "playground" for the kayakers is beneath the covered bridge at West Cornwall, built in 1837.

▶ *Stay on* **Route 7** *north for 4½ miles (7km), bearing left on* **Route 112** *for ¾ mile (1km) to Lime Rock Park.*

9 Lime Rock Park

Deep in the rural idyll, the self-styled "Road Racing Center of the East," comes as a surprise. The deceptively simple 1½-mile (2.4km) track has tested the best from every category of motorsport. Drivers from Formula 1 to NASCAR and sports car racing have all taken the wheel here. Actor Paul Newman, still highly capable and competitive, is often seen here.

▶ *Continue west for 3¾ miles (6km) on* **Route 112**. *Climbing out of the Housatonic Valley, grand views open up of magnificent farms. To the north and west, the Berkshire Hills continue and blend into the Catskill Mountains of New York and the Green Mountains of Vermont. Turn north onto* **Route 41** *and drive for 1½ miles (2.4km) to Lakeville.*

10 Lakeville

St. Mary's Church spire can be seen on the right on the way into town. Pocketknife Square, just ahead on the left is worth a stop. The handsome four-story brick mill was the site of the Salisbury Forge, known as the "Arsenal of the Revolution." A rich seam of pure iron ore was used to manufacture cannon, shot and weaponry to fight the British. So vital was production that laborers were given special rations of rum and meat. Later, in 1844, the Holley family turned the forge into America's first cutlery factory, and Holley knives with their hand-forged blades became as famous as their more murderous predecessors.

▶ *Continue north on* **Routes 41** *and* **44** *for 2 miles (3km) to Salisbury.*

11 Salisbury

Though Lakeville almost overlaps with its neighbor, Salisbury has its own special merits. It has unofficially become the "Tea Capital" of Connecticut thanks to Chaiwalla, a specialty tea room, and Harney & Sons, master tea blenders and manufacturers found on Main Street. Nearby is the venerable Salisbury Ski Jump, where the annual winter festival in February brings competitors from as far as Norway and Finland.

i Chamber of Commerce, Main Street

▶ *Follow* **Route 44** *for 7 miles (11km) to Canaan and on for another 7 miles (11km) to Norfolk.*

12 Norfolk

Connecticut's highest town, tucked away in the northwestern corner, has an elevation of 1,770 feet (550m). Here, the Battell Chapel, with its Tiffany glass windows, faces the central Green which sits atop the hill. Each summer, the Norfolk Chamber Music Festival, with the Yale Summer School of Music, attracts music fans as it has for almost a century. Rachmaninov, Caruso and Paderewski are among the legends who have performed during the season. Many of the street signs, painted by hand, have been brightened up with pictures of animals.

▶ *From the Green take the tranquil country drive back to Torrington on* **Route 272**. *This is a peaceful stretch of hilly evergreen and oak forest, dotted with lovely homes and farms. Return to Hartford.*

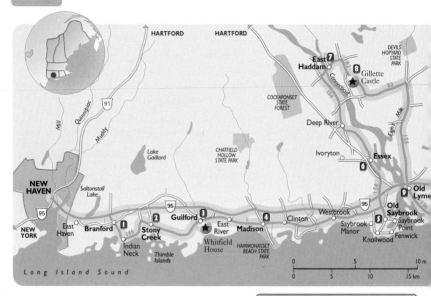

HARTFORD   HARTFORD

DEVILS HOPYARD STATE PARK

East Haddam

Gillette Castle

COCKAPONSET STATE FOREST

Deep River

CHATFIELD HOLLOW STATE PARK

Lake Gaillard

Ivoryton

Essex

NEW HAVEN

Saltonstall Lake

Old Lyme

Westbrook   Old Saybrook

NEW YORK   East Haven   Branford   Stony Creek   Guilford   East River   Madison   Clinton   Saybrook Manor   Saybrook Point   Knollwood   Fenwick

Indian Neck   Thimble Islands   Whitfield House   HAMMONASSET BEACH STATE PARK

Long Island Sound

0   5   10 m
0   5   10   15 km

The
Connecticut
Shore

2 DAYS • 158 MILES • 254KM

New Haven is a mixture of industry and academia. Some areas are grimy survivors of the Industrial Revolution that had its roots here; other areas are a delight, thanks to the ivied walls and grassy quadrangles of Yale University. East of New Haven, the Connecticut shore is dotted with some surprisingly sleepy villages, sheltered from traffic by I–95, the interstate highway that speeds traffic on its way and diverts it from the coast.

ℹ️ *City Hall, Church Street*

▶ *Start in New Haven on **Route** **95** east. Take exit 53 and at the rotary take **Route 146** east to Branford (7miles/11km).*

❶ Branford

The pleasant town of Branford has an old-fashioned green with an unusually opulent library, church and school nearby. The only historic mansion open to the public is the Nathaniel Harrison House on South Main Street, a restored 1724 "saltbox" with beautiful period furnishings and flower and herb gardens.

▶ *Stay on **Route 146** for 6 miles (10km), following the shoreline through Indian Neck to Stony Creek.*

❷ Stony Creek

Millions of Americans and foreigners have seen the pink granite produced from the local quarry: it was used in Grand Central Station and for the pedestal of the Statue of Liberty. Just off shore, the water is speckled by the tiny Thimble Islands. Called the "Hundred Islands" by the Colonists, there are actually over 300 islands scattered throughout Long Island Sound. Some are barely big enough to

accommodate the cottages built on them, often on stilts. With names like Treasure Island and Money Island, it is no surprise that the pirate Captain Kidd supposedly hid out here. Small boats are ready at Stony Creek harbor to give tours.

▶ *Continue on **Route 146** for 4 miles (6km) to Guilford.·*

❸ Guilford

There is a particularly English feeling about this town, founded in 1639 and built around an unusually large green. Luckily, it escaped serious damage during the War of Independence, and around 80 pre-Revolutionary houses still stand.

The oldest, the 1639 Henry Whitfield State Museum, is also the oldest stone building in New England. Sitting on a slight rise in the middle of a large lot, this originally looked more like a fortified manor house, but the steeply-pitched roof and small, leaded, lattice windows reflect its remarkable age.

Other homes with history include the 1660 red saltbox Hyland House, and the 1774 Thomas Griswold House, occupied by Griswold descendants until 1958. Harriet Beecher Stowe, who later wrote *Uncle*

Tom's Cabin, stayed in Guilford on her grandmother's farm where she got to know the black servants.

▶ *Continue on **Route 146** and turn onto **Route 1** east.*

❹ Madison

On the Green at the entrance to the town is the late 17th-century Deacon John Grave House. It has been a school, infirmary, arsenal, tavern and courtroom in its time and is undergoing extensive restorations. Madison also has one of the few beaches on this shore that is open to all. Located in the enormous Hammonasset Beach State Park, the area also includes a nature reserve.

▶ *Continue on **Route 1** east, then turn right to Old Saybrook.*

❺ Old Saybrook

Though busy and commercially developed, Saybrook still has many fine Colonial homes, including the General William Hart House (1767), with its corner fireplaces and herb garden. Saybrook's most famous son is David Bushnell (1742–1824), credited with building the first "sub-marine."

▶ *Return north on **Route 154** and drive for 5 miles (8km) to Essex.*

FOR HISTORY BUFFS

In the 1770s, Yale student David Bushnell was fascinated by explosives. Tests of his limpet mine, in Otter Cove near Old Saybrook, impressed George Washington and renowned inventor Benjamin Franklin. But Bushnell's pride and joy was his *American Turtle*. Reconstructed at the Connecticut River Museum in Essex, this self-propelled underwater capsule is considered the first "sub-marine." It was lost in battle against the British.

⑥ Essex

In a 1996 book called *The 100 Best Small Towns in America*, Essex came out number one. Founded in 1648, it became quite wealthy due to the skill of its carpenters and shipwrights. The splendid Colonial, Georgian and Federal homes on Main Street were built by their bosses, the shipbuilders and sea captains. The town's social hub is the 200-year-old Griswold Inn. Here, collections of marine art and 19th-century firearms add to the atmosphere of "the 'Gris,'" a busy, though jolly, hotel-restaurant. At the end of the street, in an old warehouse on Steamboat Landing, is the Connecticut River Museum. This tells the story of Essex and of the Connecticut River, from its source in northeastern New Hampshire to the mouth. Star attraction is the reproduction of

Cruising on the Connecticut River near East Haddam

David Bushnell's remarkable underwater craft, *American Turtle*. A stone's-throw away, the keel was laid for the *Oliver Cromwell*, the colony's first custom-built warship, back in 1776. From then on, Essex was an important ship-building center. The tradition continues nearby at the Brewers Dauntless Shipyard, which produces sleek modern yachts. The 1732 Pratt

House is well-preserved in the style of 1800, with a herb garden.

▶ Return to *Route 154* and drive 8 miles (13km) north to *Route 82* east. Turn right and cross the Connecticut River on the turntable bridge to East Haddam.

SCENIC ROUTES

The Essex Steam Train and Riverboat is organized by the Valley Railroad Company, whose volunteers restore, maintain and operate old steam engines and cars. They puff through the countryside for the two-and-a-half hour trip up to Haddam, stopping at Deep River, and connect with a river boat for an hour-long cruise.

SPECIAL TO...

No prizes for guessing how Ivoryton, 2 miles (3km) west of Essex, got its name. In the old days, ivory from Africa was unloaded in Essex and driven here in horse-drawn carts. It was then cut and polished into piano keys, buttons and combs. Although a factory nearby is now the world's largest producer of piano and organ keyboards, ivory is no longer used. The hamlet itself is tranquil, with huge beech trees on its main street, a general store and a summer theater.

7 East Haddam

Just at the end of the bridge, high above the river, stands the Goodspeed Opera House. This six-story, white "wedding cake" is a grand reminder of the late 19th century, when East Haddam was a resort town, used by Mr. William Goodspeed's very own steam ships. Restored in the 1960s, the house's specialty is musical comedies. It hosted pre-Broadway runs for brand-new shows such as *Man of La Mancha*, in 1966, and *Annie*, in 1977. Now, new musicals are presented in a second theater in Chester, while this house concentrates on revivals. Land for East Haddam's original 17th-century settlement was sold to the English by local Indians in exchange for 30 coats. The one-room schoolhouse, where hero Nathan Hale once taught, is preserved next to the church.

▶ *Continue on* **Route 82** *south to Gillette Castle.*

Typical two-story New England Colonial house, Old Lyme

8 Gillette Castle

At the turn of the century, actor William Gillette (1853–1937) had superstar status, drawing huge audiences to see his 1,300 performances portraying Sherlock Holmes, complete with deerstalker and cape. By 1919, he had poured a million dollars into this extraordinary fake medieval stone castle. An amateur inventor with an odd sense of humor, he made many of the "puzzle locks" on its doors and designed a system of mirrors to be able to see who was visiting. Now owned by the state, the 122-acre (48.8-hectare) grounds make a fine picnic spot, high on the bank overlooking the river.

▶ *Continue on* **Route 82** *for 5 miles (8km) to* **Route 156** *south. Drive a further 9 miles (14km) to Old Lyme.*

9 Old Lyme

Old Lyme, one of America's first art colonies, is the unofficial home of American Impressionism, thanks to Florence Griswold. At the turn of the century, "Miss Florence" decided to take in boarders; first one, then more artists moved into her fine, Greek Revival home, drawn by the light and the serenity of the surrounding beaches and marshes. Instead of signing the visitors book, guests

such as Willard Metcalf, Childe Hassam and William Chadwick painted scenes on their land-lady's doors and wall panels. The dining room is profusely decorated. This 1817 house, in the heart of the Old Lyme Historic District, is now a museum with a fine collection of the *plein air* movement. Next door, the Lyme Academy of Fine Arts is one of America's leading art schools.

▶ *Leave town and follow* **Route 156** *east, crossing Niantic Bay with a view of the Millstone Energy Center, a nuclear power plant. After 16 miles (26km), arrive in New London.*

> #### FOR HISTORY BUFFS
>
> Called the "Fresh River" by Dutch explorer Adriaen Block and the "Great River" by English settlers, the waterway for which the state of Connecticut is named was always the Quinnetukut to the Indians. The name means "the long river whose waters are driven by wind and tide." It starts in the three Connecticut Lakes, way up in the northeastern corner of New Hampshire, near the Canadian border.

New London

Although New London is slowly renewing its image, it still remains a working town, just as it has been for 300 years. While not as attractive as smaller, more gentrified places in New England, the history here is just as important. The deep harbor made this an important port in the early 18th century, not just for fishing boats, but also for trade with British colonies as far south as the West Indies. During the American Revolution, New London was the headquarters of the patriots' naval resistance, which made it a target for the British Army. Later, the port became one of the world's biggest and busiest whaling ports, with as many as 80 ships in its fleet. Whale Oil Row has four splendid 1832 mansions, grandiose Greek Revival temples of affluence.

The town's nautical history was boosted further in 1876 when the U.S. Coast Guard Academy opened. Its 60-year-old German barque, the US *Eagle*, was confiscated from Germany by the US Navy after World War II. Now, this 295-foot-long (109m) sailing ship welcomes visitors on Friday afternoons, during spring and autumn, unless it is out at sea on a training cruise. Across from the Coast Guard Academy is the Lyman-Allyn Art Museum which offers something for everyone: toys and a doll's house, Indian artifacts and paintings by Connecticut artists.

New London also has a cultural legacy. Playwright Eugene O'Neill spent unhappy boyhood summers at Monte Cristo Cottage, to the south on Pequot Avenue. The cottage is now a research library, but bleak family events there a century ago are recalled in three O'Neill plays, including *Long Day's Journey into Night*. On Route 213, 6 miles (10km) south, is the Eugene O'Neill Theater Center, well known for its theatrical workshops. Performances are presented throughout the season.

▶ Follow signs to *I–95* east and cross the Thames river. Exit 86 leads 1½ miles (2km) north on *Route 12* to the Nautilus Memorial.

USS *Nautilus*

The USS *Nautilus*, dating from 1954, is the world's first nuclear-powered sub and the first to venture under the ice cap at the North Pole. Now open for visitors, it shows just how crowded conditions are when living underwater in a "sub."

▶ Return on *Route 12* and take *Route 1* east for 4 miles (6.4km). Turn right on *Route 215* and drive to Noank.

Noank

Noank, meaning "neck of land" in Indian, is as salty and undiscovered a town as there is on the Connecticut shoreline. A fishing and shipbuilding community in the past, it now looks as if every house might have a retired lobsterman or sea captain sitting out on the front porch. Pearl Street is the main thoroughfare and provides all the high points, from the Deacon Robert Palmer House with its whimsical gingerbread architecture and wild colors to Abbott's Lobster-in-the-Rough. This is a lobster house of the sort found in Maine – informal, with picnic-style eating.

▶ Continue on *Route 215*, then *Route 1* for 2½ miles (5km) to Mystic.

Mystic

The town itself is attractive, but often overlooked by the visitors who swarm to Mystic Seaport,

Monte Cristo Cottage, named after O'Neill's actor-father's greatest role

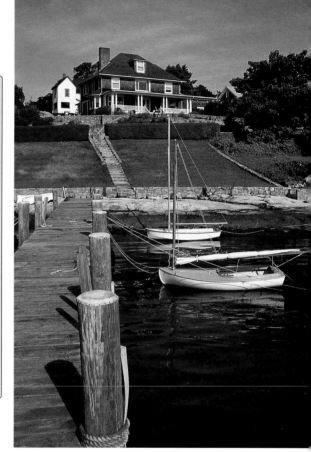

the re-creation of a 19th-century fishing village. A mixture of real and replica, this is much more than a conventional open-air museum, with the largest and most complete maritime collection in the country. Taking full advantage of its waterside location, it has sailing vessels and models of every description and size on display. The 1841 *Charles W. Morgan*, the last wooden whaling vessel ever to be built, and the *L. A. Dunton*, a sleek 123-foot (45.5m) Gloucester fishing schooner which looks more like an America's Cup race competitor, can be seen.

Every possible craft and trade associated with seafaring life can be found and studied somewhere on the 17-acre (6.8-hectare) site. Active craftsmen re-create the workaday world of an early 19th-century fishing village. Nautical terms such as "sandbaggers," "smacks," "chandlers," "coopers" and "cordage" are all explained, while the bank and blacksmith, even the remedies at the pharmacy, all show life as it was way back then. You can even board a steam-

boat for a trip out onto the river.

Also in town is the Mystic Marinelife Aquarium, where dolphins and whales are put through gymnastic routines. Another popular landmark is the after-school teenage hangout, Mystic Pizza. The 1988 movie of the same name gave actress Julia Roberts one of her early breaks on the way to becoming a superstar. The filming, however, took place in the neighboring town of Stonington.

▶ Take **Route 1** towards Stonington. After 3 miles (5km), turn onto **Route 1A** for the village.

14 Stonington

Stonington Borough, a peninsula covered in old houses, remains peaceful and untouristy. The docks of this working fishing port, which has Connecticut's largest commercial fleet, provide an atmospheric place to stroll and watch the dragger fleet and

The sleepy little town of Noank, near Mystic

lobster boats come in each afternoon. At the end of the long narrow main street is the Land Battery, with two of the cannons which helped repulse a British naval attack in the War of 1812. A few steps further is the Old Lighthouse Museum (1823), the first Government-operated lighthouse in Connecticut with gear for whaling and "ice harvesting" displayed in the "pocket-sized" lighthouse. A stroll around town takes you past noteworthy buildings such as the Thomas Ash House and the club house of the Portuguese Holy Ghost Society, for expatriate fishermen from the Azores. The pizza parlor in the film *Mystic Pizza* was re-created in an old lobster warehouse here in town.

▶ Return to **Route 1**, then join **I–95** west and return to New Haven.

THE MARITIME TRADITION

The Atlantic Ocean has had a profound affect on the development of New England. Five of the six states in the region are adjacent to the coastline and the Europeans who first arrived all had to cross the stormy North Atlantic. Once they arrived, ships maintained the umbilical cord linking them with the Mother Countries, and permanent communities grew up around safe harbors. The abundance of fish offshore made fishing an easy and reliable means of finding food, and it became so vital to the early settlers that fishermen were exempt from military service.

Once the Colonies were established, shipping became an important part of the economy, though strict laws from London insisted that all manufactured goods had to be imported from England alone. Enforcement was another matter, and not only were "illegal" cargoes landed, customs duties were, on occasion, evaded.

Ships were a necessity for England and the navy increasingly relied on timber from Maine. Soon, the boats themselves were being constructed in the Colonies, since shipbuilding costs were from 20 to 50 percent less than in the Mother Country. Shipbuilding thrived and by 1760, one-third of the total British merchant tonnage was produced in the American Colonies.

By this time, the patterns of triangular trade routes were established. Merchant ships sailed from New England with grain, timber and fish for the West Indies. These were traded for fruit, sugar and molasses, which were taken on to England. There, the holds were loaded up with manufactured goods to be transported back home. Similar routes connected New England with Africa and the Mediterranean.

After years of lax enforcement, Britain decided to toughen up its policing of the trade laws in order to raise more revenue from the Colonies. Not only did this hurt the New England economy, but it fostered anti-London feelings. The major ports of Boston and Portland, along with New York to the south, were targets before and during the Revolution.

Shipping again became a contentious issue during the Napoleonic Wars in Europe. Although the U.S. remained neutral, Britain interfered with American shipping, hoping to deprive the French of supplies. In addition, seamen were taken off captured ships and forced to sail for Britain. Eventually, these grievances led to the War of 1812.

From their early days, Colonists learned from the Indians how to catch whales when the mammals swam near shore, and towns such as New London and Mystic in Connecticut and New Bedford and Provincetown in Massachusetts thrived at the expense of the whale. In 1774, 360 whaling ships sailed from Nantucket. Rhode Island developed a huge candle-making industry based on whale products. The oil was used to light streets and homes in Europe, while bones and baleen were used to make anything from umbrella spokes to corset stays. Only the discovery of oil (made into kerosene) in Pennsylvania in 1859 ended the bloody trade. The business of whaling was epitomized in Herman Melville's novel, *Moby Dick*, based on his own experiences

Above: humpback whales can reach 40 to 50 feet

aboard ship. Today, museums such as Nantucket's Whaling Museum, housed in a former whale oil refinery, record the exploits of American sailors who roamed the oceans in the early 19th century.

Apart from their heavy involvement in the slave trade, "Yankee traders" sailed round South America to do business with China and the Pacific islands, bringing back huge wealth to towns such as Boston, Salem and Portsmouth. Along the Maine coast, at Kennebunkport and Kittery, Bath, Camden and Belfast, shipbuilders continued traditions begun as early as 1607 when the *Virginia* was the first ship built in the Colonies, near Bath.

Today, New England's nautical traditions concentrate on the pleasure industry, with yachting keeping the shipbuilders and sail-makers of the region at the forefront of technology. For the first half of the 20th century,

Tall ships at Mystic Seaport

Newport rivalled Cowes (in England) as the sailing capital of the world. The rich and famous built ever-larger yachts and raced them. Battles in the wind-swept seas off Newport for the legendary America's Cup were a feature of the town between 1930 and 1983.

In Bristol, Rhode Island, the Herreshoff Marine Museum recalls the Herreshoff Company's contribution to sailing. Between 1893 and 1934, eight consecutive winners in the America's Cup competition were built on the site, as well as the first torpedo boats for the U.S. Navy. In Newport, the Naval War College Museum emphasizes America's rise to power as a world force on the high seas. Out at Fort Adams State Park, at the Museum of Yachting, is the breathtaking *Shamrock V*, Sir Thomas Lighton's 1930 challenger for the America's Cup.

"Windjammers," old sailing ships, are now a popular way of spending a vacation, afloat along the coast. In Maine, Rockland and Camden are the best-known centers, while summer festivals such as Windjammer Days in the Boothbays and the finish of the Great Schooner Race at the Rockland Breakwater celebrate the nautical tradition.

Nowhere records New England's tradition better than Mystic Seaport on the Mystic River in Connecticut. An American whaler, the *Charles W. Morgan*, built of wood in 1841, is one of several sailing vessels ready for visitors to explore.

RHODE ISLAND

Rhode Island, "Little Rhody," is the smallest state, yet it also boasts the longest name: officially, it is The State of Rhode Island and Providence Plantations. This densely populated and heavily industrialized state received its title back in 1644, when two colonies were combined. A mere 48 miles by 37 miles (77km by 59km), it is nicknamed the "Ocean State" because of its 400 miles (640km) of shoreline, which includes some 100 beaches with public access. Not all the coast runs along the Atlantic Ocean; it also borders Narragansett Bay, which bites into the southeast corner of the state and stretches 28 miles (45km) inland, to the capital city of Providence.

Although the Vikings may have visited North America in the 11th century, Giovanni da Verrazano, the Italian explorer, is on record for sailing past what is now Block Island in 1524. He named it after the Island of Rhodes in Greece. When Roger Williams and a band of followers fled the intolerance of the Puritan colony in Massachusetts in 1636, they settled in what is now Providence. Two years later, Anne Hutchinson was similarly banished, and led another group to Aquidneck Island, now better known for the town of Newport. Both communities believed in religious freedom, for Christians as well as non-Christians. The first synagogue in the U.S. was built in Newport, while the first Baptist church was founded in Providence.

Sailboats reflecting in Newport's harbor

Rhode Island has been a holiday destination for almost two centuries. In the early 1800s, the seashore attracted wealthy Southerners, keen to escape the summer heat of the plantations. Families such as the Astors and Vanderbilts spent the summer social season in their "cottages," whose magnificence rivalled European palaces. Tennis, then the sport of the rich, made its American debut at the casino in Newport, and the International Tennis Hall of Fame now has its home here.

But it is sailing, rather than tennis, that is most associated with Newport. For some 50 years, the town hosted the America's Cup challenges, until 1983 when Australia broke the home team's winning streak and took the Cup "down under." Nevertheless, Newport remains the sailing capital of the East Coast.

Tour 12

Providence, the capital of Rhode Island, is a gem of a city, all too often overlooked by visitors to New England. The riverfront and downtown area have been successfully restored and revitalized, while the historic district around Benefit Street is full of 18th- and 19th-century houses, now used for offices and museums, classrooms and private homes. Nearby is Brown University, the seventh oldest in the country, founded in 1764, and the Rhode Island School of Design, one of the country's leading art schools. Not surprisingly, this area is known as College Hill. Across the river is Federal Hill, where Little Italy is full of delicatessens and cafés. With its ethnic mix and large student population, Providence is a lively city, with a thriving music scene, art galleries and numerous restaurants. The *haute cuisine* is a by-product of Johnson and Wales University, which specializes in the culinary arts and hospitality business.

Tour 13

Newport is situated at the southern tip of an island, with a harbor on one side and beaches stretching along the other. This town of contrasts has its share of plain pre-Revolutionary houses as well as opulent summer homes, such as Château-sur-Mer and The Breakers. A century ago, entrance was only for the privileged few; today, visitors are welcome to see the priceless art and grandiose architecture.

Marble House, Newport, was modeled on the Grand and Petit Trianon at Versailles

Sailing has long been popular here, with the most famous race of all, the America's Cup, a long tradition. Even though the Cup has been lost to Australians and, most recently, New Zealanders, Narragansett Bay still brings in the sailing crowd. Newport also attracts tennis fans, who visit the Hall of Fame. In summer you can see one of the few professional tournaments outside the British Isles that is still played on grass. The town also draws music lovers. Since the first Newport Jazz Festival in 1954, the outdoor summer concerts have become important fixtures on the U.S. music calendar.

Providence

Providence, the third largest city in New England, is only now getting the credit and attention it deserves as one of New England's most approachable destinations. Compact and walkable, with fine examples of pre- and post-Revolutionary architecture, it has a lively and artistic student body as well as high-quality restaurants, thanks to the influence of one of America's leading culinary schools.

HALF A DAY

Native American monument, Narragansett

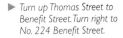

i *30 Exchange Terrace, downtown*

▶ *Start at the Convention Center (park the car here, or in one of the public parking lots nearby). Walk to Memorial Boulevard.*

❶ Waterplace Park

This gem of design is the focal point of Providence's extensive riverfront redevelopment. Cobbled walks, brick paths, planted terraces, amphitheaters, gleaming wrought ironwork and graceful bridges make the Providence River area a model of downtown urban beauty. This is the perfect place to view the State Capitol, sitting imperially on the hill. Built in 1904 of Georgia marble, its dome is second in size only to St. Peter's in Rome. On top, the gilded statue *Independent Man* symbolizes the free-thinking founders of Rhode Island. Inside hangs one of the most famous paint-

ings in the country: the full-length portrait of George Washington, which appears on dollar bills, painted by Rhode Islander Gilbert Stuart.

▶ *Continue along Memorial Boulevard, cross the Providence River on Steeple Street Bridge; follow Steeple Street up the hill to No. 75 North Main Street.*

❷ First Baptist Meeting House

Although Roger Williams founded the Baptist congregation in 1638, the first church was not built for 50 years. This house of worship dates from 1775. A plan for St. Martin-in-the-Fields in London provided the inspiration for architect Joseph Brown, but the ability of the 185-foot steeple (56m) to withstand storms was due to the carpenters' extensive shipbuilding experience.

▶ *Turn up Thomas Street to Benefit Street. Turn right to No. 224 Benefit Street.*

❸ Rhode Island School of Design

Rhode Island School of Design, always abbreviated to "Ris-dee," is one of America's leading art schools. The museum's modern entrance is in the Daphne Farago Wing where the focus is *Mantled Figure*, Howard Ben Tre's sculpture in solid cast glass. Works by Monet and Picasso, an Egyptian mummy, and a 9-foot (2.7m) tall Buddha, dating back ten centuries, are among the rich and varied 100,000-piece collection.

▶ *Continue on Benefit Street to College Street. Turn left and walk up the hill to No. 42.*

❹ Handicraft Club

Members of this private club are painters and craftspeople, but their restored headquarters, the Truman-Beckwith House, is open to the public. When it was built in 1825, the furnishings must have set tongues wagging, particularly the Parisian wallpaper in the front corner sitting-room, with its fanciful scenes of the Far East and India.

▶ *On the opposite corner is the Providence Athenaeum.*

❺ Providence Athenaeum

In the old days, a club for learned men was often called an "athenaeum," in honor of Athena, the goddess of wisdom. This Greek Revival building was finished in 1838 and its stern exterior contrasts with the warm intimacy of the main reading room with its tiers of books. Here, poet Edgar Allen Poe wooed local widow Sarah Whitman, who accepted, then rejected him. Today, anyone in need of inspiration needs only look up to busts of the Greek historian, Homer, the English

Providence has undergone massive renewal and revitalization in recent years authors Milton and Keats, and the American statesman, Daniel Webster. Among the fine bindings and rare editions is an original portfolio of illustrations of American birds by the 19th-century naturalist, John James Audubon.

▶ *Continue up College Street. On the left is the List Art Center where exhibitions of works by Brown students are shown in the David Winton Bell Gallery. Continue to the corner of College and Prospect streets.*

Libraries

This could be called "library corner." On the right is "the Rock," the bustling J. D. Rockefeller Library, open only to Brown students. Opposite is the "Hay," the hushed John Hay Library, where the public may explore the vast book collection and the small gallery in the lobby. John Hay graduated from

The famous *Brown Bear* statue at Brown University

the university in 1858. A poet and historian, he was also the U.S. Secretary of State at the turn of the century.

▶ *Cross Prospect Street and enter the campus of Brown University.*

FOR HISTORY BUFFS

Roger Williams founded Providence, but the city's success in the late 18th and early 19th centuries followed the fortunes of the four Brown brothers. John was a merchant. Joseph, the architect, designed the Market House, First Baptist Church, and a mansion for brother John. Moses founded the Providence Bank and financed the mill at Pawtucket, which started the Industrial Revolution in New England. Nicholas gave land and money to Rhode Island College, which was to be later renamed Brown University in 1804.

Brown University

The Van Wickle Gates, leading to the quadrangle, open just twice a year: to let new students in and graduates out. Founded in 1764, it is the seventh-oldest university in the country, and became co-ed in 1971. The main quadrangle boasts a variety of architecture, with the oldest building, University Hall (1771), being used as a barracks for French and American troops during the Revolution. The larger-than-life bronze *Brown Bear* statue rearing up, with its rather kindly expression, supposedly stands on a slate from the rock where Roger Williams first set foot on his arrival from Massachusetts in 1636. At the upper end of the college's grounds is the Carrie Tower, built by Paul Bajnotti of Turin in memory of his wife. It is inscribed: "Love is as strong as death."

▶ *Return down the hill on College Street and turn left on Benefit Street.*

FOR HISTORY BUFFS

Which Civil War general gave his name to a fashion trend? General Ambrose Burnside, whose statue stands in City Hall Park. So well-known were his side whiskers that the style became known as "sideburns." He went on to be governor and senator for Rhode Island and lived at No. 314 Benefit Street.

Benefit Street

Originally known as Back Street, because it ran behind the houses facing the main street, Benefit Street was transformed from a path into a proper road in 1758 "for the common benefit of all." Now it is known as the "Mile of History," with its many 18th- and 19th-century houses: note details such as the old-fashioned street lights and boot scrapers. At No. 43 Benefit Street, on the corner of Hopkins Street, stands the clapboard Governor

GIVEN BY ALVMNI AND VNDERGRADVATES

Stephen Hopkins House. This delightful example of early 1700s architecture was the home of the ten-time Governor of the state and signer of the Declaration of Independence.

▶ *Continue along Benefit Street.*

9 First Unitarian Church

John Holden Greene, the architect, rated this 1816 church his finest achievement. High in its steeple hangs the largest ever bell cast by the Paul Revere Foundry. Better known now as the messenger who rode from Boston to Lexington in 1775 to warn the Colonists that the British were approaching, Revere was a silversmith and bell-maker.

▶ *Continue on Benefit to the corner of Power Street.*

10 John Brown House

John Brown was a successful merchant who opened up trade with China after the American Revolution. His brother, Joseph, designed this imposing brick house, whose entrance is at No. 52 Power Street. President John Quincy Adams once called it "the most magnificent and elegant" mansion of any in North America. Filled with fine examples of Rhode Island's furniture-making tradition, it

exemplifies the gracious living of the 18th century.

▶ *Continue a few steps further along Benefit Street to No. 357.*

11 Joseph Nightingale House

Supposedly the country's largest wood-frame house, this 200-year-old ochre and cream merchant's home has been restored so completely, it could have been built yesterday.

▶ *Return to Power Street and walk down the hill. Turn right on South Main Street and walk 1½ blocks to the Old Stone Bank.*

12 Old Stone Bank

After the geometric simplicity of most of the buildings on this walk, the art nouveau-style gilt and green dome seems extravagant. It is planned to be the new home of Brown's Haffenreffer Museum of Anthropology.

▶ *Continue to Westminster Street, then cross the river to The Arcade.*

13 The Arcade

Shopaholics in the early 19th century had their own indoor shopping malls. This was the

Brown University's first building, University Hall, is now a National Historic Landmark

U.S.A.'s first, built back in 1828. Note the contrasting styles of the two ends; supposedly, the two architects employed could not agree on a uniform design. The stores and goods may have changed, but it is still popular with visitors as well as locals. The cantilevered stairways and ironwork are still remarkable today.

▶ *Continue on Westminster Street to Dorrance Street. Turn right, heading towards the restored Union Station. At Exchange Street, turn left and return to the Convention Center.*

SPECIAL TO...

Quahogs, often pronounced *ko-hogs* in Rhode Island, are the local clams. The shells were once used as *wampum*, or currency, by the Native Americans. Nowadays, big shells are often saved for a dish or ashtray. Baby quahogs, called cherrystones or littlenecks, are eaten raw, on the half shell, while mature quahogs are used in chowder.

Newport

The original settlement of Newport was founded on the principles of religious tolerance, attracting Jews, Quakers, Baptists and followers of the established Church of England. With its safe, deep-water harbor it rivalled Boston and Philadelphia by the middle of the 18th century. The city tour route starts with a walk through the Newport of the early days and finishes with a drive past the grand mansions of the late 19th century, referred to as the "Gilded Age." As well as fine museums, Newport offers wide, flat beaches, making this an appealing destination for families. **HALF A DAY**

ⓘ *Gateway Visitors Center, 23 America's Cup Avenue*

▶ *Park in the parking lot behind the Visitors Center. Walk south along the avenue for one block to Long Wharf. Cross the avenue and proceed through Brick Market Place, a tree-lined mall of small shops, to the Brick Market building.*

❶ Brick Market Building

This handsome three-story building, built in the late 1770s, was the commercial hub of Colonial Newport. Its arches and columns were radical features in their day, marking a move away from the strictly geometric Georgian style. Now it is the Museum of Newport History, with furniture, tools, interactive computer displays and a fine model of the side-wheel steamer *Bristol* on display.

In the triangular Washington Square, the statue of Oliver Hazard Perry is a reminder of the naval hero who grew up in Newport. Aged 28, he defeated the British on Lake Erie in what was an important battle during the War of 1812. "We have met the enemy and they are ours," was his victory message.

▶ *Walk up the hill to the Robert and Joseph Rogers House.*

❷ Robert and Joseph Rogers House

Nearly 300 years old and still standing, this house displays the swells and bulges resulting from the settling of its foundations. The once rectangular windows have shifted into a curious variety of rhomboids and trapezoids. Closed to the public as it is now used for offices, this is one of only a handful of Federal-style houses in Newport.

▶ *Continue up the square to Old Colony House.*

❸ Old Colony House

In a town constructed primarily of wood, this brick building would have looked even more imposing in the 18th century. The oldest capitol building in the country, it was the head-quarters of government from 1739 until 1900, when the new State House was opened in Providence. Important announcements read from the central second-floor balcony range from the coronation of King George III in 1760 to the results of elections for Rhode Island governors.

FOR HISTORY BUFFS

'...Whereas George the Third ... forgetting his dignity ... instead of protecting is endeavoring to destroy the good people of this colony ...' Those words, read to a crowd waiting outside the Old Colony House, announced the repudiation of English authority in the colony of Rhode Island. The date was May 4, 1776. Two months later, on July 4, came the Declaration of Independence of all 13 colonies.

▶ *From the Old Colony House turn right and walk along Broadway to No. 17, the Wanton-Lyman-Hazard House.*

Newport is an attractive little town set dramatically against Narragansett Bay

❹ Wanton-Lyman-Hazard House

When this house was built around 1675, it was one of more than 260 in a thriving village. Notice that the chimney stack is in the middle of the steep roof, but the front door is off-center; this style was typical of the area and is known as the "Rhode Island floor plan." A century later, Tory-enthusiast Martin Howard lived here, but was forced to flee from an angry mob who were protesting against the Stamp Act.

▶ *Return to the square and turn left on Touro Street at No. 85.*

❺ Touro Synagogue

'Erected 5603'. That inscription celebrated the opening in 1763 of the first synagogue in the States, the oldest Jewish place of worship in the Americas, founded by Rabbi Touro. A community of Sephardic Jews had been in Newport since 1658, when 15 families arrived from Holland. Like the Quakers, the Jews were important in building Newport's trading links and wealth. Architect Peter Harrison, who also designed the Brick Market and the Redwood Library, included 12 pillars to represent the 12 tribes of Israel in an interior that looks much like a classic New England meeting house.

▶ *Continue to the building nextdoor.*

❻ Newport Historical Society

The Newport Historical Society, a driving force behind the preservation of Newport's historic buildings, was established in 1853, though it evolved from an even earlier club. The Seventh Day Adventist Meeting House, built in 1729, was moved here in 1887.

▶ *Return to Washington Square and turn left on Clarke Street. Walk halfway down this street of colorfully painted houses to No. 23–25, the Armory of the Artillery Company of Newport.*

The moon rises over white-steepled Trinity Church

❼ Newport Artillery Company

Uniforms worn by Field Marshall Montgomery, Prince Philip and President Anwar Sadat of Egypt are among the uniforms, flags and regalia in the museum contained in this 1836

stone building. The "1741" over the door refers to the date of the Artillery's charter, making this the oldest military organization in the country.

▶ *Walk to the corner of Clarke and Mary streets.*

❽ Vernon House

In 1781, General Washington met with French Generals Lafayette and Rochambeau to decide tactics for the next stage of the war. Rochambeau, commander of the French troops quartered in Newport, lived in this house. If you look closely you will see what appears to be weathered stone block is actually wood.

▶ *Continue up Mary Street, turn right on Spring Street and proceed to Trinity Church.*

❾ Trinity Church

Since 1726, the tall white spire has been a landmark on the hill above the harbor. In the vestibule is the church's original bell, "probably the first bell that rang over a New England church." The church's organ, made by Richard Bridge, came from London in 1733 and may have been played by composer Friedrich Handel himself. On the main floor stand box pews, which are privately owned and can be bought and sold. Note the individually chosen cushions and elaborate needlepoint covers for the kneelers. The inscriptions on Pew 81 commemorate the most famous worshippers, from George Washington to Queen Elizabeth II and Archbishop Desmond Tutu of South Africa. Stained-glass windows by Tiffany stand out against a background of white walls and green-gray woodwork. They were paid for by wealthy summer residents such as Cornelius Vanderbilt.

▶ *The next left is Mill Street. Turn left, and walk up the hill past Touro Park and the mysterious Stone Tower. Legend says that it was erected by Vikings in the*

11th century. More probably, it was a look-out for Governor Benedict Arnold (grandfather of the Revolutionary traitor) who owned much of the land. Continue up to Bellevue Avenue and cross the street to No. 50.

❿ Redwood Library

A £500 donation in 1746 bought the first books for what is the oldest continuously used library in the country. The benefactor was Abraham Redwood, a rich trader from the West Indies. The building is typical of the pre-Revolutionary era, with wood painted to look like stone. As well as books, there is a sculpture of Benjamin Franklin

by Jean-Antoine Houdin and paintings by Gilbert Stuart.

▶ *Walk next door.*

⓫ Newport Art Museum

Clipped gables, airy verandas, scroll-sawed trim and ornamental timbers, or "sticks," epitomize the "stick style" of 19th-century architecture.

Dating from 1862, this is the first of many buildings in Newport designed by Richard Morris Hunt, but it is vastly different to the extravaganzas that made him the defining architect of the later "Gilded Age."

▶ *Cross Bellevue to Touro Park and walk down Pelham Street to the harbor area. Along the way, you pass the tiny Arnold Burying Ground, where the stones date back to 1677. At the bottom, turn right and return to the Visitor's Information Center. The rest of the route is followed by car. Drive up Memorial Boulevard and turn right on Bellevue Avenue and head for No. 194.*

for "little house." The first major commission for Stanford White and the McKim, Mead and White architectural firm, its "shingle" style was another popular Victorian trend. It spreads over almost a full city block; there are shops on the ground floor, with the ever-expanding Tennis Hall of Fame above. Outside are the world's oldest continuously-used grass tennis courts, dating from 1881. (The All-England Club is older, but moved to its present Wimbledon site in 1922.) The annual professional tournament here is played each July, immediately after Wimbledon.

On entering the main gate to the Hall of Fame, there is the

view of two players volleying. If you feel so inclined, book time on one of the 13 courts and play where the U.S. Open Tennis Championships were born.

▶ *From here, drive along Bellevue Avenue. A combination ticket provides entry to eight of the Preservation Society properties.*

13 Kingscote Mansion

In 1841, the Bellevue Avenue area was only starting to develop as a residential neighborhood, and Kingscote Mansion looks positively simple compared to the grandiose designs of the 1890s. Typical of the Gothic

The Redwood Library, designed to look like a Roman temple

12 Newport Casino and the International Tennis Hall of Fame

The Casino, not a gambling casino but a gentlemen's club, was founded in 1880 as a rival to the Newport Reading Room. It takes its name from the Italian

distant roar of cheering tennis fans and the voice of an announcer calling a famous match from the past. The all-encompassing collection of tennis memorabilia ranges from an 1876 tennis racquet-bending machine right up to Monica Seles' 1995 ensemble, while state-of-the-art computer displays provide a net judge's

Revival style are the elaborate barge-boards, lancet arch casement window, and sawn cornice trim. Designed by Richard Upjohn and built for George Noble Jones, some say that the expression "Keeping up with the Joneses" originated here.

▶ *Continue on Bellevue Avenue.*

14 The Elms

When Pennsylvania coal baron Edward Berwind went to France, he was so impressed by the 18th-century Château d'Asnières, near Paris, that he made it the model for this house. The Elms, built in 1901, has furnishings that span the Louis XIV and XV styles, while the formal gardens have spacious terraces and lawns. At the top of the house, a hidden third story contains the servants' quarters. Berwind's sister lived in The Elms until her death in 1961.

▶ *Continue on Bellevue Avenue.*

15 Château-sur-Mer

In 1857, William Wetmore invited 2,500 guests to a party in his five-year-old home. He paid for those festivities, and for this lavishly-decorated mansion, with profits from trading with China.

▶ *Proceed another block on Bellevue, then turn left at Ruggles Avenue and follow the signs to The Breakers.*

16 The Breakers

This is the ultimate in extravagance and the most famous summer "cottage" of all. Two decades after Richard Morris Hunt renovated Château-sur-

SPECIAL TO...

Newport's wealthy loved racing huge yachts. Their money and patronage stimulated interest in the America's Cup, the world's oldest international sporting challenge. The first race was held in England, round the Isle of Wight, in 1851, but from 1920 onwards, Newport was the host. The American winning streak finally ended in 1983, when Australia took the cup. In recent decades, the port has also acted as the finish line for single-handed transatlantic races. The full story is told in the Museum of Yachting at Fort Adams State Park, which also has fishing, sailing and swimming exhibits.

Mer, he created this mock 16th-century Italian palace for the railroad tycoon, Cornelius Vanderbilt II. Hundreds of craftsmen were employed, many brought over from Europe, but the grand salon was actually built in France, disassembled,

FOR HISTORY BUFFS

Just over a century ago, Newport was the hub of the New York social set, perhaps the wealthiest group of friends in the world. Each summer would be spent in what were called "summer cottages." Built along Bellevue Avenue, Ocean Drive and Harrison Avenue, these deliberately rivalled Europe's palaces in size and splendor, as families such as the Vanderbilts and Astors vied to be America's royalty. In the two-month season, one lavish party followed another, with no expense spared.

shipped across the Atlantic, and reassembled by the same French craftsmen. In the dining room, a painted ceiling is two stories above the life-sized figures and gigantic marble columns. Guides delight in opening oak doors weighing several tons with just the touch of a finger. Although the kitchen is the size of an average house, it looks surprisingly simple and functional, hung with yard after yard of copper cooking pots and pans.

▶ *Return to Bellevue Avenue and continue.*

17 Rosecliff

The Grand Trianon of Versailles was the inspiration for the summer home of Mrs. Hermann Oerlich. Soft-white tiles cover the outside; inside, the 80-foot (24m) long ballroom is all cream and gold. Elegant and refined, Rosecliff sits near the ocean and was used for shooting the 1974 film, *The Great Gatsby* and, more recently, *True Lies* with Arnold Schwarzenegger.

▶ *Continue along Bellevue Avenue.*

18 Beechwood

At the end of the 19th century, Caroline Astor was the reigning queen of American society. To be invited to her parties meant social acceptance. Her famous list of "The Top 400" people supposedly reflected the capacity of the ballroom in her New York City residence. Today, guides show visitors round and give some idea of how the other 0.1 per cent lived.

▶ *Next door is Marble House.*

19 Marble House

Marble House is another Richard Morris Hunt creation, built in 1892 by William Vanderbilt, the brother of Cornelius. The overpowering entrance is covered in Italian marble, while the dining room boasts one-of-a-kind bronze Louis XIV chairs weighing 60 pounds (27kg) each. Most amazing of all is the ballroom, where "all that glisters" really is gold,

Cornelius Vanderbilt's Breakers,
Newport's most splendid estate
Inset: the Newport coastline

wedding reception of Jacqueline
Bouvier to John F. Kennedy.
From 1961 to 1963 it was also
the "Summer White House" for
President Kennedy, who often
vacationed here. It is still a working farm.

SCENIC ROUTES

The 3-mile (4.8km) Cliff Walk,
starting at Cliff Walk Manor on
Memorial Avenue and ending
at Bailey's Beach, is an
excellent way to see the
splendors of the mansions
from a different angle. You will
also enjoy the many varied
coastal views.

or gilded. When Alva Vanderbilt
divorced her husband, she took
the house, then married Perry
Belmont (see below).

▶ Proceed a little farther to
Belcourt Castle.

20 Belcourt Castle

Alva Vanderbilt did not move far
from her first Newport "cottage"
after she divorced William K.
Vanderbilt, and married his good
friend, Perry Belmont. Where
Vanderbilt was keen on yachts,
Belmont followed horse-racing
and helped build the Belmont
Track in New York.

▶ Ocean Drive starts here,
following a scenic stretch of
broken and rocky shoreline,
dotted by breathtaking private
homes, many of which rival
the splendor of Bellevue
Avenue. Bailey's Beach, the
first on the left, was the beach
favored by the "400". Some
5 miles (8km) farther, also on
the left, is Hammersmith
Farm.

21 Hammersmith Farm

This shingled 1888 beach house
on the Auchinloss estate gained
worldwide prominence in the
1950s as the location for the

▶ Bearing left at the next intersection will take you back to
the Newport Harbor area, via
Harrison Avenue, Halidon
Avenue, Wellington Avenue
and Thames Street.

VERMONT

Vermont has been called "every American's second state" because of the small farms with red barns, and villages with white churches that make up the traditional image of "old-fashioned America." The most rural of all states, it has only one major town, Burlington, with 40,000 inhabitants. The remainder of the half million or so Vermonters are scattered throughout the rolling hills and valleys stretching north–south between Canada and the Massachusetts border.

Although Lake Champlain lies on its western flank and the Connecticut River forms the eastern border, Vermont is the only New England state with no access to the sea. What it does have is mountains. French explorer Samuel de Champlain first remarked on the *verts monts*, the green mountains, back in the 17th century. While still a colony, Vermonters argued over land ownership with neighboring New York; the Vermonters won. When the colonies threw off the yoke of the English crown, Vermont went its own way; from 1777 to 1791 it was a republic, minting its own coins and printing its own stamps.

Vermont's gentle rolling landscape

The population has always been small. The roller-coaster landscape is difficult to farm, winters are bitter and summers are short. Despite that, Vermont has had its moments of affluence. Early in the 19th century, its wool was in demand world-wide. When that trade was lost, dairy farming took over. Although forests now cover acres of land once cleared for pasture, cattle remain a significant revenue earner. The sharp flavor of Vermont cheddar cheese is rated by gourmets, while a more recent dairy-related success is Ben and Jerry's Ice Cream. Other natural resources such as marble and granite provide a base to the economy, matched by furniture-making, paper production and computers. Most important of all, however, is tourism.

Each autumn, "leaf peepers" by the thousands invade the state, drawn by the natural phenomenon of the maple leaves turning to brilliant shades of red and gold. Since the first ski tow was set up in Woodstock in 1934, the winter season has attracted downhill and cross-country skiers.

Tour 14

The southern Vermont town of Bennington rarely rates more than a few lines in the history books, yet it played its part in the Revolution, and a 306-foot (91.8m) high stone needle commemorates the 1777 battle. Nearby is the grave of one of the country's favorite poets, the 20th-century writer Robert Frost. Bennington's museum displays a fine collection of naive paintings by Grandma Moses. These, along with handsome old houses and business buildings add up to a town worth exploring.

Tour 15

Southern Vermont looks softer than points further north and is known for its photogenic farms and villages. Weston, set on a hilltop, preserves the atmosphere of a typical 19th-century Vermont village. Ludlow offers its own ski mountain; while the center of Grafton, known for its cheese, has been preserved, scrubbed clean, painted white and seems suspended in time. The only crowded place is Manchester, full of shoppers hunting for bargains at the numerous factory outlet stores.

Tour 16

This part of Vermont is best known for the world-class ski resort of Killington. Apart from that, it is also another peaceful area where artists and craftspeople create minor masterpieces in small villages tucked away in the Green Mountains. Former U.S. President Calvin Coolidge is a local hero, his birthplace and homestead have become minor shrines. A few villages, such as Woodstock, have been deliberately "prettied up," but overall, the natural, unhustled pace of life will reward those looking for a relaxed vacation. Take time to bike the back roads.

Tour 17

Compared with the quieter regions to the south, the northern section is a bustling part of the state. Celebrities range from Ben and Jerry, whose ice creams have taken the world by storm, to the Trapp Family of *Sound of Music* fame, who run an inn near Stowe. Teddy bears and Icelandic horses, a house with secret passages and the Robert Frost Trail are some of the offbeat attractions. The Shelburne Museum is an outstanding collection of American folk art, housed in buildings that were moved here lock, stock and barrel from locations all over New England. The elongated Lake Champlain is fine for a ferry ride, water sports, or for those in search of quiet contemplation.

The first pumpkins of the season: they must be picked before the frosts arrive

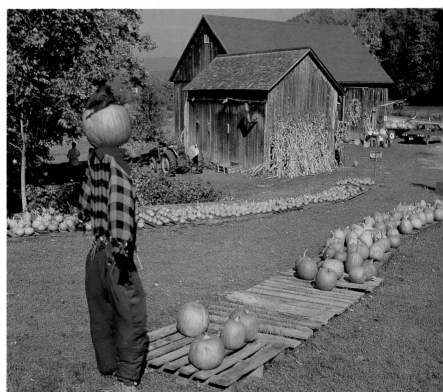

HALF A DAY

Bennington

Outside the state, Bennington is best known for Ethan Allen and his Green Mountain Boys, a group of feisty Vermonters who not only had a grievance against the British, but also against the neighboring, land-greedy "Yorkers," New Yorkers, in the state next door. The historic district and its college make this an attractive small town.

ⓘ *Veterans Memorial Drive*

▶ *Park at the Bennington Museum to start the tour.*

❶ Bennington Museum

"Grandma" Moses (1860–1961) was known as much for her longevity as for her "primitive" portrayals of rural life. This farmer's wife only started to paint when she turned 70, recording countryside activities such as haymaking and maple sugaring. Critical acclaim led to an exhibition at New York's Museum of Modern Art. Although she lived just across the state line, in Eagle Bridge, New York, this Vermont museum has the largest collection of her work, with 28 paintings shown in a special gallery. A favorite picture, often used on greetings cards, is *Over the River*, which depicts the trip to Grandmother's house for Thanksgiving. Memorabilia are found in the old schoolhouse where she, her grandchildren and her great-grandchildren all

studied. The museum also houses the 1777 Battle of Bennington flag, thought to be the oldest "Stars and Stripes" in existence. Watch for the Bennington pottery and glass collection from the 19th century and the Bennington Wasp (1920s), the only automobile ever to be manufactured in Vermont.

▶ *Walk up the hill to the small green in the center of Old Bennington. Look to your left.*

The grave of Robert Frost, a simple memorial to the poet, lies in Bennington cemetery

❷ Old First Church

*"And were an epitaph to be my story
I'd have a short one ready for my own.
I would have written of me on my stone:
I had a lover's quarrel with the world."*

The final line of Robert Frost's 1942 poem, *The Lesson for Today*, is engraved on the plain stone marking his grave in the cemetery. One of the best-loved poets of his time (1874–1963), he captured the essential sights, smells and character of New England.

Also buried here are five Vermont governors and many patriots who fell in the Battle of Bennington. The original 1763

meeting house was replaced in 1805 by this handsome church, whose stylish belfry contrasts with the usual spiked steeple.

Across the street is the old Walloomsac Inn. Here, refreshments were first served in 1766, so it claims to being the "longest-running tavern in America." It is now a private home.

▶ *Turn right on Monument Avenue and head towards the obelisk. Just on the right is a statue.*

3 Catamount Tavern

Looking ready to pounce on
unwary passers-by, this big
bronze wild cat commemorates
the site of the Catamount
Tavern, built in 1767. It was the
meeting place of Ethan Allen
and the Green Mountain Boys.
The catamount, or catamoun-
tain, is the state mascot of
Vermont. It is also called a puma,
cougar, and lynx.

▶ *Walk to the top of Monument
Avenue.*

4 Bennington Battle Monument

Confusingly, the Battle of
Bennington took place in New
York. In 1777, the British were
running low on food and arms, so
General Burgoyne sent troops to
capture the American stores
which were stashed in a depot in
Bennington. Before the
Redcoats could reach the town,
they were intercepted and over-
powered by the patriots led by
General Stark and Colonel Seth
Warner. This was a significant
victory in a regional campaign
that ended with the surrender of
Burgoyne at Saratoga a few
months later.

The statue of local hero,
Colonel Seth Warner, stands
before the simple monument on
the site of the supply depot.
Over a century old, the statue,
built of locally quarried lime-

stone, ranks as the tallest man-
made structure in Vermont,
soaring 306 feet (91.8m). Take
the elevator to the observation
levels for spectacular views of
three states – New York,
Massachusetts and Vermont.
Each year, the victory is celebrated in style on Bennington
Battle Day Weekend in mid-
August.

▶ *Return down Monument
Avenue, noting the fine examples of Federal and Georgian
houses on either side. Turn left
on West Main Street and
head down the hill into town.
On the left is a service station.*

5 Hemming's Sunoco Station

You could be forgiven for thinking this is a museum of classic
vehicles. Although it is a func-
tioning Sunoco station, the
owners are the Hemmings
family, the publishers of *Motor*

The observation platform on top
of Bennington's Battle Monument
gives excellent views over the city

News. The magazine is perhaps
the best available listing of
antique and classic automobiles
in the U.S.A. Unusual models of
restored tractors, wreckers,
steamrollers and panel trucks
from the 1920s to the 1940s are
often on display outside.

▶ *Walk on for a block, then turn
left on Depot Street. Continue
to the junction with River
Street.*

6 Historic Bennington Railroad Station

The Bennington and Rutland
Railroad was successful a
century ago, when this temple of
limestone and blue marble was
built. However, passenger trains
have not stopped here since
1933, although freight trundled
through right up to the 1950s.

The handsome building survives as a restaurant, with evocative photographs of old steam engines on the walls.

▶ *Turn left on River Street and then right onto Benmont Avenue.*

7 Holden Leonard Mill
Back in the 19th century, Bennington was a manufacturing town, using the rushing Walloomsac River to power grist and paper mills such as the Holden Leonard Mill. This massive building, with a central tower rising four stories high, has been converted to offices, but stands as a legacy to the industrial past.

▶ *Turn right on County Street. At the corner of North Street is the Hawkins House with its contemporary crafts. Cross North Street and continue to No. 324 County Street.*

8 Potters' Yard
In the 19th century, the town was known for its pottery, as the 4,000-piece collection in the museum shows. Today, around 40 potters still work in what was an old grist mill on County Street. This arts and crafts center, with small shops and a restaurant, is owned by David Gil, who has been designing his popular, colorful splatterware since 1948. As well as the jugs, pitchers and vases, his dinner services are in great demand both in restaurants and homes.

▶ *Return to North Street and turn left. This becomes South Street after the intersection with Main Street.*

9 Pennysaver Building
The houses and churches of 19th-century New England are familiar from postcards and calendars, but the commercial architecture can be just as fascinating. The former Putnam Hotel block curving round from South to Main and the Pennysaver Building at 107 South Street are typical of "downtown"

structures. The *Pennysaver*, a free newpaper, still occupies the premises. The huge, globular lights outside were originally gaslit.

▶ *Return to Main Street and turn back west, returning to the car. Now drive to Bennington College, via Route 7A and Route 67A.*

10 Bennington College
Founded in 1925 to offer further education to women, Bennington College is now co-ed. It was once the most expensive private college in America, and former students include Broadway actress Carol Channing and film star Alan Arkin, as well as a host of artists. Known for its programs of fine arts (drama, painting, sculpture and writing), the campus is an attractive blend of mock colonial and modern buildings in a rural setting.

▶ *Continue on Route 67A to North Bennington (2 miles/ 3km). Three covered bridges arch the Walloomsac River on the left: the Silk Road, Papermill Village and the Bert Henry Bridge on Murphy Road. On the right, entering the town, is a fine complex of water-driven mills on Paran Creek. This is a convenient place to park. Cross Main Street, and bear left up West Street. At the corner of Park Street is the Park-McCullough House.*

11 Park-McCullough House
With its handsome curving veranda, this early example of an American Second Empire-style mansion (1865) gives an idea of how the wealthy lived in the latter half of the 19th century. The name combines that of lawyer Trenor Park, who built the house, and his son-in-law, John McCullough, one of the two Vermont governors who lived here. The 35-room house has a collection of early photographs by Carlton Watkins, who recorded life in the Wild West. Out in the stables are old sleighs and carriages. Open to the public, there is a small replica of the mansion on the front lawn.

▶ *Return to Main Street and turn left up the hill, past the imposing Greek columns of Powers Market. It is no more than a country store inside, but at the top of the hill is the station.*

12 Old Train Station
This delightful Victorian railroad station, decorated in shades of green and barn-red trim, dates back to 1880. Today it is a popular dining venue.

▶ *Return to car at the bottom of the hill.*

Taking a quiet moment in Bennington, once a center of Revolutionary action

While most of the world experiences a dull, even sad end to the year, New England's landscape goes out in a blaze of glory. Due to a combination of soil and trees, sun and rain, the hillsides change from green to a tapestry of scarlet and gold, purple and orange. This is the "foliage season." Rudyard Kipling, who lived for a while in Vermont, felt almost powerless to depict the transformation. "No pen can describe the turning of the leaves – the insurrection of the tree people against the waning year. A little maple began it, flaming blood-red of a sudden where he stood against the dark green of a pine-belt. Next morning there was an answering signal from the swamp where the sumacs grow. Three days later, the hill-sides as far as the eye could range were afire, and the roads paved with crimson and gold." (*Leaves from a Winter Notebook*, 1900.)

Photographs cannot prepare you for your first sight of New England in September and October. Millions of visitors, "leaf peepers," visit the region every year, with cameras at the ready. Most go by car or on bus tours, but hot-air balloons and river cruise boats also provide a spectacular experience.

Science

Scientists have a clinical explana-tion for the changes. They say that sunny days, allied with chilly nights, stop the production of chlorophyll, the chemical that turns leaves green. This, in turn, allows other pigments such as anthocyanin (red) or carotenoids (orange, yellow) to show through in the leaves. The Native American explanation is far more entertaining: the Great Bear (in the sky) was killed in a hunt, and its blood dripped down onto the leaves. As for the yellow, that was attributed to the fat of the bear splashing out of the cooking pot.

The time

The leaves change color in a tide that sweeps down from north to south, usually starting in late September in Maine, northern Vermont and New Hampshire and reaching Connecticut in the south, around the middle of October. The most intense period is, by tradition, the first two weeks in October, especially

in Vermont and New Hampshire. The Columbus Day holiday (second weekend of October) is the most crowded of the year in those tiny states. Hotels and inns tend to have "foliage season rates" that start in mid-September and carry on through mid-October. Of course, there is no promise from Mother Nature that she'll get her paint-brushes out at this time: a dry summer and the leaves could change earlier; a wet summer and the "foliage" could be delayed. To avoid the inevitable

The dazzling colors of fall

crowds, a few visitors gamble and go north to Maine, where the weather might not be so gentle, but the roads are almost certainly quiet. Otherwise, the trick is stay off the main roads, and drift along the twisting country lanes which often have poor or even no signs at all. Take warm clothing; leaf watching is warm in the sun, but can turn chilly at the end of the day.

The trees

The dark green is usually provided by fir and spruce.
Scarlet and crimson: dogwood, red (or swamp) maple, sassafras and red oak.
Gold and yellow: poplar, elm, birch and gingko.
Orange: hickory, mountain maple and mountain ash.
Brown: oak.
Purple: sumac.

Hotlines

The New England states have special telephone numbers with up-to-date information on the progression of the color, and where to find it.

Connecticut (tel: 203/566–5348 or 800/CT–BOUND)
Maine (tel: 207/582–9300 or 800/533–9595)
Massachusetts (tel: 617/727–3201 or 800/632–8038)
New Hampshire (tel: 603/271–2343 or 800/258–3608)
Rhode Island (tel: 401/277–2601 or 800/556–2484)
Vermont (tel: 802/828–3239.

2 DAYS • 151 MILES • 244KM

Southern
Vermont

"The Switzerland of North America" was a British ambassador's description of Vermont, yet the southern part is softer than the rest of this rugged state, with hamlets and houses scattered across the landscape. Almost every village has a green, a white steepled church and an inn, and roadside stands selling maple syrup.

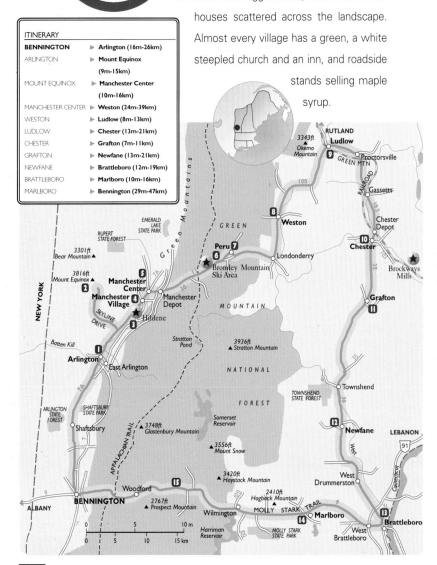

---

i *Veterans Memorial Drive*

▶ *Start in Bennington and drive north on **Route 7A**, passing through the town of Shaftsbury and the Vermont Pipe Shop before reaching Arlington.*

❶ Arlington

Illustrator Norman Rockwell, famous for his *Saturday Evening Post* magazine covers, spent the middle part of his life here, from 1939 to 1953, using local people as models for his countless views of everyday life. Some of them still live in the village today. Although the most complete record of his work is further south in Stockbridge, Massachusetts, a church here in Arlington also has a permanent record, though these are all reproductions. The country doctor who appeared in a Rockwell picture popular in many waiting rooms was one Dr. Russell, whose vast collection of Vermontiana is housed behind the library. Vermont's first grist mill was built here in 1764 by the splendidly named Remember Baker. Only a plaque remains to mark the site.

▶ *Proceed north on **Route 7A** for 4 miles (6km) to the foot of Mount Equinox.*

❷ Mount Equinox

The Carthusian order has a monastery here on the 3,816-foot (1,163m) Big Equinox peak, the highest point in the Taconic Range. The 5-mile (8km) Skyline Drive toll road climbs steeply to the Equinox

Covered bridges are now recognized as historic landmarks. This example is at West Arlington

Mountain Inn with memorable views across to Quebec, New York, New Hampshire and Massachusetts. Cars are warned to have good "brakes, radiators and transmissions" before attempting the drive. Cyclists and sports-car racers fequently test themselves on "hill climbs." The record ascent is just over 8 minutes by racing car.

▶ *Continue on **Route 7A** to Hildene.*

❸ Hildene

Robert Todd Lincoln was the son of President Abraham Lincoln. As a child, he visited the Equinox Hotel with his mother, just before his father was assassinated, but only returned to the area many years later. Hildene, Lincoln's summer home, was built in 1904, and it was here that he died in 1926. Lincoln descendants lived here until 1975; the house is filled with authentic memorabilia of the Civil War leader, including Abe's "stovepipe" hat. The stately 24-room Georgian Revival home boasts a huge pipe organ and magnificent grounds. Polo matches are played on summer Sundays and, in winter, the former carriage house is a base for visitors who cross-country ski the 13 miles (21km) of trails. Candlelight tours of the interior are particularly evocative.

▶ *Continue for 2 miles (3km) to Manchester Village.*

❹ Manchester Village

There are three Manchesters: Center, Depot, and the oldest and highest, the Village. This is where the rich and powerful summered, either in their own luxury mansions, or at the legendary resort hotel, the Equinox. Dating back to 1769, this splendid Victorian hotel has been expanded and renovated over the years and today has 163 rooms and the renowned par-71 Gleneagles golf course.

▶ *Drive a further ¹/₂ mile (800m) into Manchester Center.*

❺ Manchester Center

Amid this rural bliss, outlet shopping comes as a shock to some visitors. Despite the out-of-the-place presence of Armani, Burberry and Calvin Klein, some small-town charm remains. Down-home favorites such as the Quality Restaurant have served up genuine Vermont cooking for years.

▶ *Drive 2 miles (3km) and turn onto **Route 11** east.*

❻ Bromley Mountain Ski Area

The road climbs steadily for 8 miles (13km) to Bromley Ski resort, a pioneer among resorts since 1937. Visitors also come in summer to try out the mile-long alpine slide, the longest concrete slide of its kind in the U.S.

▶ *Continue on **Route 11** east, then turn off to Peru.*

❼ Peru

Peru, one of the state's little-known hamlets, was featured in the 1987 film *Baby Boom*, with Diane Keaton. A small woodworking shop shares the street with a church, an antique shop and several lovely homes.

▶ *Return to **Route 11**, east, and drive to Londonderry. Turn left onto **Route 100**, north for Weston.*

❽ Weston

Weston is well known, not only for its prettiness, but also for the two rival stores across the street from one another. The Vermont

The Old Tavern Inn, in the pristine village of Grafton

comfortable Inn at Long Last, pleasant shops and a narrow green. The only business of note is the National Survey, a map-making company and shop which has everything to do with cartography.

Chester Depot, the site of the old railway station, is now home to the *Green Mountain Flyer*, a summer tourist train with nice old carriages. The *Flyer* runs up to Bellows Falls through the impressive Brockway Mills Gorge.

▶ Take **Route 35** south for 7 miles (11km) to Grafton.

11 Grafton

In a state of many lovely villages, Grafton is probably the most photogenic of them all. It was once an affluent town on the Boston to Albany post road, with soapstone quarries and a thriving woolen industry, but after the Civil War, its economy collapsed. There was a revival in 1801, when the handsome Old Tavern was built with a California gold miner's money, but by the middle of the century, the village had all but died yet again. Help was at hand, however. In her will, Pauline Fisk instructed her nephews to use her fortune for a good cause of their choice. They came up with the idea of reviving Grafton.

In 1963, the Windham Foundation began the restoration of Grafton's historic charm that draws admiring visitors. For some, the houses are almost too pretty, too perfect for such a rural setting. The village has also revived a former industry: a nutty cheddar-style cheese, made by the Cheese Factory. The tiny Village Store also has locally made preserves and hand-knit treasures, and there is a working blacksmith's shop. Two covered bridges complete the scene. On Sunday evenings in summer, the cornet band plays on the green, a tradition dating back to 1867.

Country Store and the Weston Village Store both do everything but bottle the nostalgia, and both offer an incredible variety of 'country' and 'Vermont' items that will bring visitors and their wallets to their knees. The circular town green, with its bandstand, inn and brick church on the hill above, is extremely photogenic. The Weston Playhouse is one of New England's oldest and most popular summer theaters.

Just north of the village is the Benedictine monks' religious community of Weston Priory, a tranquil place where visitors are welcome to join in services and walk in the grounds.

▶ Continue for 8 miles (13km) to Ludlow.

9 Ludlow

In contrast to Weston, Ludlow may seem somber at first sight, but there is a gritty charm to this former mill town on the banks of the Black River. Here, wool was recycled into inexpensive cloth called 'shoddy', which has become a pejorative description for anything cheap. The mill on Main Street is now an inn and the area has been revitalized. The successful Okemo Mountain resort, with its 3,343-foot (1,000m) hill, is widely acknowledged as having the best snow-making and grooming facilities in Vermont.

▶ Take **Route 103** south for 13 miles (21km) to Chester.

10 Chester

Hidden away in the woods on the way to Chester was the home of Russian Nobel Prize-winner, Alexander Solzhenitsyn. He lived here in isolation in Chester during his exile from the Soviet Union. The Stone Village on North Street has, unusually for Vermont, some 30 cottages built of local stone. Dating from before the Civil War, these had hiding places for slaves escaping from the southern states on the so-called Underground Railroad to Canada.

The heart of Chester is the broad main street, with the

▶ *Leave Grafton on **Route 35**
south, which turns briefly into a
dirt road after 6 miles (10km).
At Townsend, take **Route 30**
south for 5 miles (8km) to
Newfane.*

🔢 Newfane

In summer, Newfane shows off
its classic white Courthouse,
church and inns, all of which
have gleaming Greek Revival
columns. The long-established
air of the place is deceptive. Two
hundred years ago, the buildings
stood 2 miles (3km) away, on
Newfane Hill. In 1825, the residents moved the town, using the
slippery snow and ice of winter
to slide the beams and boards to
today's site. Jail accommodations
were so comfortable and the
food so palatable that paying
guests were allowed to enjoy
"good pies and oyster soup"
along with the inmates.
Excellent fare is still a tradition,
with both of the town's inns
renowned for their cuisine. On
summer Sundays, the flea
market on the green is one of
Vermont's biggest and best.

The local museum is easy to
spot, with its early 19th-century
bell standing outside. Inside are
simple memorabilia from the
area – Victorian dresses, old
maps and a variety of household
items.

Beyond town, Route 30 runs
parallel to the West River, where
rafters and paddlers take up the
challenge of high water in
spring. A local map of the river,
produced by the eighth-grade
class at the junior high school,
shows all the rapids, covered
bridges, dams and swimming-
holes ... even the ones where
'skinny-dipping' or nude swimming, is common.

▶ *Continue on **Route 30** to
Brattleboro.*

🔢 Brattleboro

Fort Dummer, the first site in
the state to be settled by
Europeans, has now been
covered by the waters of the
nearby dam. Originally this was
the western frontier of the Bay
Colony, used in defense against
the French and the Indians.

Brattleboro is situated just
down the road. In recent years,
there has been a clean-up of the
town's industrial infrastructure,
centered about the main thoroughfare, Elliott Street. The
former Union Railroad Station is
now the Museum and Art
Center with five galleries. One is
devoted to the history of the
Estey Organ Co, the local firm
that cheered up Victorian parlors
across the nation.

Just north of the town at
Dummerston, in a house called
Naulakha, author Rudyard
Kipling lived and worked from
1892 to 1896, after marrying a
local girl, Carrie Balestier. Books
such as *Captains Courageous*, the
Jungle Books and the *Just So
Stories* were all written here. One
celebrity who never left town
was the notorious 19th-century
swindler, Jubilee Jim Fisk.
"Jubilee Jim," who once
cornered the New York gold
market, is buried in the cemetery, with a monument by local
sculptor Larken Mead. Mead
gained true recognition for his
memorial honoring a more
reputable man: he carved the
statue that graces Abraham

Lincoln's tomb in Springfield, Illinois.

▶ *Take **Route 9** west and start climbing into the hills. Pass Whetstone Valley Farm, known for maple sugaring in early spring, to Marlboro (10 miles/16km).*

🄸 Marlboro

The countryside looks attractive today, but back in 1763 it must have been daunting for the European settlers. Two families

Newfane's County Courthouse offers a touch of grandeur

are credited with founding Marlboro, but neither pioneer family knew the other was nearby for over a year. The focus of town is Marlboro College, with its music school founded by pianist Rudolf Serkin. The six-week-long summer chamber music festival is a well established highlight, due to the long residency and efforts of cellist Pablo Casals in its early years.

▶ *Continue west on **Route 9**. After 15 miles (24km), there is a panoramic view from one of the highest points on the road. Continue to Wilmington.*

🄸 Wilmington and Woodford

The alpine-looking village of Wilmington is at the crossroads with Route 100, the north–south route that winds its way through the villages and ski resorts of the Green Mountains. Haystack Mountain and Mount Snow are just to the north.

Route 9 climbs on into the Green Mountain National Forest, passing through Woodford, Vermont's highest village. Prospect Mountain offers hiking opportunities.

▶ *Return to Bennington.*

Central
Vermont

The central part of the state gets busy in winter due to the appeal of internationally known ski resorts such as Killington. In summer, attractions range from the Quechee Gorge, a sudden tear in the landscape, to Plymouth, the home of Calvin Coolidge. Rutland is nicknamed the "Marble City," because local quarries have provided floors and walls for many of America's grand civic buildings.

1 DAY • 109 MILES • 175KM

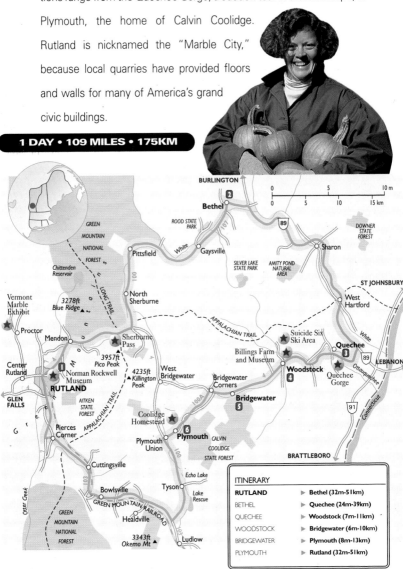

ITINERARY		
RUTLAND	▶	**Bethel (32m-51km)**
BETHEL	▶	**Quechee (24m-39km)**
QUECHEE	▶	**Woodstock (7m-11km)**
WOODSTOCK	▶	**Bridgewater (6m-10km)**
BRIDGEWATER	▶	**Plymouth (8m-13km)**
PLYMOUTH	▶	**Rutland (32m-51km)**

i *256 North Main Street*

▶ *Leave Rutland on **Route 4**
east. After 2 miles (3km) is the
Norman Rockwell Museum on
the right.*

❶ Norman Rockwell Museum

Better known collections of the
popular illustrator's work can
be found in Stockbridge
(Massachusetts) and Arlington
(Vermont), but you'll find 2,000
reproductions of well-loved
covers from magazines such as
Saturday Evening Post, Life and
Literary Digest here. There is
enough to keep nostalgia
hunters interested for an hour or
more; some of his illustrations
from children's books are also on
display. After the Museum, the
road starts its long climb into the
Green Mountain National
Forest. Pico Peak ski area is on
the right. Near the summit,
there is a sign for the Long Trail.
In summer, the Pico Alpine
Slide is a thrill for youngsters
and brave adults.

▶ *Continue on **Route 4** over the
Sherburne Pass, turn onto
Route 100 north, then take
Route 107 to Bethel.*

❷ Bethel

In the new showrooms of
Vermont Castings are their
popular wood-burning stoves,
seemingly essential to any
Vermont home. An exhibition at
the White River National Fish
Hatchery explains an ambitious
project to bring back the
Atlantic salmon to the
Connecticut River. Abundant
when the Colonists arrived, the
fish have been virtually wiped
out by dams, over-fishing and
pollution.

▶ *Follow **Route 107** and turn
onto **I–89** south. After 18
miles (29km) take exit 1.
Route 4 leads to Quechee.*

❸ Quechee and Quechee Gorge

Quechee (Kwee-chy) Gorge is
162 feet (49m) deep. Jagged
chunks of schist rock protrude
from the walls. While the best
view of Vermont's "Little Grand
Canyon" is from the old railway
bridge that spans the ravine,
there is also a half-mile (800m)
hike to the bottom. The
Ottauquechee River that used
to drive the woolen mills of
Quechee now powers the
converted Downer's Mill. It is

Quechee Falls, on the
Ottauquechee River

here that Simon Pearce's well-
known glass is made. Visitors can
watch his craftsmen at work
blowing glass. The Irishman
opened his studios in 1981 and
has since added a restaurant. All
round town are retirement
communities.

RECOMMENDED WALKS

Two of the Northeast's most
famous hiking trails part company near Pico Peak. The Long
Trail runs the length of the
state, some 260 miles (416km)
from the Massachusetts line to
Quebec. This "Footpath in the
Wilderness," which touches
some of the main peaks in the
Green Mountains, opened in
1926. The southern part of it
overlaps with the even longer
Appalachian Trail, which runs
from Maine down to Georgia.
Be warned! These hikes are
only for the hearty. They are
administered by the Green
Mountain Club, in Waterbury
(tel: 802 244 7037) and have
simple accommodations on
the trails.

▶ *Continue on **Route 4** to Woodstock.*

FOR HISTORY BUFFS

Although Joseph Smith is always connected with Salt Lake City and Utah, the founder of the Mormons (Church of Jesus Christ of the Latter Day Saints) was actually born in 1805 on a farm near Sharon, 10 miles (16km) southeast of Bethel. His family left the state in 1816, but a huge granite monument at the top of a steep hill is a tribute to the prophet. Each foot of the 38.5-foot-high (11.4m) obelisk represents a year of his short life.

From Thanksgiving to Christmas, 85,000 decorative lights brighten the visitor center. Brigham Young, the other great Mormon leader, was another Vermonter, born in Whitingham, near the Massachusetts border.

4 Woodstock

This is New England as most people imagine it: a covered bridge, bandstand on the green, shuttered Colonial homes and an elegant inn. Regularly voted one of America's prettiest towns, Woodstock was one of the first in the state to develop as a two-season resort. Visitors used to arrive in the summer at the end of the last century, but in 1934 came a breakthrough that made skiing fun – a Model T Ford car engine, set up at the bottom of a hill, was hooked up to a piece of cable on a wheel and Woodstock had the first ski tow in the U.S.A. The colorfully named Suicide Six Ski Area still tests even the most competent of skiers.

Woodstock has been a cultural center from its early days. Musicians and silversmiths, tailors and newspaper publishers have been prominent among its inhabitants. One of the most intellectual of all its sons was George Marsh (1801–82), the lawyer, diplomat

SPECIAL TO...

The sentimental book and film *The Bridges of Madison County* revived interest in covered bridges everywhere in the early 1990s. Although the movie was set in Iowa, New England is renowned for its bridges. They are most often painted red, and there are three in and around Stockbridge, on the way to Bethel. Roofed over in order to give the boards extra protection, covered bridges have acquired a number of uses, from a chance for a kiss in the dark to a sheltered place to hang post boxes, as they do in Wilmington, Vermont.

and fervent conservationist. He wrote *Man and Nature* in 1864. He also had a hand in the design of the Washington Monument, sending plans for the obelisk from Rome, based on his studies of classical architecture. His

Everyday exhibits at the Billings Museum, Woodstock
Right: red barns and silos are a common sight in Vermont

friend, Frederick Billings, promoted modern farming techniques. Billings' methods and buildings are preserved at the Billings Farm and Museum. The museum remains a working dairy farm where visitors can watch butter and cheese making, maple sugaring and even ice cutting.

Four of Vermont's eight bells cast by patriotic hero Paul Revere are here: one is silent, on show at the Congregational Church, but the other three still ring out across the town.

▶ *Continue for 6 miles (10km) to Bridgewater.*

5 Bridgewater

Bridgewater and its namesakes further upstream, West Bridgewater and Bridgewater Corners, were all mill towns. In

One of the dozens of Victorian stained-glass windows in Wilson Castle, northwest of Rutland

Bridgewater itself, one old mill has been turned into an outlet center for designer clothes, with a crafts center. Mountain Brewers produce a Long Trail Ale, which has a special appeal to thirsty hikers.

▶ *Continue west on* **Route 4**. *After 2 miles (3km), turn left on* **Route 100A** *south for Plymouth.*

⑥ Plymouth

Calvin Coolidge (1872–1933), the 30th president of the United States, was born here in Plymouth. There is a small shrine to the only president born on the Fourth of July. The five-room Coolidge Birthplace, his father's general store next door, the Coolidge Homestead and the Wilder House, his mother's childhood home, have been kept much as they would have been when Coolidge was a boy. The summer White House, used in 1924 by Coolidge, has been re-created nearby. He and many other Coolidges are buried in Plymouth cemetery. The President's father founded the Plymouth Cheese Company over a century ago; in 1960, a descendant revived the tradition which continues to make cheese on the site.

▶ *Continue on* **Route 100A**, *then turn left on* **Route 100** *towards Ludlow, passing the Green Mountain Sugar House. Set on the shore of Echo Lake, the Sugar House is a good place for maple-related products and gifts. Turn right on* **Route 103** *and return to Rutland.*

FOR HISTORY BUFFS

Vermont farms are built to cope with the extremely cold weather. The early settlers soon realized that the less they went outside in winter, the warmer they would stay. The farmhouses were often joined to the barn with a small hallway, an idea developed by the Dutch. In this way, the farmer could tend to his animals without having to go outside.

FOR HISTORY BUFFS

Despite the esteem with which he is held in his native state, Coolidge made his political career in Massachusetts, where he was Governor. Coolidge was visiting his father on the family farm in Plymouth when President Warren Harding died suddenly on August 3, 1923. At 2.47am, Col. John Coolidge took up the old family Bible and, in his role as a justice of the peace, administered the presidential oath to his son. Harding's administration had been tainted by corruption, so Coolidge's frugal New England virtues were welcomed. Famous for his quote that "the business of America is business," Coolidge believed that government should not interfere with industry.

Northern Vermont

In this sparsely-populated part of the state, there are a surprising number of attractions.

2 DAYS • 134 MILES • 215KM

ST ALBANS

4393ft
Mount Mansfield

Mount Mansfield
Ski Area

Winooski

BURLINGTON

South Burlington

Williston

Stowe

MOUNT
MANSFIELD
STATE
FOREST

Richmond

Jonesville

Waterbury
Reservoir

**NEW
YORK**

Shelburne
Museum

Shelburne

Lake
Iroqois

Ben and Jerry's

Colbyville

Waterbury

CAMEL'S
HUMP
STATE
PARK

Duxbury

Essex

Cedar
Beach

Charlotte

MT PHILO
STATE PARK

4083ft
Camel's Hump

LEBANON

Vermont
Wildflower
Farm

Lewis Creek

Rokeby Museum

Moretown

Ferrisburgh

Mad River
Glen

Waitsfield

Irasville

BUTTON BAY
STATE PARK

Vergennes

4135ft
Mount Ellen

CHIMNEY
POINT
STATE
PARK

Sugarbush Valley
Ski Area

Warren

3975ft
Lincoln Peak

ROXBURY
STATE
FOREST

Morgan
Horse Farm

3661ft
Mount Grant

Moss Glen
Falls

Vermont State
Craft Center

GREEN

MOUNTAIN

Middlebury

3823ft
Bread Loaf
Mt

White

Granville

Lower Granville

6 Ripton

Robert Frost Trail

**East
Middlebury**

Bread Loaf

Texas
Falls

Hancock

Middlebury
Gap

NATIONAL

Lake
Dunmore

FOREST

0   5   10 m
0   5   10   15 km

RUTLAND

ITINERARY

BURLINGTON	▶ **Charlotte** (10 m-16km)
CHARLOTTE	▶ **Vergennes** (11m-18km)
VERGENNES	▶ **Middlebury** (13m-21km)
MIDDLEBURY	▶ **Ripton** (8m-13km)
RIPTON	▶ **Warren** (27m-43km)
WARREN	▶ **Waitsfield** (5m-8km)
WAITSFIELD	▶ **Waterbury** (15m-24km)
WATERBURY	▶ **Stowe** (9m-14km)
STOWE	▶ **Burlington** (36m-58km)

i   *209 Battery Street*

▶ *From Burlington, take **Route 7** south for 5 miles (8 km) and turn right for Shelburne Farms.*

❶ Shelburne

Most Vermont farms are humble affairs, with red barns, a white silo and a low-slung farmhouse. Shelburne Farms is the opposite, a millionaire's toy built in the 1880s and 1890s on a giant scale and using all the latest technical equipment available. After William Webb married Lila Vanderbilt, daughter of the rail-road tycoon, they created a European-style estate.

Farms, married Electra Havemeyer, they began collecting art objects, large and small. The 37 buildings in which the quilts, paintings, toys and farm equipment are displayed, are themselves collector's items. These buildings, each a historical landmark, have been rescued from all over New England and reassembled on the 45-acre (18-hectare) site. You'll find a schoolhouse, railroad station, general store, barn, jailhouse and inn, now serving as galleries. Most arresting of all is a boat – the 220-foot-long (66m) side-

Apothecary store, one of the exhibits at Shelburne Museum

The Webbs called upon Frederick Law Olmsted, the man who landscaped New York's Central Park, to map out their property. Like so many millionaires of late last century, the Webb's "summer cottage" was extraordinary – a 110-room Queen Anne-style manor house. It is now the Inn at Shelburne Farms. The farm continues to be an experimental and working farm, where visitors can watch cheese-making, bread-baking and furniture-making. Old-fashioned pleasures such as hay rides will entertain the small children.

When J. Watson Webb, the son of the Webbs of Shelburne

SPECIAL TO...

Lake Champlain is shaped like a sausage, 120 miles (192km) long and anything from 400 yards (400m) to 12 miles (19km) wide. Samuel de Champlain, the 17th-century French explorer, recorded seeing a 20-foot-long (6m) serpent with a head like a horse, and visitors have been trying to spot "Champ" ever since. Lake Champlain has four ferry services that cross from Vermont to the New York shores: from Grand Isle to Cumberland Head (12 minutes), from Burlington to Port Kent (an hour), from Charlotte to Essex (20 minutes) and from Larrabee's Point to Ticonderoga (6 minutes).

wheel steamer *Ticonderoga*. It was hauled for 2 miles (3km) from Lake Champlain to its final landlocked berth here on the farm. Although the folk art collection is justifiably highlighted as one of the finest in the world, the Shelburne art collection is equally impressive. Pieces by American painters Andrew Wyeth and Winslow Homer are on display, as are European artists Rembrandt and Goya. After this exhaustive and exhausting museum visit, linger a while in the farm's delightful formal gardens.

The town of Shelburne has a more recent industry: the Vermont Teddy Bear Company, which exports its furry friends world-wide. Children can decorate and stuff the "new born" bears.

Church Street market, Burlington

▷ *Continue to Ferrisburgh. On a hill to the left is the Rokeby Museum.*

❸ Ferrisburgh
One of the state's underrated museums is the Rokeby, home of the Robinson family for generations. Beautifully furnished, the house is a tribute to their own artistic talents, with portraits and landscapes they have personally painted lining the walls. Rokeby was also one of the last stops on the Underground Railroad, the escape route for black slaves from the American South to Canada. It contains a secret passage and hiding room.

▷ *Continue south to Vergennes.*

❹ Vergennes
Vergennes was named after France's foreign minister and a great supporter of the Americans in the Revolution. It claims to be the smallest city in the country, just one square mile (259 hectares) with 2,500 inhabitants. On Basin Harbor Road, in a 19th-century stone schoolhouse, you'll find Lake Champlain Maritime Museum. During both the Revolution and the War of 1812, American and British warships battled for supremacy on this elongated strip of water. Benedict Arnold (see page 80), later a notorious traitor, delayed the British in 1776 with a series of clever ploys, as explained in the museum. A full-size replica of his gunboat, the *Philadelphia II*, is the highlight of the visit.

▷ *Continue on **Route 7** south to Middlebury.*

❺ Middlebury
Middlebury is best known for its college, founded in 1800. Visitors who come to admire the old houses and museums such as the Sheldon and Painter Hall use it as a base. For more contemporary culture, the Vermont State Craft Center, in Frog Hollow, on Otter Creek

FOR CHILDREN
Holy Cow Studios in Middlebury is a must for visitors. Artist Woody Jackson explored the "relationships and geometrics" of cows and came up with the omnipresent silhouettes of Holstein cows. They have become a trademark for Vermont. His studios create everything from the original large plywood cut-out cows to coffee mugs and handkerchiefs with the black and white logo. The symbol is also used on Ben and Jerry's ice cream cartons.

Falls, is a modern showcase for the talents of some 300 artists and craftspeople from all over the state. Across the creek are the old marble works, filled with shops. The railway offers scenic rides up to Burlington and back.

Middlebury College claims to be the birthplace of the Frisbee in 1938. Yale students may dispute this (see page 68), but the Vermonters have a handsome statue of a dog leaping to catch a flying disk. It was unveiled in front of Monroe Hall on what they insist was the 50th anniversary of spinning pie dishes at one another.

ⓘ *2 Court Street*

▷ *Follow **Route 7** south, then turn onto **Route 125** for East Middlebury.*

RECOMMENDED WALKS
Split by the Mad River and the cascading Moss Glen Falls, Granville Gulf State Park borders the eastern boundary of the Green Mountains National Forest. There is a 6-mile (10km) scenic drive, as well as two hiking trails. The easy 1-mile (1.6km) loop on the east side of the road contrasts with the shorter, but tougher, ½-mile (0.8km) hike to the west.

▷ *Continue on **Route 7** to Charlotte (5 miles/8km).*

❷ Charlotte
Pronounced char-LOT, the town's heyday was in the early 19th century, when it was a stage-coach stop on the journey from Burlington to Troy. The old houses in the historic district remain, along with three covered bridges.

Slightly further along Route 7 is the Vermont Wildflower Farm with 6 acres (2.4 hectares) of woodland and flower fields. Self-guided trails explain the legends of wildflowers and how Native Americans used them for herbal remedies. Visitors can also buy seeds. This stretch of Route 7 has magnificent views across Lake Champlain to the Adirondack Mountains.

❻ East Middlebury

Two hundred years ago the hamlet of East Middlebury was little more than a spot for stage coaches to Boston to change horses. Then the television cameras arrived to film the hit TV comedy series *Newhart*, starring comedian Bob Newhart, at the Waybury Inn. Rooms in this quaint 1810 inn have been refurbished in period style.

▶ *Continue for 4 miles (6km) to Ripton on* **Route 125**, *the Robert Frost Memorial Drive.*

❼ Ripton

The poet Robert Frost summered in the woods near

The densely wooded Green Mountains clothed in fall foliage

Ripton for 23 years, and today the mountain to the north is named after him. Just after the hamlet of Ripton is a picnic area on the left, and a rough track leading to his cabin. On the other side of the road is the Robert Frost Interpretative Trail, a ¾-mile (1.2km) walk studded with plaques of quotes by the great man.

Seven miles (11km) after leaving Middlebury is the Bread Loaf Campus of Middlebury College. Once a hotel in the shadow of Bread Loaf Mountain, the campus is now well known for its summer writing schools and conferences. In winter it is a base for cross-country skiing.

▶ **Route 125** *climbs steadily, passing Bread Loaf and the*

Snow Bowl, a local but chal-
lenging ski area. Beyond the
summit of Middlebury Gap
the road drops down to
Hancock, passing Texas Falls
recreation area. At Hancock,
turn left on **Route 100** north,
alongside the White River. After
4 miles (6km) is Granville, and
another 10 miles (16km)
further turn right to Warren.

8 Warren

Despite the popularity of the
neighboring Sugarbush Valley
ski area, Warren has changed
little. The simple exterior of the
Warren Store belies a sophisticated little emporium of
gourmet foods and fine wines
for the city folk who visit.
Simpler pleasures survive, with
a wind chime artisan and glider

rides from the little airport.

Just north of Warren is the
left turn for Sugarbush, the heart
of one of Vermont's premier ski
destinations. Opened in 1958,
this affluent resort has expensive
condominiums and a busy
restaurant scene. Vermont's third
highest peak, Mt. Ellen (4,135
feet/1,211m), and Lincoln Peak
(3,975 feet/1,192m) are the two
mountains that provide the ski
thrills. In summer, golfers test
themselves on the course
designed by Robert Trent Jones,
Sr. There are also tennis courts.

▶ Continue to Waitsfield.

9 Waitsfield

The Mad River Glen ski resort
has boosted what was once a
lumber and dairy town. It is

smaller, older and less formal
than the nearby Sugarbush
resort, but offers more challeng-
ing runs for the advanced skier.
It has given a boost to what was
once a lumber and dairy town.
Now arts, crafts and chic shopping thrive. In contrast, the old
covered bridge and the Mad
River Canoe Company, the
famous makers of recreational
canoes, add a more down-to-
earth element. Nearby, the
Vermont Icelandic Horse Farm
is a treat for small children.

▶ Take **Route 100** north to
Waterbury (15miles/24km).
Ben and Jerry's is 1 mile
(1.6km) north of I–89.

10 Waterbury

Waterbury means just one thing
to ice cream aficionados: Ben
and Jerry's. Ben Cohen and Jerry
Greenfield's rags-to-riches story
is the American dream, set deep
in the Vermont countryside. In
1977 they started by producing
home-made ice cream in
Burlington, in a disused and
dismantled service station.
These days, the factory is in
Waterbury, where tours with free
tastings are a constant draw. In
summer, old-fashioned ice
cream machines and real cows,
ready for milking, keep children
entertained.

Waterbury has expanded to
include other tasty attractions:
the Cabot Creamery Annex,
Green Mountain Chocolate Co.,
and the Cold Hollow Cider Mill,
with its excellent pure pressed
apple juices. The Green
Mountain Club, half way to
Stowe, administers the Long
Trail and other outdoor activities.

▶ Continue for 11 miles (18km)
to Stowe, then follow **Route
108** to the Mount Mansfield
Ski Area.

11 Stowe

Near Stowe is Mount Mansfield
Ski Area, one of New England's
premier ski resorts, built on
Mount Mansfield, Vermont's
highest peak (4,393 feet/

COLD HOLLOW CIDER MILL

Low mist over Stowe, the main skiing and recreation center for this popular area

grown substantially over the years. It is all very atmospheric and *gemütlich*, with staff in Austrian costume, though some find it a little overdone.

[i] *Main Street, Stowe*

1,318m). In summer, a gravel toll road, the Stowe Auto Road, leads to the summit, a 4½-mile (7km) journey. This steep route, with numerous steep, tight curves, is a test of both car and driver. For a more relaxed journey use the Stowe Gondola, a half-hour scenic swing over the forested slopes. With tennis courts, a golf course and an In-Line Skate Park, this is a summer destination for the active.

Another attraction is the Trapp Family Lodge in Stowe, built by the real-life family of *The Sound of Music* fame. A sign "invites you to share a little of Austria, a lot of Vermont." Actually, they offer quite a lot of everything since this resort has

▶ *Return on **Route 100** to I–89 and drive northwest to Burlington.*

NEW HAMPSHIRE

New Hampshire's nickname is the "Granite State." Some say it refers to the rocky scenery, others maintain it describes the implacable nature of the residents. Certainly, the terrain is the very opposite of the English county that lent it its name. Although New Hampshire has only an 18-mile (29km) strip of Atlantic coastline, a mere 80 miles (128km) away are the White Mountains, the tallest in New England. Hundreds of lakes, often bearing the Indian names given by earlier residents – Sunapee, Winnipesaukee and Squam – are scattered throughout the thick pine forests. Sixty covered bridges stretch across tumbling streams.

The early settlers were "economic refugees," leaving Europe to make a better life rather than to find religious freedom. The land and climate made the early days a struggle. Later, the Scots-Irish added their resolute character to the New Hampshire men and women. Today, car license plates bear the state motto: "Live Free or Die." The rest of this Revolutionary rallying cry is "death is not the worst of evils." The fiery words are attributed to farmer-turned-general, John Stark, one of the New Hampshire men who formed the backbone of the American troops in the early days of the Revolution.

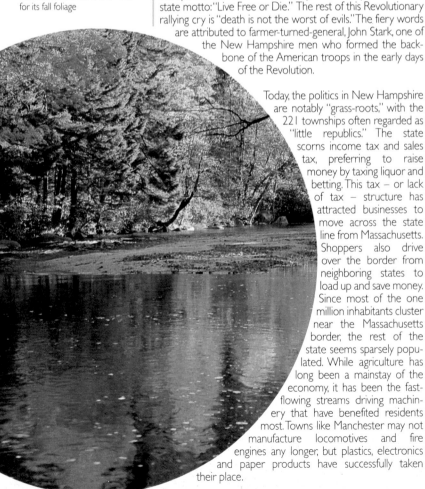

The Kancamagus Highway, in the White Mountains, is famous for its fall foliage

Today, the politics in New Hampshire are notably "grass-roots," with the 221 townships often regarded as "little republics." The state scorns income tax and sales tax, preferring to raise money by taxing liquor and betting. This tax – or lack of tax – structure has attracted businesses to move across the state line from Massachusetts. Shoppers also drive over the border from neighboring states to load up and save money. Since most of the one million inhabitants cluster near the Massachusetts border, the rest of the state seems sparsely populated. While agriculture has long been a mainstay of the economy, it has been the fast-flowing streams driving machinery that have benefited residents most. Towns like Manchester may not manufacture locomotives and fire engines any longer, but plastics, electronics and paper products have successfully taken their place.

Tour 18

Portsmouth, New Hampshire's port, is wedged between Massachusetts and Maine. Forty years ago it was a rundown city, a place to escape rather than a tourist destination. However, the residents recognized the rich history beneath the dirt – instead of tearing down the old buildings, they started a major restoration project. Now the merchants' houses and warehouses, meeting houses and bankers' offices are the attractive heart of the city and a source of civic pride. Small parks and museums reflect Portsmouth's role as a ship-building center, others are filled with fine antique American furniture. Best known is Strawbery Banke, a collection of houses that show what everyday life was like over a period of four centuries.

Above: Strawbery Banke
Below: The Flume, a giant chasm where a mountain stream tumbles in a series of waterfalls

Tour 19

The White Mountains are a popular destination all year round. The focus is Mount Washington, first climbed by a European 350 years ago. It is now deluged by 250,000 enthusiastic tourists every summer. A cog railroad crawls its way up to the top. Those wanting to avoid the "madding crowds" can explore the numerous well-marked trails throughout the mountains, either for a day hike or a longer trek. In winter, "the Whites" attract both downhill and cross-country skiers. The spectacular scenery on this route includes "the Kanc," the Kancamagus Highway, one of America's prettiest drives.

Tour 20

Since 1981, Squam Lake has become a "must see" for fans of the film *On Golden Pond*. Nearby, larger Lake Winnipesaukee has long been a popular destination for summer visitors wishing to escape the heat and humidity of Boston. The western shore has become over-popular and built-up, but for the most part, this is a peaceful drive, with villages, craft shops and museums en route. Anyone interested in top-quality crafts should plan to spend time in Center Sandwich, while Meredith is best known for its dolls.

Portsmouth

Portsmouth has one of New England's finest natural harbors and became wealthy on the timber trade, exporting lumber to Britain and the West Indies. Huge fortunes were made and spent on grandiose mansions, many of which still stand. A massive preservation program over recent decades has saved numerous fine buildings, making this a city for anyone interested in the architecture and craftsmanship of 18th- and 19th-century America.

HALF A DAY

i *500 Market Street*

▶ *Start at Market Square, the heart of the city for nearly 300 years.*

❶ Market Square

The lottery may seem a new idea but it has long been a means of raising money. Back in 1762, the militia's training ground was paved with funds from a public lottery. The Athenaeum, at No. 9, was originally the headquarters of a fire and marine insurance company, but became a private library in 1823. Ironically, it was built *after* the Portsmouth fire of 1802. The classic pointed spire of North Church can be seen from anywhere in the downtown area, especially when it is illuminated at night. On the east side of the

The John Paul Jones House, where the Scots-born Navy officer lived

square stands the impressive wall of Bankers Row, the guardians of civic wealth for nearly 200 years. No. 24/26 is thought to be the oldest bank in America, and it was extensively rebuilt in 1904.

▶ *Leave Market Square, heading south on Pleasant Street. Turn right on State Street.*

❷ State Street

Contrasting with the elegant white spire of North Church is the squat tower of South Church, at No. 292. This solid-looking granite building dates from 1826 and is still used for worship by the Unitarian Universalists. Nearby was the starting point of the 1813 fire, which blazed towards the water-front. Some houses survived, only to be lost to a 1950s urban planning project. Still standing is the Abraham Shaw House

(1810) at No. 379. A few doors further on is the Rockingham Hotel (No. 401), whose lions became the personal emblem of Frank Jones, a flamboyant brewer and entrepreneur whose bust is on the right. He turned the hotel into "the most elegant and superbly furnished estab-lishment ... outside of Boston."

▶ *At the corner of State and Middle streets is Haymarket Square, with its enclave of elegant homes. At No. 43 Middle Street is the John Paul Jones House.*

❸ John Paul Jones House

Scottish-born John Paul Jones is known as the "father of the US Navy." He did not own this handsome clapboard house, but rented rooms from Mrs. Sarah Purcell. The naval hero was in Portsmouth in 1777 to supervise the fitting out of the *Ranger*, and once again in 1781 for the build-ing of the *America*. The house is now the headquarters of the local historical society.

▶ *Turn south on Middle Street. Cross the square to No. 18 Court Street.*

❹ John Peirce Mansion

"The best" of the city's 19th-century houses, according to some critics. No expense was spared when Peirce built this home in 1799. It was handed down through the family for generations until 1955, when the Baptist Church bought the prop-erty.

▶ *Two blocks further along Middle Street is No. 364.*

5 Rundlet-May House

James Rundlet started out as a farm boy but ended up a wealthy man. With the money he made from importing textiles and wallpaper, he built this mansion in 1807. The garden, pet cemetery and stables add an extra dimension to the period furniture.

▶ *Retrace your steps to Court Street; bear right and walk two blocks to Pleasant Street. On the corner of Pleasant and Court is No. 93 Pleasant Street.*

6 Ann Treadwell Mansion

This house was built to comply with the 1814 law specifying that structures of more than one story had to be made of brick. The previous year, yet another fire had taken its toll, this time along Court Street, with hundreds of houses ruined.

▶ *Retrace your steps. Cross Court Street, then go south on Pleasant Street to No. 143.*

7 Governor Langdon House

John Langdon was one of New Hampshire's founding fathers who made his money in ship-building and buying and selling goods captured from the British.

Langdon became President of the Senate, delegate to the Constitutional Convention of 1787 and finally state governor for three terms. He built this mansion, one of the finest in New England, and the garden to impress, and it still does today. Note the exquisitely carved pale green fireplace in the drawing-room, where Langdon hosted parties. One guest was President George Washington, who commented that, among the town's houses "Col. Langdon's may be esteemed the first."

▶ *Walk next door to No. 145.*

8 Thomas Thompson House

Portsmouth's importance to the New Hampshire economy is reflected in the state seal and flag, which show shipbuilders at work on a frigate. The first frigate was the *Raleigh*, often called the "first ship in the U.S. Navy." Its owner, Thomas Thompson, erected this house in 1784, and his business partner, John Langdon, put up his mansion next door a year later.

▶ *Continue on Pleasant Street, then bear left on Gate Street.*

Portsmouth lies on the banks of the Piscataqua River

9 Gate Street

James T. Fields (1817–81), the publisher of *The Atlantic Monthly* magazine, gave American writers a boost onto the world literary stage. He was born and lived in the house at 83/85 Gates Street. A few doors down, No. 130 is another fine old place, built as early as 1731 by the Peirce family. This street was one of the first to be saved back in the 1960s rebirth of Portsmouth.

▶ *Turn right on Manning Street, then left at South Ward Meeting House. Cross Marcy Street to Hunking Street. Turn left on Mechanic Street and walk to No. 50.*

FOR CHILDREN

Portsmouth has a long history of building warships. At Albacore Park, there is a rare chance to explore a submarine, the 205-foot (61m) long USS *Albacore*. The cramped space did not allow room for beds for each of the crew, so, men "hot bunked:" when one shift finished, they slept in the bunks of those going on duty. The submarine never fired a shot in anger.

10 Wentworth Gardner House

Tiled fireplaces, fine carving and paneling, make this a "must" for those interested in 18th-century craftsmanship. The owner, Thomas Wentworth, was the younger brother of the last royal governor of New Hampshire.

▶ Continue on Mechanic Street which bears left; turn right on Marcy Street.

11 Liberty Pole

Colonials showed dissent by putting up a Liberty Pole on their village or town green. The residents of Portsmouth first did this in 1766, to protest against the infamous Stamp Act. The pole became a permanent reminder of that feisty spirit in 1824. Each season, the gardens of Portsmouth are planted with experimental varieties developed by botanists from the University of New Hampshire.

▶ Right behind the liberty pole is Strawbery Banke.

12 Strawbery Banke

Close to the waterfront, the site of the original 1630 settlement is now one of America's finest outdoor museums. Some 40 buildings, examples of Portsmouth's architecture from 1695 to World War II, have been moved and rebuilt on this 10-acre (4-hectare) site, once a slum. It all comes colorfully to life, with the blacksmith, potter and boatbuilder working at their trades. A favorite spot is the 1766 William Pitt Tavern, which

---

SPECIAL TO...

When English settlers arrived in 1623, the meadows running down to the Piscataqua River were so thick with strawberries, they called their new home Strawbery Banke. Thirty years later, with shipbuilding becoming the established industry, they changed the name to the more appropriate Portsmouth.

---

shows the role of the pub in every day life. The newest building is Abbott's Market (1943), complete with products on the shelves from that era.

▶ Continue on Marcy Street to the end. Turn left, then right across the parking lot to No. 150 Daniel Street.

13 Warner House

The oldest brick house in town was once part of a row of splendid brick mansions built around 1716. The museum-quality furniture behind the 18-inch (45cm) walls was used by the same family for two centuries, while the hall staircase is covered with extensive murals. These murals, possibly the oldest in the country, date from 1720, and include biblical scenes and portraits of two Mohawk Indians. A lightning conductor set into the west wall was supposedly installed by the inventor Benjamin Franklin.

▶ Turn right on Chapel Street.

14 St. John's Church

Designed by Alexander Parris to replace a church burned in the fire of 1806, St. John's boasts America's oldest working organ,

---

The Old Country Store at Strawbery Banke

the Brattle Organ, as well as splendid *trompe-l'oeil* paintings of biblical scenes.

▶ Continue on Chapel Street to Bow Street. Turn left, then right on Ceres Street. At the end, take the steps to No. 154 Market Street.

15 Moffatt-Ladd House

Little imagination is needed here to visualize the life of a wealthy Portsmouth family. The Moffatts built their home in 1763 directly across from their warehouses. The counting house next door, with its wall safe, was a more recent addition – in 1830. Now a museum, family mementos range from wedding dresses and portraits, to jewelry and silver. Two inventories of household goods in the late 18th century provided the curators with the details to re-create the Moffatt home, where the family lived until 1913. The beautiful gardens are a highlight: the plan is 18th-century but the interpretation is 19th-century.

▶ Return to Market Square via Market Street.

The White
Mountains

Weekend hikers and serious climbers come to test themselves against the mountains, of which Mount Washington is only one of 86 named peaks.

VERMONT

WHITE MOUNTAIN
NATIONAL FOREST

MOOSE
BROOK
STATE PARK

Androscoggin

Connecticut

Six Gun
City

Jefferson
Highlands

Randolph

Gorham 5

Meadows

ST JOHNSBURY

93

Bethlehem 4

Pierce
Bridge

Carroll

Twin Mountain

5798ft
Mount Adams

Presidential Range

Glen House

4397ft
▲ Wildcat Mountain

Sugar
Hill

Franconia 3

Bretton
Woods

6288ft
Mt Washington 6

Cog Railway

Glen Ellis
Falls

3303ft
▲ Black Mountain

MAINE

W H I T E   M O U N T A I N

Crawford
Notch

2032ft
Pinkham
Notch

APPALACHIAN TRAIL

4060ft
Cannon Mt ▲

5249ft
▲ Mount Lafayette

Old Man of
the Mountains

N A T I O N A L

CRAWFORD
NOTCH
STATE PARK

Jackson 7

Story Land

Franconia
Notch 2

F O R E S T

Heritage New
Hampshire

The Flume

Pemigewasset

4647ft
Mount Carrigan

302

Glen 8

Whale's Tale Water Park

Clark's Trading
Post

Loon Mountain

Saco

Lower Bartlett

93

Bartlett

**North
Conway** 9

**North
Woodstock** 1

Lincoln

KANCAMAGUS

Pemi
Overlook

10

HIGHWAY

Passaconaway
Historic
Site

Lower Falls
Scenic Area

Redstone

Woodstock

3728ft
Mount Kancamagus

112

Rocky
Gorge
Scenic Area

Swift

112

Conway

CONWAY SCENIC RAILROAD

West
Thornton

Mill Brook

W H I T E
M O U N T A I N
N A T I O N A L   F O R E S T

Sabbaday
Falls

Albany

Conway
Lake

Thornton

Mod

Campton

0   5   10 m

West
Campton

0   5   10   15 km

Squam
Lake

PLYMOUTH 93

CONCORD

2 DAYS • 188 MILES • 302KM

The Old Man of the Mountains, the craggy, enduring symbol of New Hampshire, is as impressive now as it must have been in 1805 when first spotted by road builders. This rock formation inspired the clever Nathaniel Hawthorne short story, *The Great Stone Face*. When the glib New Hampshire senator Daniel Webster saw it, he reportedly said that "Men hang out their signs indicative of their respective trades; shoemakers hang out a gigantic shoe; jewelers a monster watch ... but up in the mountains of New Hampshire, God Almighty has hung out a sign to show that there He makes man." One family, the Nielsens, have made it their mission to preserve the face from crumbling. Three generations have worked on it since 1960.

i *Chamber of Commerce booth, exit 28, off I–83*

▶ *Starting in Plymouth, proceed north on I–93, noting the frequency of the "moose crossing" signs and warnings. After 25 miles (40km), exit 32 heads off for North Woodstock and Lincoln.*

❶ North Woodstock

With storefronts that look like film sets for Hollywood westerns, North Woodstock is not your typical New England village. The main attraction is Clark's Trading Post, a theme park from the days before theme parks were a "dime-a-dozen." Florence Clark took the unlikely title of "first woman to reach the summit of Mount Washington using a dog sled." The Clark family still runs the show after 70 years. The attraction, which began as a dog ranch now features performing bears, Merlin's Mystical Mansion, a garage from yesteryear, an old fire station and other eccentric and eclectic Americana. Clark's

Trading Post also claims to have the world's last remaining Howetruss railroad bridge in the world, a covered, 120-foot (36m) long affair.

▶ *At this point I–93 becomes the Franconia Notch State Parkway. Continue north to The Flume and Franconia Notch Pass.*

❷ Franconia Notch

The Notch is the best-known high pass in New England. Ever since the first Europeans saw its towering granite walls 200 years ago, tourists have come to admire the gorge, formed by a massive prehistoric glacier. Preserved and protected in their own privately-funded State Park, these natural wonders are easily accessible and the Park is geared for those who wish to see the sights without much fight. The Flume Visitor Center has information on all the attractions in the Notch, as well as a shuttle bus to the Flume itself. Gravel paths and wooden walkways lead through a narrow gorge, 800 feet (240m) long. Its sheer walls stretch 90 feet (27m) straight up on both sides. Through the Notch, the Flume Brook bounces down the side of Mount Liberty and into the glacial pool.

Further along the road is the viewpoint for The Old Man of

Clark's Trading Post includes a reconstructed New England street

the Mountains, also called the Great Stone Face or Profile. Towering high above Profile Lake, and measuring 40 feet (12m) from forehead to chin, the five ledges of granite look like the silhouette of a man's face.

About ¹⁄₂ mile (800m) along is the Cannon Mountain Aerial Tramway II. Gondolas whisk 80 passengers at a time up to the top of Cannon Mountain (4,060feet/1,237m), climbing some 2,022 feet (606m) in just 7¹⁄₂ minutes. The view is well worth the fee, and there are plentiful, marked walks around the Summit Observatory Platform. Refreshments are available here.

FOR HISTORY BUFFS

New Hampshire claims many firsts in skiing: the first ski club, in Berlin in 1872; the first ski school, in Sugar Hill, in 1929; the first overhead cable ski tow at Black Mountain, in 1935; and the first trail cut for skiing, right here on Cannon Mountain in 1930. These historic moments are all described at the New England Ski Museum.

The Presidential Range, the most famous part of the White Mountains, is a backbone of high peaks running south from Gorham. The peaks are named predominantly after U.S. presidents (Madison, Adams, Jefferson, Washington, Monroe, Franklin, Eisenhower, Pierce and Jackson). Five of them exceed 5,000 feet (1,500m). Henry Clay and New Hampshire hero Daniel Webster have also given their names to peaks in the range.

Seats are limited on the Mount Washington Cog Railway, so advance booking is recommended

Next to the base of the tramway is the New England Ski Museum. Echo Lake, a little further on, is a natural mirror, reflecting Cannon Mountain and Mount Lafayette in its still waters. The energetic can cycle through the Notch on the 9-mile (15km) bike path which passes most of the attractions.

▶ Continue on Franconia Notch State Parkway, which becomes I–93 again. Take exit 38 for Franconia.

8 Franconia

Once a flourishing resort, Franconia has seemingly gone back to sleep. It has been overtaken by the more ambitious towns south of the Notch. Poetry lovers drop by the Robert Frost Place, the 150-year-old, white clapboard hillside farmhouse to which Frost returned in 1915, upon his homecoming from England. Aged 40 and still virtually unknown, he farmed the land, wrote three books of verse and won a Pulitzer prize, all in the next five years. Visitors can see his writing desk, signed first editions and a rare collection of his Christmas card

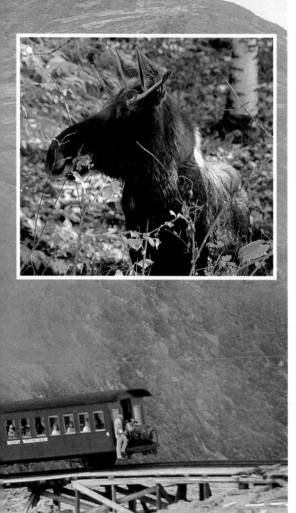

🔟 Gorham

Gorham is a useful stop for those who are keen on wildlife. At dawn and dusk, guides take visitors on a two-hour explanatory Moose Tour in search of these big beasts, which are abundant in the woods.

ⓘ *Information Booth, The Common*

▶ *Leave town on **Route 16** south to Glen House, at the foot of Mount Washington.*

poems. In summer, there are readings by a poet in residence and a Festival of Poetry in late July and early August. A ½-mile (800m) nature trail, highlighted with plaques along the way, presents 15 of Frost's favorite poems.

▶ *Return to **I–93** and drive 6 miles (10km) to exit 40 for Bethlehem. Turn on to **Route 302** east.*

🔟 Bethlehem

The little town of Bethlehem is more Victorian-looking than Colonial, reflecting its heyday as a vacation destination a century

Inset: a young moose

ago. Back then, thousands flocked here by train. The air was so clean and clear of pollution that the National Hay Fever Relief Association was started here in the 1920s. Now, apart from its antique shops, Bethlehem is a base for touring and hiking.

▶ *Stay on **Route 302** east for 8 miles (13km) to Twin Mountain. Turn left onto **Route 3**. At Carroll, take the **115** through Meadows, then join **Route 2** and head east to Gorham.*

6 Mount Washington

Mount Washington is the tallest mountain in the East at 6,288 feet (1,886m). A road and railway allow visitors access to the bare granite summit. On the eastern face of the mountain, at Glen House, about 8 miles (13km) south of Gorham, is the start of the 8-mile (13km) toll road to the top. Built back in 1861, the road is advertised as America's first man-made attraction. Six horses used to pull a wagon full of tourists up the grade, which still averages 12 percent. Today, large vans provide the same service. Bolder folk drive up, a test of their automobiles and their nerves.

The top is surprisingly busy with radio and TV transmitters, an observatory and the Summit Building, with its glassed-in viewing area. At the peak is the old Tip Top House, a hotel built in 1853. There is also a museum of mountain memorabilia and local wildlife.

Summer skiers willing to endure the tough hike can test

▶ *Continue for 13 miles (21km), then take the lefthand turn on* **Route 16A** *to detour into the little village of Jackson.*

7 Jackson

Jackson, a town with a mere 700 inhabitants, offers skiing – downhill and cross-country. The Attitash, Black, Wildcat and Cranmore mountains offer more than 100 trails, enough to satisfy all levels of ability from mogul masters to modest beginners.

SPECIAL TO...

The Jackson Ski Touring Foundation is dedicated to cross-country skiers. An unusual co-operative effort by the towns of Jackson and Bartlett has produced a network of some 100 miles (160km). The Ellis River Trail (5 miles/8km) is ideally flat for beginners. By contrast, the Wildcat ski area offers 11 miles (18km) of expert cross-country runs.

---

come into their own in unfriendly weather. Heritage New Hampshire, a museum/ theme park, is a 300-year journey through the state's history, from the first European settlements in 1634, through two revolutions – the American and the industrial. Actors explain their lives and simulated train rides add to the interest. Story Land, a well thought-out theme park, is aimed at a younger audience. There is a Mexican Village, re-creations of fairy-tales and rides and flumes.

▶ *Continue for 5 miles (8km) to North Conway.*

9 North Conway

With no sales tax and an outlet strip mall 3 miles (5km) long, shopping is the number one sport in this popular small town. Music festivals, a football game played in knee-deep mud and theater are just some of the diversions apart from hiking and climbing. It's all a far cry from the days when artists would

themselves on the dangerous chutes and headwall of the legendary Tuckerman's Ravine nearby. Skiing on July 4 is a traditional challenge among the hard-core skiers. At the base of the mountain is the recently opened Great Glen Trails recreation area with a lodge and a vast trail system for cross-country skiing, mountain-biking and hiking. Reserve accommodation well ahead at peak season.

Fun and fantasy at Story Land

Strict controls on building have kept this a picturesque village, with an emphasis on lodging and dining, rather than shopping, motels and fast food.

▶ *Continue south to Glen.*

8 Glen

As well as being a resort town, Glen has two attractions that flock to paint Thompson's Falls. The 1874 railway station, North Conway Depot, has survived with much of its Victorian ambience, including the wind-up brass clock, the Telegraph Office and the separate men's and women's waiting rooms. Now the Conway Scenic Railroad, with its Pullman carriages, runs from here for 11 miles (18km) alongside the Saco River to Conway.

▶ *Continue south and turn west onto **Route 112**, the 37-mile (59km) long Kancamagus Highway to Lincoln.*

⑩ Kancamagus Highway

Following alongside the rushing Swift River, "the Kanc" was only a primitive back road until 1964, and was not plowed in winter until 1968. It is New England's only designated National Scenic Byway – there are no private homes, service stations or other encroachments to spoil the views. The 37-mile (56km) stretch of road, from Conway to

the Pemigewasset River, climbs to 3,000 feet (900m) on the way, and honors New Hampshire's legendary Indian chief, Kancamagus (The Fearless One). He was the grandson of Passaconaway (Child of the Bear) who united and ruled the local tribes from 1627 to 1669. All along the road are Scenic Areas, places to stop. The best known spots include Sabbaday Falls, a short walk from the road, and the Lower Falls and Rocky Gorge, where bathing in the pools and sunbathing on the small beaches is most enjoyable on a hot summer's day.

⑪ Lincoln

The ski resort of Loon Mountain has transformed Lincoln into a busy year-round resort. The skyride, with its four-passenger gondola, is as attractive in summer as in winter, rising 7,000 feet (2,100m) to the summit and its walking trails and glacial caves. Other popular attractions include the Whale's Tale Waterpark, with its

variety of rides on land and in water, and the less frantic Hobo Railroad, which trundles through the Pemi River Valley for 15 miles (24km).

▶ *Return on **Route 93** south, 25 miles (40km) to Plymouth.*

The Kancamagus Highway, named after the Indian chief who strove for peace with the white man

> **SPECIAL TO...**
>
> Mount Washington has a meteorological record to rival the North Pole. Nowhere in the world that is visited by as many as 250,000 people a year has such terrible weather. The highest wind speed ever recorded in the world was here, in April 1934. Scientists clocked gusts of 231mph (370km/h). Year round, the average temperature at the summit is below freezing: fog is common.

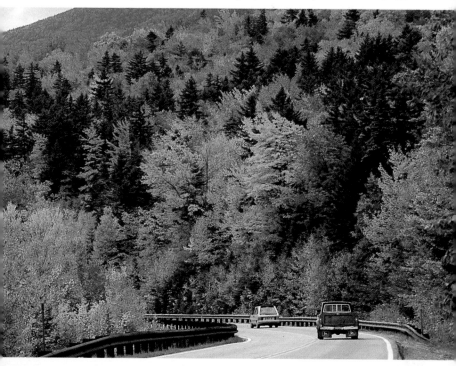

1 DAY • 106 MILES • 169KM

Around Lake
Winnipesaukee

Lake Winnipesaukee is huge, the sixth largest body of water inside the country. The Native American name is "The Smile of the Great Spirit," though some experts prefer the more prosaic translation of "Beautiful Water in a High Place."

ITINERARY		
PLYMOUTH	▶	**Ashland (7m-11km)**
ASHLAND	▶	**Holderness (4m-6km)**
HOLDERNESS	▶	**Center Sandwich (12m-19km)**
CENTER SANDWICH	▶	**Moultonborough (5m-8km)**
MOULTONBOROUGH	▶	**Wolfeboro (17m-27km)**
WOLFEBORO	▶	**Alton Bay (13m-21km)**
ALTON BAY	▶	**Weir's Beach (22m-35km)**
WEIR'S BEACH	▶	**Meredith (8m-13km)**
MEREDITH	▶	**Plymouth (18m-29km)**

i *Chamber of Commerce booth, exit 28, off I-83*

► *Start in Plymouth and take I–93 south to exit 24 for Ashland.*

❶ Ashland
The small town of Ashland, once an important stop on the old Boston, Concord and Montreal Railroad line, retains the character of an old mill town. The Ashland Historical Society is based in the former home of Dr. George Whipple, the pathologist who won the Nobel prize for medicine in 1934. Nextdoor, the Pauline Glidden Toy Museum has over 1,000 early toys, and the Vintage Fret Shop in town carries a variety of stringed instruments. A local resident, the late Milton Graton, was one of New England's experts on the restoration and building of covered bridges. His last was built here in his home town, where his son Arnold continues the tradition.

► *Continue on **Route 3** to Holderness.*

❷ Holderness
Holderness sits on Little Squam Lake; to the east is the much larger Squam Lake. The

Academy Award-winning 1981 film, *On Golden Pond*, starring Katherine Hepburn and Henry Fonda, was filmed here, catapulting Squam Lake to fame, even though the film was supposedly set in Maine. Small boats cruise the peaceful lake and delight in showing visitors where the scenes were shot. It is a favorite nesting place for loons.

► *Follow **Route 113** for Center Sandwich (12 miles/19km). Pass Squam Lake.*

❸ Center Sandwich
Sitting between the Squam Mountains and Squam Lake, this is one of several Sandwich villages in the area. New England poet John Greenleaf Whittier (1807–92) spent time in Center Sandwich. This crusading Quaker championed the anti-slavery cause and used poetry in his emotional campaigns:
"What! mothers from their children riven!
What! God's own image bought and sold!
Americans to market driven,
And bartered as the brute for gold!"
Whittier wrote *Sunset* on the Bearcamp, the river which runs through Bearcamp Pond between Center Sandwich and

North Sandwich. The Whittier covered bridge crosses the river in West Ossipee.

► *Drive south on **Route 109** for 5 miles (8km) to Moultonborough.*

❹ Moultonborough
This typical New England village has the bonus of the lake as a backdrop. Apart from its idyllic setting, the big attraction is "Castle in the Clouds," a reminder of the astonishing

Aerial view of the turreted hilltop Castle in the Clouds

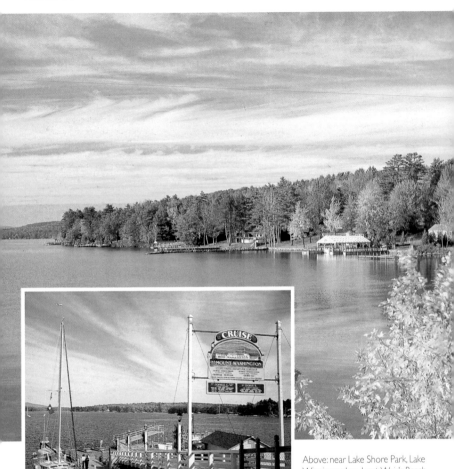

Above: near Lake Shore Park, Lake Winnipesaukee. Inset: Weir's Beach

wealth garnered a century ago. Set 750 feet (225m) up in the Ossipee Mountains, this mock castle offers spectacular views. Millionaire Thomas Plant, who made his money from shoes, owned the land for miles around, and today's visitors may enjoy the woods and meadows of the estate. This $7 million house was designed by Plant himself, explaining the variety of architectural styles, from Swiss chalet to Norman castle. A touch of English Tudor is the *coup de grâce*. It was built by hundreds of craftsmen, including Italian stone masons brought over from Europe. Water from a spring in the grounds is bottled commercially.

▶ *Continue south on **Route 109** for 17 miles (27km) to Wolfeboro. The route passes through Melvin Village, known for its antiques shops. Continue along the shores of Winnipesaukee, through Mirror Lake.*

🞱 Wolfeboro

Just before Wolfeboro, on the edge of Mirror Lake, is the Libby Museum which explains the story of this hamlet and America's oldest resort. Back in 1768, Massachusetts Governor John Wentworth ordered a summer house here. To reach the house from Portsmouth, he even had the "Governor's Road" built. The retreat burned down in 1820 and is now the site of an archeological dig in Wentworth State Park, 6 miles (10km) east of town. Everyday life in the second half of the 19th century is on view at the Historical Society's Americana Museum. Displays include a one-room schoolhouse (1868), a fire house and a farmhouse. Cruise boats use the town docks.

▶ *Take **Routes 28** and **28A** south for 13 miles (21km) to Alton Bay, right at the foot of Lake Winnipesaukee.*

6 Alton Bay

The little town of Alton Bay looks much as it must have in its summer heydays. There is a floating bandstand out in the bay, and the railroad station has been spruced up. Scenic lake cruises depart from the nearby docks.

▶ Follow *Route 11 northwest. This side of the lake is much more open, affording great views of the water and to the White Mountains in the north. Weir's Beach is 22 miles (35km) farther on via the Ellacoya State Beach, where you get a sense of how large Lake Winnipesaukee really is. Continue to Weir's Beach.*

7 Weir's Beach

Weir's Beach is the Coney Island of the region with amusement parks, boardwalks, beaches and weekly fireworks. It is especially busy when the motorbike races take place in nearby Loudun. There are two waterslide parks, but tamer rides are also available, on the railway or cruising on the lake. One of New England's last drive-in movie theaters is here too.

SPECIAL TO...

West of Alton Bay on Route 140 (12miles/19km) is the town that shocked America in 1956. Gilmanton was the home of *Peyton Place* author Grace Metalious. This high-school teacher's wife had been unable to achieve success with her writing ... until her account of life and love in small town America topped the best-seller lists. Today, the town shows no signs of the steamy passions described in the book, film and TV series. "You live in a small town and there are patterns. The minute you deviate from the pattern you are a freak," she said, "I wrote a book and that made me a freak." She died, aged 39, in 1964.

SCENIC RIDES

Apart from the 70-passenger M/V *Judge David Sewall*, based in Wolfeboro, there are several passenger boats that run out of Weir's Beach. The venerable 1,250 passenger M/S *Mount Washington*, popular for dinner cruises and moonlight cruises, is the largest. The *Washington* runs across to Wolfeboro and, on alternate days, either up to Center Harbor or down to Alton Bay. The M/V *Sophie* doubles up as a floating postman, delivering mail to the little island communities. The Winnipesaukee Railroad is yet another railway nostalgia trip, conjuring up the 1920s and 1930s, and runs from Weir's Beach to Meredith.

▶ Take *Route 3 north to Meredith (8 miles/13km).*

FOR HISTORY BUFFS

Sport is a high-profile, major ingredient of today's U.S. college life. The first inter-collegiate sporting event, however, was very low key. It took place in 1852, at Center Harbor on Lake Winnipesaukee. Harvard took on Yale in a rowing race over "two miles to windward and straight away," and beat them by two lengths. The ten-minute duel began a rivalry that remains intense nearly 150 years later.

---

8 Meredith

Quieter than Weir's Beach, with pretty docks and landings on the lake, Meredith is the home of the popular felt Annalee Dolls. Annalee Thorndike created these cutesy dolls in 1934 and now the factory is a major local employer. The dolls are bought by fans and collectors from all over the world. There is also a museum dedicated to them.

A second museum in the town is in the old Oak Hill church, where local enthusiasts have amassed old photographs and clothing, farming and household implements, especially those made locally. Small but fun.

▶ Return to Plymouth via *Route 3 through Holderness and I–93.*

BACK TO NATURE

The Science Center of New Hampshire is just to the east of Holderness and enables visitors to observe wild animals such as otters, deer, bears and various birds of prey. All are unable to live in their natural habitats, due to injury. Follow the ¾-mile (1,200m) nature trail and try the hands-on puzzles in the children's activity center.

MAINE

The Algonquin Indians called this region the "Land of the Frozen Ground" and the summer season is certainly the shortest here in New England, barely covering June through September. No-one knows how or why Maine received its present name. What is known is that it could swallow up the rest of the New England states. One single county, Aroostook, is bigger than the states of Connecticut and Rhode Island combined. Yet the population is only 1,200,000, mostly in the south and along the coast.

Residents and visitors alike come to Maine to enjoy the unspoiled natural beauty. Geographers estimate that the 230-mile (368km) long coastline would stretch to 3,500 miles (5,600km) if every cove and inlet were measured. Drive down the fingers of land that jut into the sea to find old fishing villages, quiet inlets and rocky cliffs. Offshore lie around 2,000 islands, some linked to the mainland by ferry, the majority barely habitable, and all surrounded by treacherous rocks and ice-cold water.

View over Camden Harbor

The coast is the biggest draw and some parts, such as Oqunquit and Boothbay Harbor, become quite crowded in season. Getting away from it all, however, is easy since 90 percent of the state is wilderness and forest. Maine attracts hikers and canoeists into its hinterland with 32,000 miles (51,200km) of river and 6,000 ponds and lakes dotted around. There are few people, but thousands of moose.

Although many experts assume that the Vikings could have paid a visit a thousand years ago, it was the French and English who first settled here. In 1677, the territory was assigned to Massachusetts, but in the early 19th century, when that state began to struggle economically, it cut the ties and Maine became a state in its own right.

Maine's nickname, the "Pine Tree State," is appropriate. Not only is the coastline wooded, there are vast forests inland. The tall, strong pines once provided masts for the British Navy; now, they are made into paper and pulp. Shipbuilding started in 1607, in Bath, and continues there today.

Lighthouses stand as symbols of New England's maritime history
Left: L. L. Bean, Freeport

galleries. "Park and Shop," for example, allows visitors free parking in exchange for a stamp showing proof of purchase from local shops and restaurants. Much of the handsome brick and granite architecture post-dates the devastating fire of 1866, and some earlier buildings remain. Included among these is the home of the writer Henry Wadsworth Longfellow, dating back to 1785.

Tour 23

Getting away from it all is easy when you head for the lakes and mountains of Maine. This long drive explores the state's remote beauty, while also passing through some charming villages. The famous Shaker religious community lives in a village at Sabbathday Lake. Their pious faith still arouses admiration, even though only a handful of the sect survives. By contrast, the nearby Sunday River ski area is one of the liveliest in Maine. Winter temperatures will test a visitor's fortitude. Rangeley is not only the mid-point of this drive, but the town also boasts being precisely halfway between the North Pole and the Equator.

Tour 21

For many, the "real Maine" begins north of Portland. Here, the coastline breaks up into long skeletal fingers of granite, pointing out to form bays dotted with pine-covered islands. The sea has always been the focus of this region and the earliest Europeans who spent time here were transient fisher folk. Seafaring and boat-building are long traditions that have continued with the U.S. Navy in Brunswick, the huge shipyard in Bath, and numerous smaller boat-builders and museums.

Although tourism is a major industry, towns such as Camden, Wiscasset and Damariscotta have been able to retain their charm.

Tour 22

Portland is often rated as one of the best cities in which to live: small enough to feel friendly, but with a lively cultural scene and innovative restaurants. In recent years, it has made a conscious and successful effort to brighten up its downtown and old harbor by recycling historic buildings and employing novel methods of attracting locals to the shops and

The Mid-Coast
of Maine

2 DAYS • 260 MILES • 418KM

Rocky bays, cliff-top lighthouses and peaceful harbors give the mid-coast of Maine its character. This route leads to busy towns and quiet hamlets, past historic houses and old forts. Artists and craftspeople have long been attracted by the area, so there are festivals and fine art galleries as well.

WATERVILLE

95

Augusta

Togus

Windsor

Searsmon

Appleton

Coopers
Mills

Stickney
Corner

Union

Randolph

Pittston

DAMARISCOTTA
LAKE STATE
PARK

Sheepscot

Dresden
Mills

Damariscotta
Lake

Waldoboro

Thomas

495

Pownalborough
Courthouse

Newcastle

95

4

Damariscotta

Merrymeeting
Bay

Days
Ferry

3

Wiscasset

BRADBURY
MOUNTAIN
STATE PARK

Topsham

Bristol

Round
Pond

*Muscongus
Bay*

Bath 2

Woolwich

Colonial Pemaquid
Restoration

Kennebec

Brunswick 1

Cooks
Corner

Maine
Maritime
Museum

Fort
William Henry

5

7 **New Harbor**

Freeport

Pemaquid Point

Yarmouth

WOLF NECK
WOODS
STATE PARK

Pemaquid Light and
Fisherman's Museum
6

Cumberland

REID
STATE PARK

Monhegan
Island

Falmouth
Foreside

POPHAM BEACH
STATE PARK

0   5   10 m

95   295

*Casco
Bay*

0   5   10   15 km

PORTLAND

ℹ 305 Commercial Street

▶ Leave Portland on I–295
north, which becomes I–95.
Take exit 22 for **Coastal Route
1** to downtown Brunswick. Turn
right on Maine Street, then left
on **Route 24** to Brunswick.

SPECIAL TO...

Shopaholics take exit 19 from I-95 for the ultimate experience: 24-hour shopping, seven days a week at L. L. Bean, the well-known camping and sports equipment store. Go after midnight and you're on your own among the flannel sheets and the fishing flies, the hiking boots and hats. The other 100 stores keep regular hours and offer a surprising range, from designer clothes to household goods, all at a discount. Please do not, however, throw money into the trout pond in the store. It kills the fish. Minutes away is the Desert of Maine, complete with sand dunes.

❶ Brunswick

Brunswick is an attractive town, centered on Bowdoin College. Originally founded in 1794 as a men's college, Bowdoin has admitted women since the 1960s. Famous graduates range from 19th-century authors Nathaniel Hawthorne and Henry Wadsworth Longfellow to explorers Robert Peary, the first man to reach the North Pole, in 1909, and his colleague, Donald MacMillan.

Memorabilia from their expeditions is the focus of the Peary-MacMillan Arctic Museum in Hubbard Hall, decorated with the only gargoyle in the whole of Maine (spot it on the left side of the building). The art museum, located in the imposing Walker Art Building, has a varied collection including Gilbert Stuart's familiar portrait of Thomas Jefferson, author of the Declaration of Independence and third President of the United States.

ℹ 59 Pleasant Street

SPECIAL TO...

Old-fashioned diners and drive-in restaurants were once part of everyday life throughout the U.S.A. They still exist in Maine. On Route 24, just north of Brunswick, is Ernie's Drive-In. Turn in and park, flash the car lights for service, order, and the food will be brought out to you by a "car hop." Further east, at the intersection of Routes 1 and 220 near Waldoboro, is Moody's. Here, vacationing New Yorkers rub elbows at the counter with local lobstermen. You can order up meatloaf, burgers and peanut butter pie better than Grandma ever made. Bargain prices.

FOR CHILDREN

The Bowdoin Pines found along Route 24 are an example of Maine's importance to the British in colonial times. These tall, straight trees were made into ships' masts for the exclusive use of the Royal Navy by the King's Mast Agent. Illegal felling was punishable by death. The White Pine is the State Tree, and the Floral Emblem is the white pine cone and tassel.

▶ Leave the campus and turn
right on **Route 24** north.
Continue to Cooks Corner and
rejoin **Route 1** north. Drive 5
miles (8km) to Bath.

❷ Bath

The town may be 18 miles (29km) from the Atlantic Ocean, but boats have been launched on the deep Kennebec River since 1607. Bath's glory days were in the 19th century, when sailing ships made fortunes for the merchants, many of whose graceful homes still line Washington Street in the Historic District. Since 1891, the Bath Iron Works and Shipyard, the largest civilian employer in Maine, has built ships for the U.S. Navy. Right on the river, with the tallest crane (400 feet/120m) on the East Coast, it's impossible to miss.

Downriver from the shipyard is the Maine Maritime Museum, a collection of buildings with seafaring memorabilia and hands-on exhibitions. This is the place to learn the history of lobstering, understand how the many-masted schooners were constructed, and watch boats in the Apprenticeshop being built or restored. Warning: avoid going to or through Bath during the shipyard's rush hour, between 3:30 and 4:15pm.

ℹ 45 Front Street

▶ Leave Bath on **Route 1** northeast and continue for 10 miles
(16km) to Wiscasset.

BANGOR

⑫ Belfast

Belmont Corner

East Northport

Northport

Isleboro

Lincolnville

CAMDEN HILLS STATE PARK

WARREN ISLAND STATE PARK

⑪ Camden

Penobscot Bay

⑩ Rockport

North Haven Island

Glen Cove

Rockland

⑨ Owls Head

Vinalhaven Island

3 Wiscasset

The Indian name means "coming out of the harbor but you don't see where." Today, "the Prettiest Village in Maine" is found easily by visitors, who flock to the antique shops, historic houses and quirky museums. Wiscasset is the seat of Lincoln County, which once stretched to the Canadian border. Throughout the original colonies, towns pride themselves on the fact that "George Washington slept here." Here, the claim is that General Lafayette of France ate ice cream at the apothecary shop that predated today's store, now called the Wizard of Odds and Ends. That was in 1824, long after Lafayette had helped the Americans during the Revolution.

On High Street is the Musical Wonder House. This is the private collection of Danilo Konvalinka, who calls it "the world's finest museum of restored international antique music boxes and mechanical instruments." The full tour is fascinating, though expensive; but it costs nothing to look round the front hall and look at the 19th-century coin-operated music boxes, hurdy gurdies and perforated metal disc players.

At the end of High Street, in a commanding position above the harbor and Sheepscot River, stands Castle Tucker. Built in 1807, it was bought by Captain Tucker in 1858, after he retired from the sea and settled down to married life. From its free-standing switchback staircase to the dramatic southeast façade with its huge windows, the house is one of a kind, and remains much as Captain Tucker left it. The wallpaper is original, as are the furnishings. A descendant of the captain still lives here.

The Nickels-Sortwell House, on the corner of Route 1 and Federal Street, is another ship-captain's home. Built in the same year as Castle Tucker, it exemplifies the Federal period. Just along Federal Street is Lincoln County Museum and Old Jail. This large and foreboding granite building served as the county jail from 1811 to 1953. Below the tiny barred windows, the cold walls, 41 inches (105cm) thick in places, are covered with graffiti, such as the painstakingly detailed schooner under full sail.

▶ Continue on **Route 1** north-east to Newcastle and turn right for Damariscotta.

4 Damariscotta

This attractive yet unpretentious riverside community has plenty of old wood-frame and brick homes. The restored 1754 Chapman-Hall House on Main and Church streets is the oldest in the region. In summer, guides in period dress conduct you round the 18th-century kitchen and herb garden.

i *Damariscotta Region Information Bureau, Route 1*

Typical wood frame house, near the township of Damariscotta

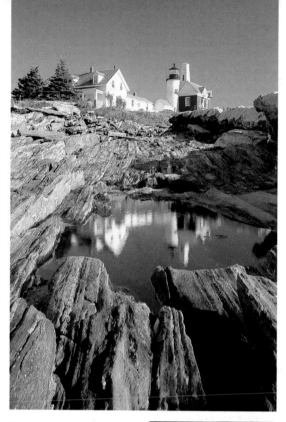

Pemaquid Point Lighthouse juts out on rocky ledges carved by ancient glaciers

FOR HISTORY BUFFS

"Damariscotta" means "the meeting place of alewives." This has nothing to do with women involved in brewing. It refers to a member of the herring family that was popular with Indians. The Indians also relished the local oysters and would congregate for "oyster festivals," leaving heaps of shells behind on the banks of the Damariscotta River. These "middens," an Old English word for "rubbish dumps," contain shells as large as plates.
Ask at the Damariscotta Region Information Bureau for maps and permission to visit them.

▶ *Leave town on Route 130 south for 11 miles (18km). Turn right on Huddle Road at signs for Historic Pemaquid and Pemaquid Point. Service stations are few and far between off the main highways, so be sure to fill up before heading down any of the numerous peninsulas.*

❺ Fort William Henry and Colonial Pemaquid Restoration

The re-creation of Fort William Henry stands guard over the water, as did four earlier fortresses. Nearby, an on-going archeological dig has uncovered a 17th-century British settlement of houses plus a tavern, jail, burying ground and customs house. It is thought to have been one of the first European settlements in the New World. Although fishing and trapping were productive in the area, raids by the French and their Indian allies, and long, hard winters took their toll.

▶ *Follow Snowball Hill Road to Route 32 and drive south to Pemaquid Point.*

❻ Pemaquid Light and Fisherman's Museum

There are 63 lighthouses in the state, but this is one of the most romantic and most photographed. The layers of rock show the geological formation of this distinctive coastline. When climbing upon the rocks near the ocean, be careful. The waters are dangerous; the undertow is strong, too.

▶ *Take Route 130 north, then turn onto Route 32 to New Harbor.*

❼ New Harbor

New Harbor is a truly picturesque and unspoiled Maine fishing village. A memorial here honors Chief Samoset of the local Pemaquid tribe. The chief learned English from British fishermen, and had travelled south to explore the Massachusetts coast in March, 1621, where he discovered the Pilgrim community. Imagine their surprise when he greeted them with the words "Welcome Englishmen."

FOR HISTORY BUFFS

Just off Route 32 is Round Pond, another fishing harbor. This once supposedly hid the notorious Captain Kidd, who buried treasure under a huge boulder on a nearby island. Some say it was on Devil's Oven, others on Otter Island. The mystery remains.

RECOMMENDED TRIPS

From New Harbor, take a daytrip out to tiny Monhegan Island, only 1½ miles (2.5km) across at its widest, with the highest cliffs on the East Coast. The energetic can hike through a wildlife sanctuary with hundreds of species of wildflowers and birds, while the less energetic can visit the artists' studios. There are also cruises for watching seals and Atlantic puffins, now a protected species.

▶ Continue on **Route 32** north
to Waldoboro (20 miles/
32km). Just before town is the
1772 Old German Meeting
House, noted for its wineglass
pulpit and square benched
pews. In the cemetery nearby,
a stone recounts the disappointment of Germans who
settled here in 1748 "with the
promise and expectation of
finding a prosperous city,
instead of which they found
nothing but wilderness." Turn
onto **Route 1** northeast and
drive 12 miles (19km) to
Thomaston.

8 Thomaston

This is another ship captain and
ship owners' town, although the
most imposing house in
Thomaston was built by a
general, Henry Knox. He was an
important figure in the
Revolution and the country's
first Secretary of War. He retired
here in 1795 and built his
mansion high on a hill overlooking the town. Still filled with its
original furnishings, this building, with its white-painted
façade and its two-story bay,
looks remarkably like the south
front of the White House in
Washington D.C., designed in
1792.

▶ Continue on **Route 1** to
Rockland.

9 Rockland

The "Lobster Capital of the
World" boasts a gem of a
museum, the result of a 1935
legacy left by an eccentric 96-
year-old. Lucy Farnsworth left
money to the city for the upkeep
of her family home, now a
museum, and to found an art
gallery in memory of her father.
The William A. Farnsworth Art
Museum specializes in American
painters from the 18th, 19th and
20th centuries, such as Fitz
Hugh Lane, Thomas Cole,
Maurice Prendergast and Childe
Hassam. Also represented are
three generations of Wyeths:
Andrew, Jamie and N.C.

i Harbor Park

FOR CHILDREN

South of Rockland, in the state
park off Route 73, is Owl's
Head Light. The 52-step climb
is worth it for the view over
Penobscot Bay, but vertigo-
sufferers should not peer over
the 87-foot (26m) sheer cliff.
Nearby is the Owl's Head
Transportation Museum, a
world-class collection of
vintage cars, airplanes, motor-
cyles and carriages in working
condition. Demonstrations are
held throughout the summer,
though the museum is open
year round.

SPECIAL TO...

One of the most famous
artistic images of Maine is
Andrew Wyeth's *Christina's
World*, portraying a crippled
girl in a meadow looking
towards her house. It was just
one of his many depictions of
members of the Olson family
and their house outside
Rockland. "I just couldn't stay
away from there ... I'd always
seem to gravitate back to the
house ... It was Maine." The
house is administered by the
Farnsworth Art Museum and is
open, in season, to the public.

▶ Follow **Route 1** north to Rockport.

⑩ Rockport

The tiny village of Rockport has a tiny harbor with lots of cultural activities. The musically minded book into chamber music and jazz concerts at the opera house. Photographers head for the internationally known Maine Photographic Workshop, while craftsmen in silver, wood or enamel take classes at Adventures in Art. Anyone can watch apprentices at work building wooden boats at The

Below: yachts in Camden Harbor
Right: lobsters at Boothbay Harbor

Artisans School. In the little park down by the harbor is a statue of André the Seal. A children's book and film were based on the story of André, who lived here for 20 years.

▶ Leave Rockport on scenic Russell Avenue, going north, with sudden glimpses of the Camden Hills and Penobscot Bay. This becomes Chestnut Street in Camden.

⑪ Camden

*"All I could see from where I stood
Was three long mountains and a wood;
I turned and looked another way,
and saw three islands in a bay."*

The panorama from the top of Mount Battie inspired Maine poet Edna St. Vincent Millay to compose this poem in 1917. The views today are still the same of the Camden Hills, Penobscot Bay and, on a clear day, Monhegan Island. In the town, below the hill, Millay's statue stands by the harbor in what is, arguably, the state's most popular year-round resort. Historic houses have been converted into stylish bed-and-breakfast inns along Route 1. There are also attractive shops and galleries here, as well as opportunities from hiking, sailing and sea kayaking in summer, and skiing and tobogganing in winter.

SPECIAL TO...

Lobsters, the speciality of Maine, are caught in the millions of traps set in the cold waters offshore. Traditionally, these box-like contraptions consist of an oak frame with cotton netting. Many visitors take them as souvenirs. However, don't be tempted to pick up any washed on to a beach by the tide: that counts as "molesting a trap" and carries a fine. Buy one from a road-side stand or, better still, stop at a fishing village, look for a pile on the dock or by a house, and make an offer to the owner.

BACK TO NATURE

Formed by the confluence of five rivers, the tidal marshes of Merrymeeting Bay were popular with the Indians for both fishing and hunting. Wild rice provides food for huge flocks of birds who stop here on what is one of the major migration routes to and from Canada. Fishing is a year-round sport here; in winter, there are ice-fishing shacks on the frozen reaches.

[i] *Public Landing*

▶ *Follow **Route 1** north 6 miles (10km) to Lincolnville, then on 13 miles (21km) to Belfast.*

🔟 Belfast

Belfast or Londonderry? A flip of a coin decided the name back in 1765. As usual in New England, a town's name pinpoints the home in the Old World. In this case, the Scots-Irish had come from what is now Northern Ireland. Over the centuries, Belfast has produced ships, axes, pantaloons, sarsaparilla, chickens, rum and shoes. More useful, but less glamorous, was the invention of the flush tank for washing machines and toilets.

[i] *Main Street*

▶ *The rest of this route is rural and scenic. Take **Route 3** west to Belmont Corner for 6 miles (10km), then **Route 131** south through scenic farmland, past stone walls and hilly vistas. Pass through Searsmont, Appleton and Union. Take **Route 17** west, then before Togus, turn onto **Route 226** south to Randolph. Follow **Route 126**, then turn on **Route 27** south. This passes a cluster of privately-owned white houses moved here from various parts of the state. Turn right on **Route 128**, an old Indian trail that follows the bay. Continue on **Route 128**.*

🔟 Pownalborough Courthouse

Now a museum, this is one of only a dozen surviving pre-Revolutionary courthouses in the country. Here, a judge could dispense justice in the court on the middle floor, walk downstairs to quaff ale in the tavern, and retire to his bed on the top floor.

▶ *Join **Route 127** south at the pretty village of Day's Ferry (the original river crossing) and continue to **Route 1** southwest at Woolwich by the Bath bridge. Return to Portland.*

SPECIAL TO...

Augusta, northwest of Togus on Route 17, has been the state capital since 1827. Although the Maine State Museum tells the story of the state's development, more fun are the Children's Discovery Museum and the Old Fort Western Museum, where the 1754 blockhouse is the oldest wooden fort still standing in New England.

Portland Head Light, the oldest lighthouse in Maine

Portland

Portland aptly deserves its symbol, the phoenix, as well as its motto, *Resurgam*, "I shall rise again." In fact, the city has arisen nearly as often as the sun. Dating back to a settlement called Falmouth, it was virtually destroyed by Indian raids in 1676. After rebuilding, the community flourished until an English fleet bombarded the town in 1775 as punishment for supporting the independence movement.

Once again restored, and renamed Portland in 1786, the port buzzed with business and finance, until the Great Fire of July 4, 1866. Again, it was rebuilt, and this tour reflects the development of Portland and the contributions made by prominent citizens to the arts, business and city life.

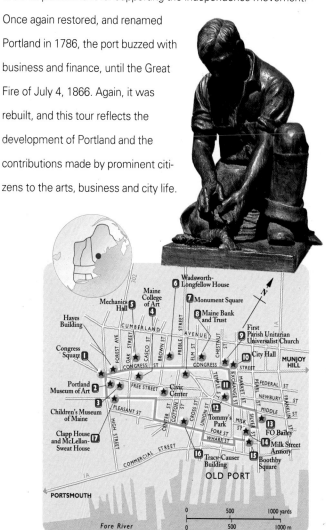

The Wadsworth-Longfellow House was the first brick house to be built in Portland

ⓘ Congress Square (summer only); Convention and Visitors Bureau of Greater Portland, 305 Commercial Street

▶ Start at Congress Square.

❶ Congress Square

This active five-street intersection is the scene of many summer events including concerts. On the corner of Congress and Free streets is the Hayes building, described as a flatiron building because of its wedge-shape. This perfectly proportioned edifice, built in 1826, is one of the recognized icons of Portland.

❷ Portland Museum of Art

The I. M. Pei firm's brick colonnaded building (1983), right on the square, makes an impressive addition to the L. D. M. Sweat Memorial Galleries and rotunda, built in 1911. It houses one of New England's finest art collections and contains pieces by well-known Maine and American painters. You will also find the Joan Whitney Payson Collection of Impressionist and Post-Impressionist works here. One of the best known is Auguste Renoir's *Confidences*. A romantic tête-à-tête, this is a sensitive portrait of one of his favorite models, Margot Legrand.

❸ Children's Museum of Maine

Nextdoor to the art museum stands this former Greek Revival church. This museum ranks among the best of its kind in New England. Star attractions range from "now" to "then." In the computer room, games start with basic ideas for pre-readers and extend the gamut to challenges for even the most computer literate. At the other end of the time scale is a wonder from the 19th century, a camera obscura, of only seven in the

world. A camera obscura is a dark room where images of objects from outside are projected onto a wall. It may sound simplistic in these days of "virtual reality," but this effective, primitive use of light and lens led to still and motion picture cameras.

▶ Leave Congress Square and walk north on Congress Street to No. 522.

❹ Maine College of Art

Cherubs still frolic on the outside of the Porteous, Mitchell and Brown department store, once the largest in town. Gutted completely in 1995, it has been rebuilt as the new Maine College of Art. There are classrooms, studios, an extensive library and workshops.

▶ Look across Congress Street.

❺ Mechanics Hall

This impressive, Italianate, granite-fronted building, with its statues of Archimedes and Vulcan, is the home of the Maine Charitable Mechanic Association. Dedicated in 1851 to "informing and cultivating the mind and training up a race of mechanics (skilled workmen)

of sound moral principle and intellectual power," it still sponsors lectures, maintains an extensive library, and offers free technical drawing classes.

▶ Continue along Congress Street to No. 485.

❻ Wadsworth-Longfellow House

Three generations of one of the city's most famous families lived here, behind the wrought-iron fence. In 1785, General Peleg Wadsworth, a Revolutionary hero and state senator, built this house, now the oldest surviving residence in Portland. The first house to be constructed of bricks in the city, its third floor was added nearly 30 years later. The bricks were shipped in from Philadelphia. Wadsworth's grandson, the poet Henry Wadsworth Longfellow, grew up here. His childhood flute is on show, and the house is furnished much as he would have remembered it as an adult. "Often I think of the beautiful town that is seated by the sea; often in thought go up and down the pleasant streets of that dear old town, and my youth comes back to me." Next door, the Maine Historical Gallery has changing exhibitions about the state.

Portland's impressive City Hall

▶ *Continue on Congress Street.*

7 Monument Square

This space, originally the town's Market Square, is named for Our Lady of Victories Monument. The monument is a Civil War memorial built in 1891 with money raised by local soldiers and sailors.

In recent years, the farmers' market has been revived, with stalls set out on Wednesdays in the summer and autumn. Summer also brings noontime concerts; in December, the city's Christmas tree lights up the square and on New Year's Eve, crowds gather to watch the fireworks.

▶ *Look to the corner of Congress and Elm streets.*

8 Maine Bank and Trust

Portland's first skyscraper, built in 1910 in the Beaux Arts style, was at that time New England's tallest building. Unlike traditional structures of the period, where the exterior walls supported the building, this was constructed with a steel skeleton, allowing greater height. Inside, the marble lobby soars to a ceiling at least three stories high. The impression is of solidity and security – perfect for a bank building.

▶ *Continue on Congress Street to No. 425.*

SPECIAL TO...

Congress Street leads to Munjoy Hill, perhaps a derivation of the French *Mont Joie*. Here, the 221-foot (66m) high Portland Observatory was erected in 1807 as a signal tower. Communication by flags announced the identity of approaching merchant ships and enabled the docks to be prepared for their arrival. Views from the top are spectacular.

Nearby is the Eastern Promenade. Turn right for the bandstand. Here, the panorama encompasses Portland Harbor, the best deep-water port north of New Jersey. Watch for an oil tanker or a cruise ferry coming from Nova Scotia. Don't try to count the islands in Casco Bay; supposedly, there are 365 of them, hence the name, the Calendar Islands.

---

9 First Parish Unitarian Universalist Church

Founded in 1674, this church predates any other house of worship in Portland. The second building on the site took several hits during the British bombardment of the town in 1775. Inside, a cannon ball still lodges within the chain supporting the magnificent 600-pound (273kg) cut-glass chandelier. The 1794 clock and 1804 bell were saved and incorporated into the present building, rebuilt of granite in 1826.

▶ *Continue on Congress Street past the Frost Gully Gallery, the oldest commercial art gallery and a useful stop for art lovers interested in living Maine artists.*

10 City Hall

The granite used to build the City Hall comes from Maine, but the design is based on the classic French *hôtel-de-ville*. Inside, the Portland Symphony Orchestra often fills the 3,000-seat auditorium with music. This is the third municipal headquarters here: the first was destroyed by the Great Fire of 1866; its successor by another blaze in 1908.

▶ *Turn right on Exchange Street.*

11 Exchange Street

Exchange Street leads into the six-square-block Old Port Exchange area, the oldest part of the city. Warehouses and offices have now become boutiques, art galleries and ethnic restaurants. Look closely and you'll see another reminder of British shelling in 1775: the cannon ball embedded in the Colesworth building, on the right, just past the entry to the parking garage. Peer through the windows of F. Parker Reidy's restaurant, almost across the street, to see the open safe and original brick walls of the Old Portland Savings Bank.

▶ *Continue to the intersection with Middle Street.*

12 Tommy's Park

The *trompe-l'oeil* by two Portland artists on the wall represents architectural elements of the 19th-century marble post office which once stood across the street in what is now the postage-stamp size Post Office

Park. In this sunny spot, the granite boulders represent the many islands of Casco Bay, just outside Portland Harbor.

▶ *Turn left on Middle Street and walk two blocks to the intersection with Pearl Street.*

13 F. O. Bailey

Now the home of a well-respected firm of antiques sellers and auctioneers, this was one of the first buildings put up after the Great Fire of 1866. Look for the architect's autograph on the base of the left corner pilaster on the Middle Street side.

▶ *Continue towards the harbor on Pearl Street. After a block, turn right on cobblestoned Milk Street. Straight ahead is the Regency Hotel.*

14 Milk Street Armory

It is no coincidence that the Regency Hotel, between Silver and Market streets, resembles a fortress. This was originally the armory, and was very active in the late 19th to mid-20th

centuries. It also had a tradition of hospitality, as it was the site of musical events and impressive balls. The contemporary dolphin fountain was originally offered to, and rejected by the city fathers. Shunted around town, it stood on a variety of sites until it was finally bought by the hotel.

▶ *Turn left on Silver Street.*

15 Boothby Square

At the intersection of Silver and Fore streets is Boothby Square. Directly in front is a row of old buildings including the 1792 Sam Butts House and Store. It is the second-oldest surviving post-revolutionary house in Portland. On your left is the 1868 granite U.S. Customs House. In the impressive interior, it is easy to imagine merchants sitting down to negotiate the tariffs on a cargo of molasses being unloaded at the wharf just down the street.

▶ *Turn right on Fore Street, pass the granite-fronted 1828 Mariner's Church and turn left*

few remaining warehouses from the "Golden Age" of the 19th and early 20th centuries. Straight ahead is Portland's second flatiron building, now full of artists' studios, used and rare book stores, and the Danforth Gallery, exhibiting alternative art.

▶ *Continue through the five-street intersection onto Pleasant Street. Immediately past the first parking garage, turn right and go up the alley and stairs to Spring Street. On the right is the Civic Center. Cross the street and turn left.*

🔟 **Clapp House and McLellan-Sweat House**
The Great Fire did not reach this area, so these two impressive merchants' homes still stand. The Maine College of Art has offices in Clapp House, a Greek Revival mansion. Major Hugh McLellan's grand Federal house was given to the Portland Society of Art in 1908 by Mrs. Lorenzo de Medici Sweat, along

with funds to build a "proper" art museum.

▶ *Turn right on High Street. Across the street is another Federal brick residence, now a private club, built by McLellan's brother, also a successful merchant and auctioneer. Return to Congress Square, at the end of the block.*

The Portland skyline at dawn, as seen from Back Cove

immediately onto the cobbled Moulton Street. Turn right on Wharf Street, go right on Union Street, then left at the light on Fore Street. On the corner of Cotton Street is the Tracy-Causer Building.

🔟 **Tracy-Causer Building**
Note the old street sign on this building, one of the few survivors of the Geat Fire of 1866. The city's Landmarks Association successfully campaigned for its preservation and restoration in 1996. On the harbor side stand some of the

2 DAYS • 268 MILES • 431KM

Mountains &
Lakes of Maine

Nature lovers and sports fans head for the lakes and mountains, just as vacationers did 150 years ago when they came by railroad to escape the summer heat of more southerly states. Winter also brings visitors, such as downhill and cross-country skiers.

i 305 Commercial Street

▶ Leave Portland on I–495 (the Maine Turnpike), turning off on Exit 11 at Gray (18m/29km). Follow **Route 26** north for 8 miles (13km) to Sabbathday Lake.

BACK TO NATURE

North of Gray is the Maine State Fish and Wildlife Visitors Center. For those who are not heading out into the wilderness areas of the state, this is a wonderful place to get a close look at moose, bears, deer and porcupines. This is not a zoo; the animals brought here were orphaned or injured.

Sabbathday Lake

A cluster of white buildings plus a large red brick house mark the home of the Shakers, the religious community founded in 1782 by Mother Ann Lee, who voyaged from Manchester, England. Some 30 years later, the Shaker movement had grown to around 7,000, with settlements in New England, Ohio and Kentucky.

Today, this is the last remaining group. Less than a dozen men and women live here, following the credo "Put your hands to work and your heart to God." They aim for self-sufficiency through farming, tending the orchards, knitting and printing. During the summer, outsiders are invited to join the Sunday services in the Meeting House, with its plain wooden benches. On other days, visitors can tour some of the buildings, including the museum, with examples of ingenious labor-saving inventions.

▶ Follow **Route 26** to Poland Spring.

Poland Spring

The popularity of bottled mineral waters may seem a recent phenomenon but Poland Spring water has been prized for over a century. When its "healing" powers became known, the spring attracted visitors, a hotel was built, and the area developed into a summer resort. The hotel is long gone but its "library" building remains. This is now the Maine State Building from the Chicago Expo in 1893, moved and reconstructed here as an attraction for visitors. It is a museum recalling the grand old days when holidaymakers came, complete with their servants, for a month or two in the summer. Poland Spring water is still bottled nearby and shipped all over New England.

▶ Continue on **Route 26** north for 17 miles (27km) through South Paris, where the Celebration Barn Theater puts on performances of vaudeville, mime and juggling in the summer. Turn right to Paris Hill.

Paris Hill

Few Americans remember Hannibal Hamlin, Vice-President during Abraham Lincoln's first term. His home is the most impressive structure in this cluster of pristine white Federal and Victorian houses on the summit of a hill. Admire the vistas across the valley and to the White Mountains to the west, then tour the tiny library in the former jail. Built in 1822, it is entirely of granite, including the floors. Ask to see the jail door keys, and to hear how a fat prisoner became stuck while trying to escape.

▶ Continue and rejoin **Route 26** and drive north to the junction of **Routes 26** and **219**. On the east side of the road is a turn-off for Snow Falls Gorge, where there is a picturesque waterfall, picnic tables and nature trails.

Trap Corner

"Rockhounds" and gemologists from all over New England know Oxford County because it is rich in minerals and gemstones such as tourmaline, amethyst and quartz.

At the junction of Routes 26 and 219 is Perham's, a landmark since 1919. As well as the shop selling local finds, and the museum, this is where modern-day prospectors can get maps of nearby quarries and information about panning for gold in the Rangeley area.

▶ Continue on **Route 26**.

Bryant Pond

The people of Maine are renowned for their stubbornness. This town enjoyed making telephone calls the old-fashioned way and made national headlines with its campaign to keep its hand-cranked phone system, the last one in the country. They lost their battle in 1983, but the anti-

Reflections at Bryant Pond

quated telephone technology is the focus of what must be one of the smallest museums in New England.

▶ Take **Route 26** to Bethel.

❻ Bethel
Founded on the Androscoggin River, the community nearly died after the Revolution. Railroads brought revitalization in the mid-19th century. As well as benefiting agriculture and timber businesses, the trains

Main picture: the covered bridge at Newry
Inset: one of Bethel's attractive houses; blueberry leaves in Acadia National Park

carried tourists. Now, vacationers come by car to what is a four-season resort. In winter, cross-country and downhill skiers head for Mount Abram and Sunday River, with its 110-trail network over eight different peaks. In summer, the chairlift up the slope provides bird's-eye views of the White Mountains as well as a great hike down. There is also camping, canoeing, mountain biking, fishing and swimming.

ℹ️ Bethel Area Chamber of Commerce, Cross Street, Town Station

▶ Leave Bethel on **Routes 26** and **2**, and drive 5 miles (8km) north to Newry.

SCENIC ROUTES

About 10m (16km) northwest of Newry is Grafton Notch State Park, where the park road has been designated a "Maine Scenic Highway." Moose can be sighted during dawn and dusk hours, while views of Bald Pate Mountain, plus Screw Augur Falls epitomize the beauties of the Carrabassett region. The Appalachian Trail crosses the road here. This hiking route starts in Georgia and follows the Appalachian Mountains all the way to Mount Katahdin in northeast Maine.

7 Newry

Just off the road is the Artist's Covered Bridge, much-painted and photographed long before the film *The Bridges of Madison County* lent cachet to similar bridges in Iowa. This one was built in 1872, over the Sunday River. More than just a scenic spot, it has popular swimming holes as well.

▶ Continue on scenic **Route 2** north to the paper mill town of Rumford and cross the river at the mighty Pennacook Falls to Mexico, where much of the country's paper for books is made. Take **Route 17** north towards Oquossoc, then turn east on **Route 4** to Rangeley.

8 Rangeley

Wilderness and isolation are the hallmarks of the Rangeley region, surrounded by mountains and punctuated by more than 40 bodies of water. The village boasts of being halfway between the North Pole and the Equator, but there is nothing halfway about the winters. A dog-sled postal service used to deliver letters to households cut off by snow; now, snowmobiles provide access to homes and businesses, but they are also raced for fun. Other winter sports include snow-shoeing, dog-sledding and ice-fishing, as well as cross-country and downhill skiing. The slopes here are less crowded than at most other

resorts. When summer comes, there is fishing for landlocked salmon and trout, canoeing, hiking and golfing.

There are also two museums. The Rangeley Lakes Historical Society, once a jail, recalls the 19th-century era of lake steamers and lodges that catered to New Yorkers escaping the heat of the city. More unusual is the Wilhelm Reich Museum, the home of the controversial Austrian psychoanalyst who studied with, then broke from, Sigmund Freud. Reich emigrated to the U.S.A. and eventually settled in Rangeley, to pursue "orgonomy, the science of the life energy." His writings and inventions were all to do with sexual energy and personality analysis. In 1956, he was found guilty of violating Food and Drug Administration laws. He died, in prison, a year later. A museum preserves his library, memorabilia and surviving inventions.

[i] *Rangeley Lakes Region Chamber of Commerce, Main Street*

SPECIAL TO...

When shoppers pick up a pack of wild blueberries, they will be taking home some of the 64 million pounds grown every year in Maine. That represents 99 percent of the nation's crop. August is the official month of blueberries and Rangeley's festival on the third Thursday of the month is a typical celebration, with stalls selling pies and muffins, sauces and ice cream. You can even "pick your own" at the Blueberry Hill Farm outside town.

BACK TO NATURE

At the Hunter Cove Sanctuary, just west of Rangeley, on Route 4, there are marked trails through swamps, meadows and thickets where bears, moose and bobcats live. Guides take visitors out for moose-watch canoe trips – as long as they are up by 5am!

▶ *Leave Rangeley via **Route 4** south. Note that Smalls Falls, in the Sandy River Gorge, has a good swimming hole, plus a waterfall, picnic site and hiking trails. At Phillips, take **Route 142** northeast to Kingfield.*

⑨ Kingfield

What do violins, automobiles and cameras all have in common? They fascinated the ingenious minds of F. O. and F. E. Stanley, twin brothers who lived here a century ago. Their most profitable discovery was a photographic process which they sold to a company that later became Kodak. Car fans know them for their Stanley Steamers, made by the Stanley Motor Carriage Company. One of their racing cars set a speed record of 127.66mph (204.3km/h) in 1906, and it remained unbroken for many years. The brothers also made fine violins. The Stanley Museum tells their story and displays their inventions, along with photographs taken by their sister, Chansonetta Stanley Emmons.

▶ *Take **Route 27** south through New Portland, stopping to see the amazing 1841 engineering feat, the Fireproof Wire Bridge, suspended across the Carrabassett River. Rejoin **Route 4** and head for Farmington.*

⑩ Farmington

It is hard to imagine that this agricultural valley produced an international opera star. A simple farmhouse, just outside Farmington, was the birthplace in 1857 of Lillian Norton. As Madame Nordica, she triumphed in Europe and was the first American woman to take Wagnerian roles at the Bayreuth Festival. Returning to the States, her "liquid purity, exceptional range and magnificent power" charmed New York critics during numerous seasons at the Metropolitan Opera House. The Nordica Homestead displays her costumes, annotated scores and other memorabilia.

A branch of the University of Maine is here, continuing a tradition of education dating back to 1788 when the school was founded. Families of soldiers of the American Revolutionary forces moved here to receive land grants.

[i] *Greater Farmington Chamber of Commerce, 30 Main Street*

▶ *Continue on **Route 4**. At the junction with **Route 2** at Wilton is the Western Maine*

View over Step Falls, Grafton Notch State Park

SPECIAL TO...

Farmington is the home of Greenwood's Champion Ear Protectors, better-known as ear muffs. They were the brainchild of local teenager Chester Greenwood, whose ears had become painfully cold while ice-skating during the winter of 1873. His prototype was made of wire, covered with fur and velvet, but after improvements, he patented the design and opened a factory in town. Each year, the first Saturday in December is Chester Greenwood Day, complete with a parade.

---

*Mountains Chamber of Commerce. **Route 4** leads through Dryden, Jay, and Livermore Falls, recognized long before arriving by the sulphurous smell of the paper mills. Take **Route 108** east for the Norlands Living History Center.*

⑪ Norlands Living History Center

Anyone who has ever wanted to go back in time should book in for a day or a weekend on this extensive farm. With a new name and a new character, adults and children participate in 19th-century life, cooking on a cast iron stove, harvesting grain or tending the vegetable garden. They even sleep on rope beds. In the morning, breakfast is oatmeal porridge and pancakes. Those who prefer to dip, rather than immerse themselves in history, can take a guided tour to learn about farming in the old days and the Washburn family, who spawned diplomats, congressmen, journalists, and businessmen, all in one generation.

▶ *Follow **Route 4** to Auburn and then take **I–495** south (Maine Turnpike) for the return to Portland.*

PRACTICAL INFORMATION

GETTING AROUND

Whether you use your own car or a rental car, driving is perhaps the best way to see New England. The forested hills, winding river valleys and historic New England towns and villages are most accessible and best appreciated when seen from a car traveling at moderate speed on secondary roads (see **Motoring**, page 161). But other means of transportation are available as well.

By Car

Within New England you'll normally drive only an hour or two to your next destination. From Boston, it's only an hour's drive to Providence, Plymouth, Manchester, or Portsmouth; about two hours to Hartford, Portland, Mystic, or Cape Cod; about three hours to New Haven, the Berkshires, southern Vermont, Boothbay Harbor, or New Hampshire's White Mountains; and only about four hours to New York City or central Vermont. Five hours takes you from Boston to the resort and national park at Bar Harbor, Maine, and not much more than six hours' driving deposits you in beautiful Montréal.

By Recreational Vehicle

Among the most pleasant ways to tour the country is in a recreational vehicle (RV, motor home, or camper). RVs come in all sizes and shapes and in dozens of models. They usually sleep four to six people comfortably, include a full kitchen (with cooking range, refrigerator, and running water), and are air-conditioned; some even come equipped with a shower!

Hundreds of campgrounds in New England can provide electrical, water and sewer hookups for $15 to $20 per night. Some RVs are so self-sufficient that they can operate for several days without hookups. In an RV,

you're completely independent, and you can save money by cooking your own meals and not paying for expensive hotel rooms. The advantages to families with young children are obvious. Family travel in a rental RV can be a very cost-effective way to tour New England.

Renting an RV has its disadvantages as well. Rentals are fairly expensive, and you should work out estimated budgets for a trip in an RV versus a trip using a rental car and hotels before making your final decision. When figuring costs, keep in mind that RVs are heavy vehicles, and they use a lot more fuel than do passenger cars. During the busy summer months, you may not be able to find the campsite you want in the location you want, since many of New England's choicest campgrounds fill up early in the day. You may have to reserve in advance, which takes some of the fun out of footloose vagabond travel. Finally, New England is a region with many delightful country inns. If you've rented an RV at considerable expense, you may not feel that you can pay to stay in country inns very often.

For more information on RVs, contact the Recreation Vehicle Industry Association, 1896 Preston White Drive, Reston, Virginia 22090 (tel: 703/620–6003 or 800/336–0355; fax 703/591–0734); for $5 they'll send you a 40-page catalog listing locations, services, and rates of the various RV rental agencies. The Recreation Vehicle Dealers Assoociation, 3930 University Drive, Fairfax, Virginia 22030 (tel: 703/591–7130) is another good source. Call Go Gamping America (tel: 800/47–SUNNY) for a free 16-page camping vacation planner to help you to plan fun and successful camping and RV vacations.

By Plane

The larger cities, such as Boston, Providence, Hartford, Portland and Burlington, all have good air service provided by the larger domestic airlines. Numerous regional "feeder" airlines fly between the larger cities and smaller ones. There are also many connections by regional carriers to New York City.

Almost all the small regional airlines operate in conjunction with larger national and international airlines. The regional airlines' flights are included in the flight schedules of larger airlines, including American, Continental, Delta and USAir. Call these airlines for information on flights, fares and cities served.

By Train

Amtrak operates trains connecting Boston with Springfield and Pittsfield, Massachusetts, and Albany, New York; Hartford, New Haven, New London and Mystic, Connecticut; Providence, Rhode Island; and (via Springfield) Brattleboro, White River Junction, and Montpelier, Vermont; and Montréal, Québec. There is no interstate train service northeast of Boston (that is, to Maine or

central and eastern New Hampshire), but there are buses that run from Amtrak's terminus at Boston's South Station to Portsmouth, New Hampshire, and to major cities and towns in eastern Maine.

Trains on routes between Boston and points south and west are fast and frequent, but to get to points in Vermont from Boston, connections are not good and service is infrequent.

By Bus

Bus service is quite good in New England. Here are some of the major companies, their phone numbers and the areas they serve:

American Eagle (tel: 508/

993–5040), New Bedford terminal, operates frequent daily buses between Boston and New Bedford.

Bonanza Bus Lines (tel: 617/720–4110 or 800/556–3815), Back Bay Terminal, 145 Dartmouth Street, runs from Boston to Cape Cod (Falmouth and Woods Hole) and Fall River (Massachusetts), and Newport and Providence (Rhode Island). Other routes run from Providence to central and western Connecticut and the Berkshires of Massachusetts, and from Providence to Cape Cod.

Concord Trailways (tel: 617/426–8080) is the line to take to New Hampshire. Buses start at Logan Airport and the Peter Pan Trailways Terminal in Boston, then head north to Concord, Laconia and North Conway, Plymouth, Waterville Valley, and Franconia. Another route goes to Alton and Wolfboro.

Greyhound (tel: 800/231–2222, with its terminal at South Station in Boston (any Red Line subway to South Station), operates many of the long-distance routes in New England, and connects the region with the rest of the country.

Greyhound buses operate from Boston via Hartford and New Haven to New York City; from New York City via New Haven and Hartford to Springfield, Massachusetts, connecting with Vermont Transit buses for points in Vermont, and Montréal, Québec.

Another Greyhound route is from Boston via Portsmouth, New Hampshire, to the Maine coast, stopping at Portland, Freeport, Brunswick, and Bangor (with connecting services to Ellsworth for Bar Harbor); this route connects with Canadian SMT buses headed for New Brunswick and Nova Scotia.

Greyhound also connects New York City via New Haven and New London, Connecticut, with Providence, Rhode Island, and also to Plymouth and Brockton Bus Lines, which service the Cape Cod area of Massachusetts.

Greyhound also operates buses heading due west from Boston, stopping at Worcester and Springfield, Massachusetts, and Albany, New York, with connecting service to points west in both the United States and Canada.

Peter Pan Trailways (tel: 617/426–7838 or 800/237–8747), at the Peter Pan Trailways terminal in Dewey Square, opposite Amtrak's South Station, runs between Boston and Albany, Amherst, Bridgeport, Danbury, Hartford, Holyoke, Lee, Middletown,

New Britain, New Haven, New York City, Northampton, Norwalk, Pittsfield, Springfield, Sturbridge, Waterbury, and Worcester. Other routes connect Springfield, Massachusetts, with Bradley International Airport and Hartford, Connecticut.

Plymouth & Brockton Street Railway Co. (tel: 508/746–0378), Peter Pan Trailways Terminal in Dewey Square, is the one to take from Boston to Plymouth, Sagamore, Barnstable, Hyannis, and Provincetown on Cape Cod. Many P&B runs start at Logan Airport, then head into Boston for stops at Park Square, the Peter Pan Trailways Terminal, and South Station. You can take any P&B bus from Logan Airport and transfer to another one downtown.

Vermont Transit Lines (tel: 800/451–3292, or 800/642–3133 in Vermont), Greyhound Terminal, in collaboration with Greyhound Lines, operates from New York City via Albany to Bennington, Manchester, East Dorset, Rutland (with connecting service to Killington, Woodstock, and White River Junction), Middlebury, and Burlington. Connecting service from Burlington goes on to Montréal.

Another service is from Boston via Manchester, Concord, Mount Sunapee, and Hanover, New Hampshire, to White River Junction (with connecting service to Woodstock, Killington, and Rutland), then to Barre, Montpelier, Burlington, and Montréal.

Vermont Transit also runs buses between Portland, Maine; Burlington, Vermont; and Montréal, stopping at North Conway and Bretton Woods, New Hampshire; and St Johnsbury, White River Junction and Montpelier, Vermont.

Another route takes travelers from New York City or Boston to White River Junction for connections to St. Johnsbury and Newport, Vermont, and

Sherbrooke and Québec City.

To get to Stowe, Vermont, you must first go to Burlington or Newport, Vermont.

HEALTH SERVICES

All New England cities have hospitals; blue signs bearing a white H mark the way. Boston is one of the country's most renowned medical centers, with dozens of hospitals and medical facilities. To use most of these facilities, however, you'll want to have health insurance, since prices for services are astronomical.

A three-day stay in hospital can cost more than $1,000 just for the room and basic services; medical procedures and doctors' fees might cost several thousand more.

HITCHHIKING

Hitchhiking is not a good way to get around New England, either within cities or between cities and towns. It's illegal to hitchhike on expressways. Incidents of robbery and violence by driver or hitcher, though few in number, have left most motorists unwilling to stop for hitchhikers.

HOLIDAYS

1 January – New Years Day;
Third Monday in January – Martin Luther King Day (long weekend);
Second weekend in February – Lincoln's Birthday (long weekend);
Third weekend in February – Washington's Birthday (long weekend);
(Presidents Week, linking the two weekends, is often a school holiday);
First Tuesday in March – Town Meeting Day (Vermont);
Third Monday in April – Patriots' Day (Massachusetts and Maine, long weekend);
Easter;
Last weekend in May – Memorial Day (long weekend);
4 July – Independence Day;
Second Monday in August – Victory Day (Rhode Island, long weekend);

16 August – Bennington Battle
Day (Vermont);
First Monday in September –
Labor Day (long weekend);
Second Monday in October –
Columbus Day (long week-
end);
First Tuesday in November –
Election Day (some states);
11 November – Veteran's Day;
Fourth Thursday in November
– Thanksgiving Day;
25 December – Christmas Day.
(A long weekend includes
Monday.)

LIQUOR LAWS
In Maine, New Hampshire, and
Vermont, liquor is sold in
government-operated stores
only; in Connecticut,
Massachusetts, and Rhode
Island, liquor is sold privately.
Liquor is not sold on Sunday,
though most restaurants and
bars with liquor licences may
serve liquor by the drink on
Sunday. The minimum age for
drinking varies by state, but in
most it's 21 years. A few towns
in New England, such as
Rockport, Massachusetts, are
"dry," which means that no
shop, restaurant, or hotel may
sell liquor, but it's not illegal to
bring your own liquor and
serve yourself.

Restaurants have either a full
liquor license (for liquor, wines,
and beer), a wine and beer
license, or no license. At some
restaurants that have no license,
you can bring your own liquor;
others don't allow this.

It's illegal to drink alcohol in
public areas, such as streets and
parks or on benches. If it's
discreet you can usually have
wine or beer with your picnic.

MOTORING
Driving
In many places outside major
cities, cars are permitted to turn
right on a red light after stopping, if it is safe to do so.

Freeways and toll roads make
travel easy, whereas side roads
are often narrow and winding.
Use particular care in winter.

You should always have your
driving license with you.

Highway and speed limits,
licensing of drivers, and all
other rules governing automobile use are set by each state's
legislature.

Car Rental
To rent a car in New York or
New England, you must be at
least 21 years of age (though
most major agencies require you
to be at least 25) and have a
valid driver's license. A credit or
charge card is almost always a
necessity.

Some companies may insist
that non-U.S. residents have an
International Drivers Permit.

If your own auto insurance
covers damage to a rental car,
you needn't waste money on
Collision Damage Waiver
(CDW) or Loss Damage Waiver
(LDW).

For American travelers it is
worth checking their own insurance policy to see if they are
already covered.

Breakdowns
Car rental companies will advise
drivers of what to do in the case
of a breakdown. However, the
American Automobile
Association ("Triple A" or AAA)
has reciprocal arrangements
with many other motoring orga-
nizations round the world, so it
is worth checking with your
own association before leaving
home. The AAA nationwide,
toll-free number is 1–800–222-
7764. In case of a breakdown,
lift up the hood, as a signal, and
remain in the car. Only open
doors and windows to police in
a patrol car.

Accidents
All accidents should be reported
to the nearest police. Exchange
names, addresses, driver license
number, and insurance details.
Non-U.S. residents who are
held responsible or have caused
an injury, shouldinsist on
contacting their embassy or
consulate.

Safety Belts
The use of safety belts is
required by law, and every

intelligent driver knows that the
chances of surviving an accident
and avoiding injury are
increased greatly if safety belts
are worn.

Throughout the United
States, infants and small children (under 4) are required by
law to be placed in child safety
seats secured by seat belts.
Child safety seats are available
from car-rental firms at a small
extra charge.

Speed Limits
The speed limit in New
England is 55 to 65mph (88 to
105km/h). In cities and built-up
areas, it is 20 to 40mph (32 to
64km/h), and 15mph (24km/h)
in school zones. Speed limits are
strictly enforced. When a school
bus stops, all traffic behind
must do the same.

Police use radar to detect
speeding drivers, but some
drivers use radar detectors to
warn them about police speed
traps.

In Connecticut, it's illegal to
mount or to use a radar detector.
If you are caught speeding in
Connecticut and you have a
radar detector in your car
(whether or not it's connected or
in use), fines may total upward
of $300.

Road Maps
New England maps are sold in
the region's bookstores and gas
stations. Maps of each state
drawn with greater detail are
available, sometimes for free,
from official state tourism
departments by mail, or from
state roadside information
centers located on major highways near state borders.

For addresses of the state
tourism offices, see **Visitor
Information** on page 164.

NEW ENGLAND
CALENDAR OF EVENTS
For up-to-date information on
events throughout New
England, buy the Thursday
edition of the *Boston Globe*,
which carries a separate calendar section with detailed listings
on all sorts of happenings.

January
• First Night. The arrival of the new year is celebrated with festivities in Boston, Massachusetts; Providence, Rhode Island; Stamford, Connecticut; Burlington, Vermont and other cities and towns. New Year's Eve.
• Stowe Winter Carnival, Stowe, Vermont. Ski races, parties, and other festivities, many of them outdoors. Third Week.

February
• Dartmouth Winter Carnival, Hanover, New Hampshire. Dartmouth College's annual snow celebration. Second week.

March
• Maine Maple Sunday, Maple sugarhouses throughout the state open their doors to visitors. Third Sunday.

April
• Boothbay Harbor Fishermen's Festival, Boothbay Harbor, Maine. Seafood feasts, exhibits and games. Second weekend.
• Patriots Day. Reenactment of the battles between Minutemen and Redcoats at Lexington Green and Concord North Bridge, with real musket fire (but no bullets). To do it right, be at Lexington Green by dawn for the Lexington battle, then walk along Battle Road to Concord North Bridge (eight miles) for the Concord one. Where: Lexington and Concord, Massachusetts. When: Patriots Day, April 19 (celebrated on the third Monday), a holiday in Massachusetts. How: for information, contact Minuteman National Historical Park (tel: 508/369–6944) the Lexington Vistors Center (tel: 617/862–1450), or the Concord Chamber of Commerce (tel: 508/369–3120).
• Boston Marathon. Patriots Day, April 19.

May
• Brimfield Antiques Fair, Brimfield, Massachusetts. Up to 2,000 dealers fill several fields near this central Massachusetts town, with similar fairs in early or mid-July and mid-September. Mid-May.
• Lobster Weekend, Mystic Seaport, Connecticut. Lobster feasts and live entertainment. Late May.

June
• Yale-Harvard Regatta, on the Thames River in New London Connecticut. Early June.
• Taste of Block Island Seafood Festival, Block Island, Rhode Island. Chowder cook-off, games, crafts, and live entertainment. Mid-June.
• Blessing of the Fleet, Gloucester, Massachusetts. Festivities, seafood fests, dancing, and exhibits. Late June.
• Jacob's Pillow Dance Festival, Becket, Massachusetts. The region's premier summer dance festival. Contact Jacob's Pillow Dance Festival, P.O. Box 287, Lee, Massachusetts 01238 (tel: 413/243–0745. June to August.

July
• New Haven Jazz Festival. Concerts on the green in New Haven, Connecticut. Early to late July.
• Independence Week. A week of concerts, exhibits, and special events culminates in the famous Boston Pops Fourth of July concert at the Hatch Memorial Shell on the Esplanade; after Tchaikovsky's *1812 Overture* (with real cannons), a mammoth fireworks display goes off over the Charles River. Where: various locations in Boston. When: week of July 4. How: for information and schedules, contact the Greater Boston Convention & Visitors Bureau, Prudential Plaza (P.O. Box 490), Boston, Massachusetts 02199 (tel: 617/536–4100 or 800/888–5515) or phone the Special Events Group (tel: 617/267–2400).
• Great Schooner Race, Rockland, Maine. First or second Friday.
• Newport Music Festival, Newport, Rhode Island. Chamber music concerts are held in the great mansions. Second and third weeks.

• Historic Homes Tour, Litchfield, Connecticut. One day is your only opportunity to tour this beautiful town's historic houses. (Tel: 203/567–4506 for details.) Mid-July.
• Barnstable County Fair, Hatchville, Massachusetts, on Cape Cod. An old-time county fair complete with rides, food, and livestock contests. Late July.
• Friendship Sloop Boothbay Harbor Regatta, Boothbay Harbor, Maine. A three-day event, this series of boat races culminates in a parade of sloops. Last week.
• Bar Harbor Music Festival, Bar Harbor, Maine. Classical and popular concerts. July to August.
• Marlboro Music Festival, Marlboro, Vermont. Among New England's oldest and most renowned. July to August.
• Tanglewood. The summer season of the Boston Symphony Orchestra brings symphony and chamber concerts and solo recitals to the Berkshire Hills. Where: Tanglewood, near Lenox, Massachusetts. When: July to August. How: write for a program: Symphony Hall, 301 Massachusetts Avenue, Boston, MA 02115 (tel: 617/266–1492), or call the Tanglewood Concert Line (tel: 413/637–1666 in July and August only).

August
• Maine Lobster Festival, Rockland, Maine. Celebration of the lobster and the region's maritime history. Arts and crafts, entertainment, a parade, and lots of lobster (tel: 207/596–0376 for more information.) First weekend.
• Newport Folk Festival and JVC Jazz Festival. Thousands of music lovers congregate at Fort Adams State Park on alternate weekends in July and August. Performers include such big names as Suzanne Vega, Randy Newman, B. B. King, Ray Charles, and Tony Bennett. Where: Newport, Rhode Island. When: second week in August.

How: for information on schedules and tickets call the Newport Festival Office (tel: 401/847–3700) or Ticketmaster (tel: 401/331–2211). For tickets and information by mail, write to the Newport Festival Office at P.O. Box 605, Newport, RI 02840. Tickets can also be purchased at the Festival Office, at 670 Fame Street.
• League of New Hampshire Craftsmen Fair, Mount Sunapee State Park, near Newbury, New Hampshire. Craft displays and demonstrations amid other festivities. Admission is charged. (Tel: 603/224–1471 for more information.) Second week.
• Bennington Battle Days, Bennington, Vermont. Commemorates the Battle of Bennington (August 11, 1777) with exhibits, speeches, and celebrations. Second week.

September
• Blue Hill Fair, Blue Hill, Maine. A country fair with rides, games, and lots to eat. Labor Day and the four days preceding it.
• Vermont State Fair, Rutland, Vermont. Agricultural exhibits, games, rides, and entertainment. Labor Day weekend.
• Providence Waterfront Festival, Providence, Rhode Island. Performances, art exhibits, boat races, and multiethnic feasts. Early September.
• New Haven Fall Antiques Show. Among the region's largest shows. Mid-September.
• Eastern States Exposition. "The Big E" is New England's largest agricultural fair, with a midway, games, rides, agricultural judgings, lots of eats, and general fun. Where: West Springfield, Massachusetts. When: mid-September. How: Contact the Eastern States Exposition (tel: 413/737–2443) or the Greater Springfield Convention and Visitors Bureau, 34 Boland Way, Springfield, Massachusetts 01103 (tel: 413/787–1548).
• National Traditional Old-Time Fiddler's Contest, Barre,

Vermont. Lots of good music. Late September.
• Northeast Kingdom Fall Foliage Festival. Hometown church breakfasts, crafts sales, and open-house tours in the towns of Barnet, Cabot, Groton, Peacham, Plainfield, and Walden, Vermont. Late September to early October.

October
• Festival of Vermont Crafts, Montpelier, Vermont. Crafts both traditional and modern. Late October.

November
• Thanksgiving Celebration, Plymouth, Massachusetts. Authentic colonial food, dress, and festivities in town and at nearby Plimouth Plantation. Third Thursday.

December
• Boston Tea Party Reenactment, Boston, Massachusetts. At the Tea Party Ship and Museum on Boston's Museum Wharf. Mid-December.
• Christmas Eve and Christmas Day. Special festivities throughout New England. In Newport, Rhode Island, several of the great mansions have special tours; Mystic Seaport in Mystic, Connecticut, has a special program of Christmas festivities; Nantucket, Massachusetts, features carolers in Victorian garb, art exhibits, and tours of historic houses. December 24–25.

NEWSPAPERS/ MAGAZINES
Each of the larger cities in New England has its own daily newspaper. The *Boston Globe* and the *Boston Herald* are distributed throughout New England, as is the *New York Times*, and, in most cities, the *Washington Post*. The national newspapers *USA Today* and the *Christian Science Monitor* are also available. You can also buy the *International Herald Tribune* at Boston's Logan Airport and at some newsstands in large cities.

POST OFFICES
Most post offices are open Monday through Friday from 8am to 5pm and Saturday from 8am to noon or 2pm. A few major post offices stay open until 5.30 or 6pm, and the post office at Boston's Logan Airport stays open until midnight. To receive mail at a post office, have it sent to you c/o General Deliveries (Poste Restante) in the town where you'd like to pick up your mail. Specify the name of the post office where you'd like to pick up your mail; if in doubt, write "Main Post Office." You'll need to show identification, such as a passport or driver's license, to pick up your mail.

SAFETY
Whenever you're traveling in an unfamiliar city or country, stay alert and keep a close eye on your possessions.

TAXES
Taxes on hotel rooms, restaurant meals, some transportation services, and purchases in general are levied by each state and by some cities. Taxes on rooms, meals, and other purchases (which can be as high as 11 or 12 per cent) are not included in the price.

TIPS FOR SPECIAL TRAVELERS
Families
New England is a favorite destination for families on vacation, and many price breaks are available. Museums, amusement attractions, whale-watch expeditions, and most other sights offer reduced admission rates for children. Many offer even better deals in the form of family plans, whereby one admission price covers an entire family; the price is lower than the sum of two adult and two children's tickets.

Some attractions (outdoor concerts, state parks, beaches, and so forth) charge admission "per car," so families on a driving vacation pay as little as solo travelers.

Often a family of four or even five can stay in the same hotel room. Most modern hotels and motels allow children to stay for free with their parents if the parents pay the normal two-person rate (not a special discount rate) and the children use the room's existing beds. In a room with two double beds, a family of four can stay as cheaply as two. If there are three children and a rollaway bed is necessary, there'll be a small charge ($10 to $20) for it. The age permissible for children under the "family plan" varies; for some plans, there is no age limit. Some inns follow the same policy, but at many others children are not accepted.

A good source of information for family travel is *Frommer's New England with Kids*.

Seniors
Senior discounts are readily available throughout New England at museums, parks, attractions and some hotels and on Amtrak trains, so make sure to carry some convincing form or photo identification.

It's best to request discounts on hotel rates, train and plane fares, and rental-car fees when you make your reservation, not when you're paying for the services. For more information about senior discounts in general and for a good-as-gold discount card, contact the American Association of Retired Persons (AARP), 601 E Street, NW, Washington, D.C. 20049 (tel: 202/434–2277, Monday through Friday from 9am to 5pm).

Boston is the home of Elderhostel, 75 Federal Street, Boston, Massachusetts 02110–1941 (tel: 617/426–7788), with innovative educational programs throughout the world for those aged 55 years and older.

Travelers with Disabilities
All of New England's major hotels and most museums and stores, as well as other large institutions, are, at least in part, accessible to visitors in wheelchairs or on crutches. However, many of the smaller country inns and bed-and-breakfast houses are not accessible or not fully accessible. The best plan is to call ahead to determine whether the level of accessibility is sufficient.

Two states offer information about accessible facilities and events. To receive the information you need, contact the Vermont Department of Travel and Tourism and the New Hampshire Office of Travel and Tourism (see **Visitor Information** below).

Amtrak trains are accessible to travelers with disabilities, but not all Amtrak stations are; ask about this when you make your train reservations, and also inquire about help with your baggage, special seating and other assistance. There's a bonus: Amtrak grants discounts of 25 percent (off the normal coach fare) to adult disabled travelers and 50 percent (off normal children's fares) to disabled travelers aged 2 to 12. For full information, ask for a copy of Amtrak's annual Travel Planner from Amtrak, National Railroad Passenger Corp., 400 N. Capitol Street NW, Washington, D.C. 20001 (tel: 800/USA–RAIL).

VISITOR INFORMATION
There are both public and private sources of information. Each state has a tourism office that issues brochures, maps, lists of festivals and special events, and other useful material. Municipal governments have their own tourism offices as well, but the job of providing information in a town or city is done mostly by the local chamber of commerce or convention and visitors bureau.

Here are the addresses and telephone numbers of the state tourism offices:

Connecticut Department of Economic Development, Tourist Division, 865 Brook Street, Rocky Hill, Connecticut 06067–3405 (tel: 203/258–4355 or 800/282–6863);

Maine Publicity Bureau, P.O. Box 2300, Hallowell, Maine 04347 (tel: 207/623–0363 or 800/533–9595 outside Maine);

Massachusetts Office of Travel & Tourism, 100 Cambridge Street, 13th Floor, Boston, Massachusetts 02202 (tel: 617/727–3201 or 800/447–6277 for a free Massachusetts Getaway Guide and map);

New Hampshire Office of Travel & Tourism, 172 Pembroke Road (P.O. Box 1856), Concord, New Hampshire 03302 (tel: 603/271–2666);

Rhode Island Department of Economic Development, 7 Jackson Walkway, Providence, Rhode Island 02903 (tel: 401/277–2601 or 800/556–2484);

Vermont Travel & Tourism, 134 State Street, Montpelier, Vermont 05602 (tel: 802/828–3237 for general information; 802/828–3236 for a vacation packet; 800/833–9756 to access visitor information by fax).

WHEN TO GO
Climate
Without doubt, the best times to tour New England are summer (June through August) and autumn (September and October), unless you're coming for skiing. You can enjoy a visit any time of year if you prepare for the weather and are wary of the busy times when hotels, restaurants and transportation are filled to capacity.

The Seasons
Weather in New England is a much-discussed topic because it's so unpredictable. However, there are some generalizations that seem to hold true from year to year, and these may affect your plans on when to visit New England.

Coming very late and staying very briefly, spring tends to be a disappointment. The week or two of spring days in the normal year are a delight, with cool temperatures in the evening and just the perfect degree of warmth during the day. In the countryside the thaw brings "mud time," the period between frost and spring planting. Mud time is the slowest season for tourist facilities, coming after ski season and before summer warmth. Thus many country inns, resorts and amusements close for a few weeks in April or thereabouts.

By mid-June, summer is on its way and, despite the region's northerly and coastal location, it can be pretty hot and sometimes humid. When it's 85°F (or even up to 95°F) and humid, as it often is through mid-September, head for the beaches, the islands, mountains, lakes and riverbanks. Sailing, along the coast or on the rivers, is a choice activity, as is a hike to the top of Mount Washington or a week at a beach on Narragansett Bay. A drive through the Berkshires or along the Connecticut coast can also be very satisfying.

Autumn is undoubtedly New England's glory and its finest season, and if you have a choice of vacation times, this is the one to pick. Although you may have to forsake swimming, the famous fall foliage is a worthy substitute; it's at its peak usually in late September and mid-October, starting in northern Maine, New Hampshire, and Vermont and moving southward and eastward as the weeks pass. Days are still warm and very pleasant, nights a bit chilly but not uncomfortably so. City people load their bikes onto the car and head for the country, picking up fresh apple cider, pumpkins and squash from farm stands on the way home. Fresh cranberries are on sale in the markets all autumn, and although the blueberry-picking season is past, many apple orchards open so that you can "pick-your-own" and get the freshest fruit possible at a very low price.

If you're heading to New England specifically to enjoy the fall foliage, you should make sure you'll be there during "peak colour." You can call a special hotline number in each state to find out about fall-foliage (see pages 102–3).

Most tourist resorts and inns stay open through September and often to mid-October. Those that stay open all year sometimes close for two weeks or so from mid-October to early December to give the staff a break before the advent of the ski season. By Thanksgiving (November 25), everyone's getting in shape for the ski season.

After a period of chilly weather in October, New England usually gets a respite, with a short period of warm weather known as "Indian summer," which can occur in later October or November. It's not dependable and may be brief, but it's glorious all the same.

Winter, as they say, depends: snow might begin in November, which is very early, for the first flurries usually come in mid-December. Ski reports appear in newspapers and the broadcast media, and the special skiing-condition phone lines go into operation. January through March is cold and snowy, and the skiing may be quite good through April; gray snowy days alternate with brilliant, crisp, sunny days when the air is very cold but the sun's warmth makes it pleasant. Those who aren't skiing take advantage of the cities' cultural seasons or perhaps escape to an inn somewhere in the snow-clad mountains for a weekend.

None of this applies to Mount Washington in New Hampshire, of course. This "highest peak in New England" is said to have the worst weather in all 50 states, and New Englanders delight in exchanging horror stories of the latest report: winds of 150 miles per hour (the record is 231mph), temperatures of -40°F, and windchill factors that don't seem earthly.

During September and October virtually the whole of New England is given over to the "fall"

INDEX

I

International Tennis Hall of Fame 93
Ipswich 22
Ives, Charles 33, 56, 57
Ivoryton 78

J

Jackson 132
John Brown House 89
John Hancock Tower 39, 50
John Paul Jones House 125
John Peirce Mansion 125
Joseph Nightingale House 89
Josiah Dennis Manse 25

K

Kancamagus Highway 123, 133
Kent 74
Kent Falls State Park 74
Killington 97
Kingfield 156
King's Chapel 41
Kingscote Mansion 93
Kipling, Rudyard 19, 102, 108

L

Lake Champlain 96, 97, 116
Lake Champlain Maritime Museum 117
Lake Waramaug 73
Lake Winnipesaukee 123, 134–7
Lakeville 59, 75
leaf peeping 96, 102–3, 165
Lenox 35
Lexington 10–12
Libby Museum 137
Liberty Pole 127
Lime Rock Park 75
Lincoln 133
Lincoln County Museum and Old Jail 142
liquor laws 161
Litchfield 59, 72–3
literature 56–7
L. L. Bean 141
Longfellow, Henry Wadsworth 7, 55, 56, 139, 141, 148
Longfellow House 55
Ludlow 97, 107
Lyman-Allyn Art Museum 80

M

Madison 77
Maine 138–57
Maine Maritime Museum 141
Maine Photographic Workshop 145
Maine State Fish and Wild-life Visitors Center 153
Maine State Museum 146
Manchester 97, 106
Manchester-by-the-Sea 18
Marble House 94–5
Marblehead 17
Marblehead Neck 17
Mark Twain House 64
Marlboro 109
Massachusetts 6–55
The Mayflower 28
Melville, Herman 32, 35, 56, 82
Meredith 123, 137
Merrymeeting Bay 146
Middlebury 117
Moffatt-Ladd House 127
Mohawk Trail 36
Monhegan Island 143
Monomoy Islands 25
Monte Cristo Cottage 80
Monterey 31
Monument Mountain 32
Morgan Horse Farm 120
motoring 158, 161
Moultonborough 135–6
The Mount 35
Mount Equinox 105–6
Mount Mansfield Ski Area 119–20
Mount Washington 123, 131, 132, 133
Mount Washington Cog Railway 131
Mr. Steward's Museum of Art and Curiosities 61
Munroe Tavern 11
music 57
Musical Wonder House 142
Mystic 58, 59, 80–1, 83

N

Nathaniel Harrison House 77
Natural History Museums 54
Nauset Light Beach 27
Naval War College Museum 83
New England Aquarium 46
New England Fire and History Museum 25

New England Holocaust Memorial 46
New England Ski Museum 129, 130
New Hampshire 122–37
New Harbor 143–4
New Haven 66–70, 76
New London 80
New Milford 73
New Preston 73
Newburyport 22
Newfane 108
Newport 83, 84, 85, 90–5
Newport Art Museum 92–3
Newport Artillery Company 92
Newport Casino 93
Newry 155
Nichols House Museum 48
Noah Webster House 65
Noank 80
Nordica Homestead 156
Norfolk 75
Norlands Living History Center 156
Norman Rockwell Museums 33, 111
North Conway 132–3
North Woodstock 129
Northampton 37
Numkeag 33

O

Okemo Mountain resort 107
Old Colony House 91
Old First Church 99
Old Fort Western Museum 146
Old Granary Burying Ground 41
Old Lighthouse Museum 81
Old Lyme 79
Old Man of the Mountains 129
Old North Bridge 12, 14
Old North Church 44
Old Saybrook 77
Old South Meeting House 42
Old State House, Boston 42
Old State House, Hartford 61
Omni Parker House 42
O'Neill, Eugene 29, 56, 57, 80
Orchard House 13
Orleans 25–6
Owl's Head Light 144
Owl's Head Transportation Museum 144

P

Paris Hill 153
Park-McCullough House 101
Parker River Wildlife Refuge 22
passports and visas 4–5
Paul Revere's House 44
Peabody Museum 18
Peary-MacMillan Arctic Museum 141
Pemaquid Light and Fisherman's Museum 143
Pennysaver Building 101
personal safety 163
Peru 106
Pigeon Cove 21–2
Pleasant Valley Wildlife Sanctuary 35
Plum Island 22
Plymouth 114
Poland Spring 153
Portland 139, 147–51, 152
Portland Harbor 149
Portland Museum of Art 148
Portland Observatory 149
Portsmouth 123, 124–7
post offices 5, 163
Potters' Yard 101
Pownalborough Courthouse 146
Presidential Range 130
Prides Crossing 18
Providence 85, 86–9
Providence Athenaeum 87–8
Provincetown 7, 28–9
public holidays 160–1

Q

Quechee 111
Quechee Gorge 111

R

Radcliffe 55
Railroad Museum 29
Rangeley 139, 155–6
recreational vehicles (RVs) 158
Redwood Library 92
Revere, Paul 7, 11, 12, 15, 41, 44, 89, 112
Rhode Island 83, 84–95
Rhode Island School of Design 85, 87
Ripton 118
Riverside Park 31
Robert Frost Place 130–1

Index & Acknowledgments

The Automobile Association
wishes to thank the following libraries and photographers for their assistance in the preparation of this book.

MARY EVANS PICTURE LIBRARY 8a, 8b, 56a, 56/7; ROBERT HARDING PICTURE LIBRARY Front cover main pic; TOM MACKIE 5, 59, 83, 84, 92, 94/5, 95, 102/3, 103a, 118/9, 120/1, 136/7, 136, 142, 143, 144/5, 153, 154/5, 154b, 157, 165; MAINE OFFICE OF TOURISM 147, 148, 149; GENE PEACH/THE PICTURE CUBE 51; PICTURES COLOUR LIBRARY LTD 9, 10, 17, 103b, 158/9; SPECTRUM COLOUR LIBRARY F/Cover inset, 6, 11, 42, 44, 82/3, 97; THE STOCK MARKET 12 (Michele Burgess 1993), 20 (Kunio Owaki 1988), 26/7 (Jean Miele MCMXCII), 28 (B O Zaunders 1991), 31 (ChromoSohm/Sohm MCMXCIV), 32/3 (Brownie Harris 1992), 33 (Lance Nelson), 58 (O'Rourke 1986), 62b (Ed Bohon 1986), 63 (Audrey Gibson 1986), 72/3 (Lance Nelson), 72 (Sonya Jacobs 1985), 74/5 (Kunio Owaki 1987), 79 (John Madere), 81 (James Marshall), 85 (Craig Hammell 1993), 92/3 (Craig Hammell 1993), 116 (Mark E Gibson 1987), 126 (James Blank), 150/1 (Randy Ury 1992); ZEFA PICTURES LTD 34, 37, 38, 49b, 68, 86/7, 91, 96, 105, 108/9, 111, 138, 139a, 146.

All remaining pictures are held in the Association's own library (AA PHOTO LIBRARY) with contributions from: R HOLMES Inside flap, B/cover a, b, 2, 14/5, 18, 29b, 30, 34/5, 36, 39b, 40, 41, 43, 45, 47, 50a, 53, 54, 55, 60, 61, 62a, 66, 76, 78/9, 122, 123b, 124, 125, 130/1, 132/3, 140; J LYNCH 13, 19a, 19b; M LYNCH B/cover c, 4, 7, 23, 24, 25, 27, 29a, 39a, 49a, 50b, 52, 64, 65, 67, 70, 80, 86, 88, 89, 98, 99, 100, 101, 106, 106/7, 110, 112/3, 113, 114, 115, 117, 120, 123a, 127, 129, 131, 132, 135, 139b, 145, 154a; J WILLIAMS 57.

Contributors
Copy editors: Larry Dunmire, Karen Bird   **Verifier:** Sheila Hawkins   **Indexer:** Marie Lorimer